The **MOTHER-
DAUGHTER**
Relationship Makeover

The MOTHER-DAUGHTER

Relationship Makeover

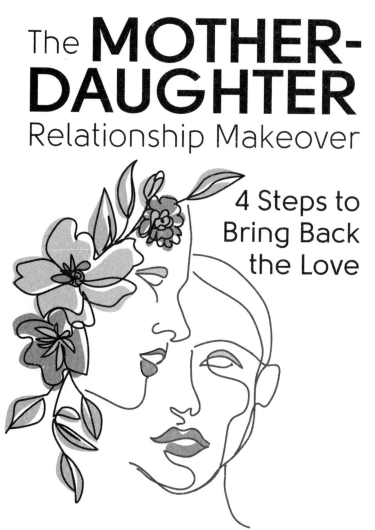

4 Steps to Bring Back the Love

Leslie and Lindsey Glass

Health Communications, Inc.
Boca Raton, Florida

www.hcibooks.com

Library of Congress Cataloging-in-Publication Data
is available through the Library of Congress

ISBN-13: 978-07573-2506-9 (Paperback)
ISBN-10: 07573-2506-8 (Paperback)
ISBN-13: 978-07573-2507-6 (ePub)
ISBN-10: 07573-2507-6 (ePub)

Publisher: Health Communications, Inc.
         301 Crawford Boulevard, Suite 200
         Boca Raton, FL 33432-3762

Cover, interior design and formatting by Larissa Hise Henoch.

To mothers and daughters
everywhere who need
a message of **HOPE**

"I think the hardest thing for a mother is to make it possible for a child to be independent and at the same time let the child know how much you love her, how much you want to take care of her, and yet how truly essential it is for her to fly on her own."

—Madeleine Albright

Contents

Acknowledgments

As journalists writing about our own experiences and those of so many others we have met over the years, we are grateful for the sharing of stories and wisdom that have inspired us to write this book of self-exploration. It's easy to blame those closest to us for our hurts and sorrows. It's an act of great courage and bravery to dig deeper and find compassion and healing for whatever went wrong. We know that positivity can bring the change you long to see. Back in 2011, Tian Dayton was the first to show us how psychodrama can change perspective. We are forever grateful to Tian for the session we filmed with her for the *Secret World of Recovery* that brought us to tears and began our quest for better communication and understanding.

So many wonderful friends and family have made great contributions to our lives, and we are grateful to everyone we have known and loved. Out of respect for their privacy, we have chosen to focus this story only on ourselves and our relationship.

Thanks to our HCI editor, Christine Belleris, for her belief in our mission and work, and for her thoughtful editing throughout the production process. Thanks to Larissa Henoch for the beautiful book cover and book design. We are so grateful to our publishing family members, Alex Glass and Sarah Pelz, for their encouragement and guidance through the development and proposal process of this book. You're the best. Special thanks to Dr. Deborah Sweet for being a mentor and participator. A huge thank-you to all the women who have been friends and supporters, too many to name, to both of us as we traveled this exciting journey.

Introduction

For all the exasperated, frustrated, raging, helpless, hopeless mothers/daughters out there, we have news for you. Whatever miseries you may be experiencing with your mother/daughter right now, the conflicts are not only about your daughter/mother. In fact, all mother-daughter conflicts originate from other people who have influenced you (and her). Wherever you are on your mother-daughter journey, your present conflicts develop from generational, familial, and cultural experiences that affect your every thought and reaction. Don't rule out other family members and the dynamic they bring to the table.

It may come as a big surprise that the things you say and do are likely the opinions and actions repeated by those who raised you and those who raised them. Traumas from generations ago such as migrations, wars, famine, persecution, genocide, economic depressions, mental illnesses, and unbearable tragedies that you have never even heard about may be ghosts of the past intruding on your relationships and feelings now. That's what we realized when we started exploring the evolution of our own conflicts and fights. How we recovered from overwhelming pain and anger is the story you will read here. Our relationship makeover became one of the greatest accomplishments of our life. We know mothers and daughters everywhere will want to share this book for aha moments that can change the way they view themselves and improve their lives. We will make you laugh and cry at our story of heartbreak and redemption.

We are going to show you how following the four steps in this book can shift negative feelings about your relationship forever. Now, it's normal to have a wide variety of mother-daughter conflicts that change over time, so we also want to make sure we're clear about what's normal fighting and the kind of behavior that crosses lines to toxic, abusive, and manipulative relationships for which you may need professional help to heal.

As we take you through the four steps of the relationship makeover, we will give you prompts along the way to think about your own mother, grandmother, and family members. The ways your loved ones influenced you will reveal the patterns that are being repeated now with your mom/daughter. How do you sound when you talk to each other? What is your tone, and what do you want to happen with your interactions and conversations? Can you listen, or do you interrupt to reinforce your point of view? With new insights you may find better ways to communicate, to stop the cycle of conflict, and to finally find your happy ending, as we did. Take that last sentence with a grain of salt. Not all relationships can or should be mended. Family members can be unsupportive, toxic, or worse. But even if you can't and shouldn't get back together again, you can heal if you understand what happened.

STEP 1

Self-Discovery

You're about to embark on **Step 1** of your relationship makeover journey. This section will be enlightening. Here are five chapters that explore who you and your mom/daughter really are. We begin this journey of self-discovery with writing. You're going to tell the story of your life through writing prompts. Why are we giving you writing prompts when you think you already know what happened and have a strong point of view? We know that writing your answers to our questions will inspire you to think about new possibilities, and this may open your mind and heart to finding peace in unexpected ways. It did for us.

Chapter 1 is about writing. Writing is the universal tool for sharing our histories, telling stories, educating, entertaining, and yes, healing. Writing is the tool that has helped us find understanding about ourselves and each other. Writing has been the outlet for saying what can't be said out loud, relieving ourselves of toxic secrets, finding self-awareness about our own behavior, and so much more. Writing is key in recovery for realizing what it was like, what happened, and how to move forward in healthier ways. In this first chapter we share what writing means to us and invite you to think about what writing has meant to you in the past and how it can help you now.

In Chapter 2 we explore our own background and stories, and we invite you to do the same. Who are you? Where do you come from? What is your history and the history of the mothers and daughters who came before you in your family. What has your life been like, and what do you know about your mother? The past reveals how we're behaving in the present and can give us the insight to make changes when necessary.

In Chapter 3 we delve into personality, mood, and emotional styles. This will show how we're different and the same and may reveal why you get along or live in conflict. When it comes to your mother-daughter relationship, what are your personality and emotional styles, and how well do they mesh? We'll give some examples of personality styles, tell you about ours, and invite you to add this component to your life story. We'll talk about mood habits here, too. This chapter may also help you identify how you are with others and your characteristics that make relationships easy or difficult.

In Chapter 4 we'll move from personality styles to communication styles. Here we'll look at the way you communicate and how it is developed by your culture and family. What does comfort sound like? Culture plays a part. In Africa, for example, being called fat is a compliment. In other places, it's the opposite. Words destroy self-esteem or bolster it. Communication affects who you are and the ways your mom-daughter relationship may be supportive, or not so much. We'll give some examples of how you may speak to each other and ask you to think about words that changed your life that you'll never forget.

In Chapter 5 we will explore the secrets we keep and the lies we tell. You know when you hide the truth. You may be protecting someone else or yourself. Lying is something else. All teens lie to their moms. And plenty of moms we know do their share of shading or hiding the truth about so many things. We'll explore the impact lying and hiding has on the mother-daughter relation-ship and how it damages trust and confidence. We'll ask you to think about your own experiences with secrets and lies.

CHAPTER 1

For Leslie and Lindsey, Writing Can Cure Almost Anything

Many forms of self-expression can provide relief from emotional distress and pain, but none can create a portal to solutions, true healing, and the potential to restore relationships quite like writing. We live in a world of behavioral rules, family rules, cultural rules, and relationship rules. Each rule can profoundly hurt us in unexpected ways. Loyalty and fear can teach us never to speak our true minds or speak from the heart because telling can get us in trouble. There is political censorship, and there is censorship we learn from family experience. Self-censorship shuts us up and shuts us down, often before we have a chance to know who we really are. We develop verbal behavior habits that disguise our feelings or blast them out in ways that don't serve us well.

Blurting negative feelings out loud to those we love does terrible damage every day. We all have trauma around that. The words mothers and daughters let loose in anger and criticism can be deeply hurtful and destructive. Casual cruelty and outright verbal attacks are not easily forgotten or forgiven. Words and feelings written on the page, however, can transform and enlighten. Writing lets you say, *"I'm mad at Mom for holding me back. My aunt is an idiot who drinks too much. Granny doesn't know what she's talking about. You've been mean and hurt me."* You've said it, but not in a way that can come back to haunt you. It's okay to tell your journal or diary or notebook what you really think. A journal doesn't talk back or tell you that your feelings are stupid or wrong.

In fact, a journal can be the path to self-discovery, a way to see how wrong you've been about something. Angry words you write one day can seem ridiculous, or at least not so important, when you read them weeks or months later. Just letting the feelings loose on the page is enough for you to feel better in the moment. Your words don't have to strike a living target to serve their purpose. Writing also opens the door to positive memories and events that can bring back joy you may have forgotten or think you've lost forever. In writing this book I've recovered memories from the very first years of my life. Telling yourself both the good and bad sides to your story can also create a more realistic truth that you can inhabit more comfortably.

For me, writing has always been a way to figure out what was going on, to translate the world whenever it made no sense. Writing something down can change a day, a mood, a relationship, indeed one's whole life for the better. Writing can be the kiss to the hurt that makes everything feel much better. The philosopher Descartes wrote in 1637, "I think, therefore I am." That one firm and absolute certainly became the basic center, the philosophical proof of our existence. Thinking may be the first step to being oneself. But sharing thoughts through words and images is the first step to being together. We don't need to ask Hallmark if it works.

Writing gave me a way to hear myself think and know that my thoughts had value. Working through a thousand issues on the page has been the magical tool that has kept me alive during all the ups and downs of life, and there have been many. My life has been messy but wonderful. No one, no matter how perfect someone's life may seem from the outside, is spared from pain and anguish. There have been many times in my life when writing felt like my only friend. When loss and defections of family members, death of much-loved animals, career struggles, discord, financial challenges, war and difficult years for my country and the people I love the most—when all these things seemed too much to bear, the simple act of writing it down gave my feelings meaning. It helped me find fresh air to breathe and a door in the wall that seemed to shut me in.

Of all the times writing has come to my rescue, it served the best when it became the tool my daughter Lindsey and I used to restore the precious relationship we had lost in the turbulent teen years. Like so many mothers and daughters, Lindsey and I unintentionally shut each other out and felt the anguish of not being heard or loved enough. After fifteen years of serial battling when it seemed nothing could restore the love and closeness we both wanted, writing gave us the gift of understanding, acceptance, and redemption.

So to mothers and daughters who feel the perfect love, mothers and teens who think things will never get better, mothers and daughters who cannot stay in the same room for very long or agree on much of anything, to everyone who is a mother or a daughter, I dedicate our story to you. With a sense of humor, a grain of salt, and an open heart, you, too, can feel better.

Lindsey Shares What Writing Means to Her

I used to hate writing, which is funny because now I love it. But I used to hate most things at first. Then when something was forced upon me, I realized I liked it. Auto-hate, I guess. Or contempt prior to investigation, as they say in recovery circles. Definitely one of my character defects. Writing was what my mom did. That was her thing, and I didn't want to be like her. Yes, we laugh about that now that I have turned into a modified version of her. Writing was something I resented for taking my mom away from me, and I found it unpleasant as an activity. It takes a certain kind of focus that was too challenging for me back in the day. It was hard enough for me to sit still when I was young and in my early years of addiction recovery, but to sit still *and* focus my thoughts was asking a lot.

When I was a teen, I was not as into books as the other members of my family. They would sit around the dinner table discussing what they were reading, and I'd tune out remembering scenes from movies or reading a comic book. I'm more visual, and I had no patience when I was a teen and young adult. As a child, I loved reading, but the moment I graduated to TV and movies, I didn't look back for a while. In my free time I preferred physical activities, being outside, or going to the movies. My mom would do nothing but read a new book in a series over a three-day weekend while I had to exercise, shop, clean, and do a multitude of other activities.

As the years have passed, I've learned to be a reader and writer. Forced into book clubs, endless self-help, and research, I followed a path that led me back into reading. I couldn't be happier as I developed a whole new love of reading and books in recent years. Writing, on the other hand, now that's a different story. When my life hit an especially dark patch in my early twenties, something completely unexpected came to my rescue: writing. Suddenly a love and devotion to the craft that I never thought possible was ignited. Over the next twenty-four years writing has evolved into a passion and job. First, it slowly became a part of my recovery life and the tool to help mend my broken relationships with my mom and so many others. This activity that seemed extremely boring suddenly became a trusted resource. It gave me clarity and relief about what had happened in my life and the person I had become.

Writing gave me a new form of self-expression. Not everybody grows up able to identify and express their feelings in appropriate or healthy ways. What's going on? Why do I feel so bad? Am I crazy? These were questions for which I had no answers, no words to help me function well in my environment. In the old days, when life got tough, I would shut down because I didn't even know what feelings I was having. I knew I was uncomfortable and unhappy, and I acted out in various ways to relieve my misery. I didn't understand the core problems or how to fix them. Writing showed me who I wanted to be and how to reconnect with what I'd lost. It helped me learn to understand what I was feeling and ways to react appropriately. Writing gave me relief from the dysfunction in my head.

An even bigger surprise came when writing became my professional life, too. My greatest goal has been to tell stories on the screen, as my grandfather did. I'm still working on it, but I've certainly made a start. The other shock came when I started writing about recovery, and my articles on our website, Reach Out Recovery, reached millions of people all over the world. It turned out that my outlet of writing became a valuable voice in the recovery world, and I ended up doing the very thing I wanted to avoid.

Then, after years of painful conflict with my mom, including a bitter four-year separation in which we didn't see or speak to each other, writing helped repair our troubled relationship. Writing hasn't been easy for me, and I haven't reached all my goals. I often experience the same feelings of failure and worthlessness my mom experienced, but the recovery mission has given me purpose. The goal of my professional writing has been to help people, and that gives it meaning. When readers comment and let me know that I've connected with them, it makes the effort worthwhile.

I feel privileged to be able to share my experience, strength, and hope, and I enjoy receiving comments about articles. Hearing that someone didn't pick up a drink or drug because I shared a little slice of hope always makes my day. Writing can lighten dark moods, help manage relationships, and be the vessel for all those things we wish we could tell people but shouldn't ever say out loud. It has been a means for accessing everything for me. I hope writing opens those doors for you, too.

CHAPTER 2

Leslie's Story and Lindsey's Story

Born at the end of World War II, I was not given an offi-cial name. My birth certificate reads Baby Girl Gordon. For years there was some debate about what my name should be, and it changed depending on who was addressing me. Although Leslie was the name on all my school forms, no one called me Leslie. Further confusion often put me on the boys' gym list because in those days Leslie was traditionally a boy's name. My mother called me Susie, the name my three-year-old brother, Stephen, liked. My father began calling me Lucy after Peanuts was created in 1950 be-cause I reminded him of a cartoon character that had strong opin-ions and gave unsolicited advice. He also called me, "Girl-child and an ugly one."

My dad believed that praising a girl and telling her she was cute or pretty would spoil her and make her into a difficult person. This was old-school thinking. Being a difficult person was a curse for a girl designed to be unspoiled and humble, preferably a desirable wife for a good earner and solid citizen. Sound familiar? Many girls are still raised not to be troublesome or think too highly of themselves. From a privileged background but not deserving of a life and choices of my own, I grew up thinking I was nobody.

Not having a consistent name was only part of my confusion about who I really was. My family's history was murky, and that also created an unreliable definition. I was told my grandfather Julius Gordon was a Jewish scholar who emigrated from Scotland. I wore a Gordon plaid kilt throughout high school. In the course of my research, however, I found out that in fact, my grandfather's parents came from England and somewhere in Russia before that. On an Illinois census form his occupation was listed as clerk. Families have secrets, and few of us know the whole story of our parents' struggles and traumas.

My dad grew up during World War I and started his career in the Great Depression. He had been a scholarship student at the University of Chicago and editor of *The University of Chicago Law Review*. Even with stellar academic credentials, however, he was barred from joining a prominent Chicago law firm because he was Jewish. Being a Jewish entrepreneur in the entertainment business, on the other hand, was a feature.

Soon after I was born, my father reorganized United Artists in Los Angeles. He was employed at the finance company Walter Heller and traveled out to California from Chicago for a few weeks at a time to work with Charlie Chaplin, Douglas Fairbanks Jr., and Mary Pickford. He lived the Hollywood lifestyle at the Beverly Hills Hotel and loved it. He was ready to leave Chicago permanently and move to Los Angeles to become president of United Artists.

My dad never had the chance to run a movie studio. My mother, Elinor Gordon, did not want to live in Los Angeles. She was interested in social issues, people who were making a difference in the world, and intellectual achievers. She was also keenly aware of the hazards of being a studio head's wife and refused to move to California under any circumstances. That left an opening for my father's close friend Arthur Krim to become the head of United Artists.

I was six when my mom, dad, and brother Stephen left our big extended family, the new house my father had built in Glencoe on Lake Michigan, and my public school. We sailed to France on a French ocean liner with no plans of ever returning to Chicago. My mother, who didn't want to raise children in the rarified air of Hollywood, looked east and chose the European way of life instead. We lived in Paris, where my brother got us kicked out of the American school in the first week. We drove around Europe, living in high-end hotels and visiting movie sets. I still remember everything about that magical time.

A year later we moved to a townhouse in New York City, where I was allowed to roller skate around the block to Lexington Avenue by myself, and my father set up his television business in the Seagram Building. Movies were booming, TV was in its infancy, and the East Coast was the hub of finance, academia, social progress, and developing TV.

I had missed second grade and would miss part of third grade and attend two different schools in fourth grade before we finally settled in Riverdale, the Bronx. There, in our house on the Palisades, people such as Eleanor Roosevelt, General Omar Bradley, Adali Stevenson, Margret Mead, Mayor Wagner—anybody who was somebody—came to dinner. My mother knew how to make friends.

And we had a Chinese cook. Our Chinese chef from Hong Kong, Mr. Ja Fa Wei was also my caretaker and driver. We had a deal going, and by the age of eight, I was handling knives, learning cooking, and teaching Wei to read and write English so he could become an American citizen. I had a magical childhood.

Who was my mom, who didn't want to live in Hollywood and created the most wonderful life in New York? She was the first girl in her family to go to college, a beauty from a staunchly middle-class Republican family with an ambiguous religious background. The confusion about religion was another burning question for me about who I really am. There was no question about my mom's status in her family, however. The former Elinor Loeff was not valued as a girl, shy, and terrified of public speaking. Perhaps because her brothers were valued more, social justice was her passion, and her aspiration was to be someone and to improve the world. That's what she set out to do as a newcomer to New York in the early 1950s.

Going back further, my mother's middle-class mother, Esther Loeff, was born Wittenberg, Nebraska, in 1888. My grandmother lived almost a hundred years and was a housewife, mother of three, and doting grandmother to ten. I was her first girl. Esther was not permitted to drive a car or write a check or speak her mind on any subject. Her mother, Moise Rachel Schumaker, was born in France in 1848. Rachel traveled to America and married Marcus Wittenburg, who was born in Hungary in 1839 and served in the Union Army during the Civil War. How did these two immigrants from different countries get to Topeka, Kansas, meet, and marry in 1872? This is a mystery. What I do know is they settled in Sutton, Nebraska, became fundamentalist Christians, and had nine children.

My great grandfather fought in the Civil War and owned a

successful dry goods store. My mother never told me this, but maybe she didn't know. I have these few facts because a distant cousin sent me a newspaper clipping about my great grandfather accompanied by a framed photo of him in his Union Army uniform. The photo hangs in my library. My mom was born in 1916 in Chicago, and her grandfather died in 1920. What did my grandmother know about her parents' background? She never shared any stories and very little advice. My mom retained her mother's Christian beliefs about sexuality and behavior and was silent about her Jewish heritage.

In any case, a hundred years after my great grandmother was born, the powerful women philanthropists and social activists who molded my mother's thinking and behavior hired others to do almost every task for them. That trend is as old as civilization and continues today. Because my mother didn't do anything domestic, I learned to do it all. My mom attended Columbia School of Social Work. After working briefly in Harlem, she turned to social activism. She met Eleanor Roosevelt through her work at Citizens Committee for Children and became equally comfortable in homeless shelters, the White House, and the United Nations.

As president of Citizens Committee for Children, Elinor Gordon lobbied in Washington for labor laws protecting children and for Head Start. She was a freedom rider during the civil rights movement and was appointed chairman of the first-ever conference on civil rights by President Lyndon Johnson.

In 1963, right after President Kennedy's assassination, she called me from onboard Air Force One. I was a freshman at Sarah Lawrence College in my dorm room when the phone rang.

"Guess where I am?" my mother said. Naturally, the president's airplane was not my first answer.

On that occasion, my mother was part of the diplomatic mission to the independence of Kenya. I have a photo of her with a tribal chief wearing some of my old summer clothes. A few years later, in 1968, she chaired the first meeting of the first civil rights conference at our home on Martha's Vineyard. I have a photo that shows my mom as the only woman at the table. I was there and must have caused her terrible grief on the most important weekend of her life, although she never showed it. I had just shocked her by bolting and returning home from a prominent marriage that she had promoted. Only a few months later I would be the first divorcée in my family.

At the Civil Rights Conference I felt a profound failure as I watched my famous mom take her place among Black and white leaders, always knowing exactly what to say despite being painfully shy herself. You can't rise to the top from a humble background without having qualities of greatness; it just doesn't happen. I knew I was a disappointment to her and believed I would never be able to think big enough or be good enough to be worthy as her daughter. I thought I could never be my mom's equal just as years later Lindsey would watch me develop into a bestselling author and speaker and believe she could never be my equal.

As Esther's daughter, Elinor broke the mold. She graduated from the University of Chicago, attended Columbia University School of Social Work, and advocated for human rights. As Elinor's daughter, I broke her mold. I had failed to launch as a debutante, left my first marriage after eleven months, and didn't care about social activism. If you raise a girl to think she's plain, you can't take it back when you want her to wear a ball gown and prance around in hopes of attracting Prince Charles or the Aga Khan. Casual cruelty can affect a child's self-esteem forever.

After graduating from college and getting a divorce at twenty-one, I became a writer at an advertising agency during the mad men era and was the first female writer in my agency and the first working woman in my immediate family. My unmarried aunt Sophie had worked in the coat department of Marshall Field. Socialites' daughters in New York, however, did not work for pay in those days. To get me back on track, my art collector mom urged me to join the Junior Committee at the Museum of Modern Art. After a few meetings, I stopped trying to fit in. I became a full-time working woman.

Independence is a streak that runs through our family. In my case, I couldn't help thinking that my beautiful mom was socially schizophrenic—riding in a limo and picking up every homeless person she saw. If you want to know what we were like, Woody Allen's 1996 movie *Everyone Says I Love You* portrays us to a tee. Mom was like Goldie Hawn, and I was like Drew Barrymore. My mom's goal in life was to empower others and give money away but not to me. I used to torture her by telling her that I would never have children or attend charity balls; I would never have my hair done every Friday at Revlon on Fifth Avenue or beg for anything in Washington; and I would never, ever be an advocate for any social issue. Social causes will break your heart.

Education was what interested me. I wanted to understand things, especially religion since ours was so fraught with secrecy. Joseph Campbell had been my don at Sarah Lawrence and Grace Paley, my writing professor. I had tried to fit into my mom's mold. My mother had pressured me to marry the son of an English lord, the nephew of a friend to whom she introduced me when I was a sophomore in college. His mother, a real-life character in a Graham Green novel, pressured me to convert to Catholicism. I was like a character in a

Henry James or Evelyn Waugh novel, the innocent American heiress married off to an upper-class Brit with unhappy consequences. After eleven months of marriage, three days before my college graduation and just weeks before my mother's history-making event on Martha's Vineyard, I bolted with nothing but my toothbrush and graduation gown. In turn, my mom was missing in action when I needed a divorce.

After the civil rights conference was over, she and my dad went on vacation to Greece for the summer. I had to negotiate my divorce during that long summer and finally traveled to Juarez alone on Labor Day weekend to get the very last Mexican divorce recognized by New York State. Walking two steps behind a snobbish British aristocrat was not for me. How many mothers raise their daughters to be accessories to prominent or rich men? It's the second oldest vocation for girls. My first experience at marriage meant I could not have a writing career or be able to do much independent thinking, much less work in an advertising agency or a magazine. Religion had something to do with it, too. But that's another story.

Being a very young divorcée in New York in the late 1960s brought shame on two distinguished families on both sides of pond society. I was not exactly ruined but certainly damaged goods at just twenty-two. What did I want? I wanted to hang around with the crime writers in the newsroom at *New York Magazine* and be a famous author like the literati I had grown up with on Martha's Vineyard. I wanted to work, not exhibit myself.

Pretty girls exhibited; plain girls achieved. I was an achiever who wanted stability in my life, so three years later I married again and thought I would be safe from bosses and sexual predators both in and out of the office. This raises the question of what we want for ourselves and why we're afraid of life on our own. A generation later, girls have more opportunities to explore different options for a fulfilling life, and not have to marry because a culture expects it or it's safer. I married a second time at twenty-five, this time to a Wall Street litigation lawyer (and the marriage lasted for twenty-six years). I thought I was settled for life.

Only two years later, however, tragedy rocked my world. When I was twenty-seven and working at my dream job, writing the "Intelligencer" column at *New York Magazine*, my beautiful, brilliant mom was diagnosed with terminal cancer. She was fifty-four. And just like that, my mom, adversary and unwanted mentor, surprisingly turned out to be my whole world. She had been my best, if complicated, friend. I knew that nothing mattered but being with her during her illness. I quit my dream job to spend every day with my mom at Sloan Kettering for two years, writing my second novel, playing the guitar, and willing my mother to survive. I also wanted to have a little girl to keep her alive, or replace her, when she passed. Wishful thinking.

My first novel, not at all biographical, about an American girl who marries an English lord, had a complicated life getting accepted and was rejected by several publishers before I gave up and shelved It. Editors didn't think the characters were likable. I can't imagine why.

My father was a trustee of New York Hospital, so the doctors did everything they could to keep my mother alive, and so did I. I didn't want to be a failure in her eyes, so this time I wrote a novel about a female writer at *New York Magazine,* and I also had a baby. Both were successful enterprises. My son, Alex, was born three weeks after my mother died.

The mother I didn't want to tell me what to do or how to be, who was disappointed by all my life choices, passed away when I was at Bernstein's a block away having a quick deli lunch. I was left with a new baby and a Book of the Month Club Alternate Selection, achievements that my wishful thinking had secretly believed would keep her alive. My adored, feared, and disapproving mom did not live to see those achievements or to hold her grandson. Worse, now that I was free to be whoever I wanted to be, all I wanted was to have her back.

When Alex was born, I vowed to be the nurturing, accepting, tolerant, domestic diva that my mother hadn't been. But life was challenging for me with no mom, mother-in-law, or sister to encourage, support, or help me, even for an hour. Like millions of moms who don't have relatives in whom they can confide, I was alone with no female ally. And I had high expectations for myself. I thought of myself as an experiment.

Could I be a successful author and full-time mom at the same time? Nope. Life intervenes. Alex was a wonderful baby and extraordinary child, staggering around and saying, "Hi there," to everyone at the grocery store at ten months. Soon he was talking in full sentences and was an expert on dinosaurs and reading by the age of three. Still, I missed my mom every single day and more wishful thinking encouraged me to have a girl to replace her. I didn't have the support system for another baby, but I was determined to get pregnant and have a girl.

Sadly, I had a fifth-month miscarriage when Alex was two. Only a few months later, I needed emergency surgery to remove an ovary. Emotionally and physically exhausted, I felt my only chance for a daughter had passed. It's hard to write about this even now, because women weren't supposed to show weakness or pain back then. I don't like to even say the words, "I felt so alone and smothered I could hardly breathe." In fact, I dreamed about not being able to breathe and suffered from asthma.

Heartbroken, I didn't dare talk to the four males in my life about how much I missed having my mom and would miss having a daughter. My mom hadn't cooked for me but brought me bags of groceries and meat from her butcher every Friday when I was a young, working wife. You couldn't talk about miscarriage, grief, or unhappiness in those days. It wasn't allowed. I had everything, after all, and I had to keep up appearances. During this time, I kept looking for my mother everywhere. Mothers and daughters on the street brought me to tears nearly every day. Without a mom, I didn't have anyone to share my feelings of loss, my concerns about my relationship, or my yearning to have a little girl. And then the miracle happened a year later, Lindsey was born. I didn't know until the moment of Lindsey's birth that she was she. Back then, there was no early gender reveal for one of nature's best surprises.

You mothers know the joy of having a baby girl to love and pamper and adore. I was elated, and the pampering began. When Lindsey was born, I carried on the togetherness tradition and even gave her an L name so she would always be close to me. Our names, of course, confuse everyone to this day. Lindsey, Leslie. Leslie Lindsey. Which was which? Remember my grandmother and mother's names: Esther and Elinor? I didn't know I was repeating their tradition. My language of love was food and music and clothes.

It's hard to imagine now, but I knitted sweaters, sewed Lindsey's dresses, and cut both Lindsey's and Alex's hair. We had high tea every day with homemade scones and strawberry jam, apple bread, and cucumber sandwiches. Weak tea and lots of hot milk. On weekends I made crepes. Alex wouldn't eat orange food, and my husband, Edmund, wouldn't eat chicken. Every day, I was like a restaurant, cooking a different meal for each picky eater. Very different from my own mom and more like my caretaking grandmother. I was very big with books and toys and games as my mother hadn't approved of possessions or the mess that children's toys bring to a home.

Lindsey was independent from the start. She wanted to do whatever her brother did. At six, she hated being left behind when her nine-year-old brother left for camp. The following year she insisted on going away for two whole months. She was seven and the baby of the camp. Was she homesick? Not for a minute. Lindsey was an adventurer and warrior, and she had a powerful will that couldn't be denied—still does.

When my children were little, I persisted in writing even when my stories, novels, and plays were rejected by every theater and publisher in the Western world. I could wallpaper an apartment with my rejection letters. Writing was not a voluntary choice for me. I had something to say, and even when no one liked what I was saying or the way I was saying it, I kept trying. Often, I would feel the rejection was just too much, and I wanted to end my suffering by ending my life. I would take to my bed for maybe twenty-four hours. Then it was time to prepare dinner. And I moved on.

I always balanced working on a book or a play or a short story that might end in rejection with something I could accomplish, something I was good at: cooking, music, making my home beautiful. No matter how deep your sadness, beauty of your own making can lift your spirits. Some of that in me may be the pioneer spirit of my Nebraska pioneer ancestors. I'm always going to plant a seed or a tree, or an herb, or a flower and watch it grow. Mothers who use their creativity in domestic arts find great joy sharing their gifts with their family and community or use their ingenuity to develop commerce based on their ideas and talents.

As a writer, I kept trying new formats of writing and ultimately became the playwright and bestselling author I had wanted to be. But the question I had set for myself was, Could I be a great mom and author at the same time? The answer: nope. How many of us can transition well into the high school years? For Lindsey, a different kind of mother was needed as middle school loomed. This happens to many of us mothers. My personality type of nonconfrontational and people-pleasing meant I was too laissez-faire to be a stern enough mom for teens. It's not natural to transition from caretaking and guiding to letting children learn consequences, self-regulation, and ways to manage painful events, the traumas that happen to us all. And I didn't know I needed to make that transition.

Lindsey began to falter in seventh grade. Moving from a sheltered uniform-wearing, strongly supportive grade school to a demanding and largely unsupervised prep school, Lindsey entered a world where school support was lacking and multiple traumas awaited. This also is common even today. Children are taught play and kindness, creativity, and tolerance in grammar school, and then the reverse happens in middle and high school. Everyone is surprised when teens are depressed and traumatized and at risk for addiction and suicide.

Lindsey's experience decades ago mirrors that of millions of daughters today who struggle with image, emotional issues, and family dysfunction no one dares to talk about, much less address. In short, Lindsey did not have an easy adolescence, and I suffered with her. In a meeting about college applications, her dean told me that she had used drugs at school. No one had reported any incidents to me. Shocking. Would it happen now? I don't know. Fancy prep schools can keep their secrets, too.

Lindsey had not been safe in her New York high school, but she hadn't confided in me. Without knowing she was a drug user, I had let her go abroad for a semester in Rome and then summer school at Cambridge University in England. I did not know my daughter was trying to escape from trauma and pain. How would I know this if no one let me in on the secret? Teens are sneaky, and I was trusting. I have heard from hundreds of mothers who say they did not know that their daughters were drug users. If we don't ask the right questions, we won't know until it's too late.

When Lindsey was moody and weird and touchy and mean, I couldn't tell if this was classic teen behavior or signs of a real problem. What are Lindsey's personality and emotional styles, and how do they match mine? Not well sometimes. Lindsey has a stubborn streak that can be impossible to penetrate, and she has no aversion to conflict when it comes to me. Quite the contrary, she used conflict and confrontation to make me succumb to her will. She could win an academy award with all the drama she created. Funny, my mother also called me a drama queen. How many mothers are afraid of opposing their daughters? If you don't have a solid backbone, you can be bent like a pretzel. Lindsey had a strong will and the perseverance to do whatever she wanted to do. These are good qualities that can also make a person difficult and stubborn to a fault.

Despite Lindsey's lackadaisical approach (to be kind) to her studies and partying ways in high school, she was accepted at Johns Hopkins University, where her brother had gone. Alex had already graduated when she arrived. There, in her freshman year, the real trouble began. At Hopkins, there was no supervision and no faculty engagement in student well-being. In case you didn't know, more students die on college campuses every year from assaults and incidents involving drugs and alcohol than perish every year in the military. A shocking number of more than 5,000 college students die of drug and alcohol-related incidents every year. Just try to find those statistics. Not surprisingly, most go unreported. Try to tell some mothers to educate their daughters about alcohol. They don't think sexual assault or alcohol poisoning could happen to their daughters. College is supposed to be fun, after all.

Quaaludes, ecstasy, and prescription pills were among the party drugs that Lindsey struggled with most, and everything about her changed. One day she called me to say she needed to go somewhere to detox for the weekend. She had overdosed, and this wasn't the first time. Here's where our story of recovery begins. Lindsey went to rehab in Tucson a few days later and then to aftercare in Los Angeles. Then, she insisted on returning to Hopkins to graduate on time. Lindsey made it through college on sheer grit, receiving a degree in art history, and two years later she received her MA in communications from New York University.

Like many recovering addicts, however, she had lost some crucial emotional and life skills development. She was not the same person as she had been. Concentration was difficult. Her self-esteem was profoundly damaged, and it was hard for us as a mother and daughter to find a feeling of peace or any kind of common purpose. The trust and innocence were gone, and jockeying for power and control took its place. This is a very common relationship result where there is drug and alcohol addiction in the family during crucial teen and young adult years.

What was surprising to me was Lindsey's career choice. She got a job as an assistant editor at Random House, and it was her turn to go where I had gone. Writing is a scary path as anyone will tell you. My mother (and father) did everything she could to stop me. Most writers do not make much of a living, and only a few authors fulfill their dreams. It's a grind and a heartbreak, so the path is not one to undertake without a lot of resolve.

All published writing is a matter of taste and timing. Editors are not going to like everything you do. Your work may come before its time or too late to be fashionable. Quality is rarely a criterion. Being likable, and salable, and having the right timing are always factors out of every writer's control. Could Lindsey endure the inevitable rejections? Could she write and rewrite projects a dozen times to learn the trade? Turns out she could, and she did.

Where did Lindsey get her drive for achievement and unwillingness to give up? Where did my mother get hers? Where did I get mine? Daughters who don't feel good enough or appreciated just for being themselves crave affirmation and approval, especially if they feel they have disappointed and failed.

Lindsey moved to Los Angeles and wrote screenplays and TV pilots, developing her writing just the way I had so many years earlier. I told her no experience is wasted, every step and misstep are opportunities for growth. Lindsey married and divorced a short time later, just as I had. Her drive to get healthy kept her going. And here, Lindsey became the leader in our relationship. She had some wisdom that I lacked and brought me into recovery with her, which launched our advocacy work. I hadn't wanted to become my mother, but my daughter became my mentor. And I became my mother, after all.

Lindsey's Story

I used to joke that I peaked at birth. I was born in New York City on the afternoon of December 22. My grandfather Milton was with Frank Sinatra in Palm

Springs for Christmas. As a nice surprise, Frank called the hospital to congratulate Leslie on my birth. Frank Sinatra's calling my mom caused major excitement among the nurses at New York Hospital. His call made my birth memorable. While I don't remember the incident, I could say it set the tone for my young life, meaning I never felt like the most important person in the room. Call it generational low self-esteem. There were always VIPs and big personalities around, and we all kowtowed to someone. In any case, I felt awed and in the presence of greatness most of the time as I was growing up. Being surrounded by greatness is not the most empowering or self-confidence-building way to grow up. Many children of the rich and famous feel this way.

It didn't help that I was painfully shy as a child. Twenty percent of humans have a genetic tendency to be naturally shy, and I'm in that group. Just taking up space in the world was uncomfortable for me. I was the little girl who hid in my mother's skirt, who trembled with fear that I'd be called on in class, even when I knew the answers. Visiting relatives would find me hiding under the bed. What was I hiding from? What was I so scared of from the moment I was born? I've heard many other people in recovery talk about that painful shyness and fear from the start, so maybe it's a component of alcoholism. We can argue all day about where mental illness and addiction come from, but I flew the red flags from my very beginning.

As a child who struggled to feel comfortable, fantasy became my first addiction. Books, games, and toys could keep me busy for days—anything I could get my hands on that would change reality. I've always had a strong wish to escape reality and a vivid imagination, so I kept myself busy. The stuffed animals that covered my bed became friends once we were alone, and I could lose myself playing with anything; sometimes even the boxes the expensive gifts came in would be my entertainment, confounding my parents as the expensive doll would be set aside. I devoured books back then and once introduced to television, loved that too.

When I was little, my mom was my world. We were together all the time, and if she left even for an hour, I sobbed. We were like cohorts, and my goal in life was to get her approval and be in her good graces. That goal persists today if that says anything about how powerful mother-daughter dynamics are. When I was three, I would see her books, or her name, on the cover of a magazine in the grocery store. I couldn't read yet, but I knew my mom's name when I saw it.

"That's my mom!" I would announce to all shoppers.

I was proud of her. She seemed to be the queen of the world, and we had an incredible life. We traveled, we shopped, we had high tea. It was the 1980s and early '90s, and life was different. You didn't know everything about everyone—meaning life was private. Social media wasn't a part of our lives. My mom was an author, not an actress, so she had status, but our faces weren't everywhere. We didn't show off who we were or what we had to anyone who wasn't in our circle. We just existed in a very pretty, protected bubble; there were many wonderful days and happy memories.

My childhood was mixed with blessings and tragedies, and I'll get into it later. I don't want to spill all the beans now. In overview, there were wonderful, magical times—vacations, holidays, family events, and lots of luxury. My mom and I knew how to have a good time. There were trips to Europe and time in our houses on Martha's Vineyard, Upper Brookville on Long Island, and the West Coast of Florida. Even though family wasn't always easy, my mom and I always had a closeness. Maybe it's a mother-daughter thing, maybe it's a girl thing, but even when times were rough, we were close.

I was close with my father and brother as well, but it was different. My father was born in New Jersey and raised in Houston, Texas, in the fifties. My dad is a genius, which is a blessing and a curse. He skipped grades, studied at Tulane University and Science Politique in Paris. He was accepted to the Tulane Medical School in his junior year of college but chose the law instead. He was offered the Root-Tilden scholarship at NYU Law, and that's how New York became his home. My dad is multitalented and can sculpt and paint as well as he can practice law at one of the best law firms in Manhattan. On the other hand, there were struggles on the emotional side. I didn't feel we understood each other when I was growing up, even though I'm just like him in so many ways. We failed to connect until I was much older. But I love my dad dearly, and we have found our way over the years. That's the important takeaway.

Speaking of bad times, there was turbulence when our parents were fighting, we siblings were struggling, and dysfunctional dynamics often created emotional chaos. I had two passionate parents who weren't afraid to share their feelings and didn't have a lot of tools for self-soothing or de-escalation. There were terrible fights between my mom and dad, though I truly have no idea what they were fighting about. There were also awful blowups with mom and dad and me and Alex. Alex could have a temper and went through his own share of growing pains. He battled with my parents through high school and college. I became rebellious at times and could be incredibly difficult to deal with or parent. We didn't know how to be kind and compassionate to one another. As a result, we all suffered.

Funny thing about memory, I don't remember all the bad times anymore. Only the good times are imprinted in my brain. When terrible things happened, my mom used to promise me, "This will just be a story someday, something that happened in your life a long time ago. You won't feel devastated about it anymore." She was right about that and much more. Some of her other parental instincts weren't so on the money, but no one's perfect.

The most unexpected thing was that I would be sick in many ways, both physically and emotionally. No mom is ever prepared for that. Reflecting on it now, of course, any mom would want to protect her child from the dangers and stigma of mental illness and addiction. There still are a multitude of consequences associated with both physical and emotional problems. When I was a child, people didn't talk about anything; we certainly didn't air our dirty laundry. Back in the '80s, '90s, and early millennium years, it always felt as if we were hiding something about me or looking the other way. While it was in these decades that mental health awareness became popular, it was still taboo for us to admit anything publicly. Don't tell anyone, or it's not that bad. These are the things we say to keep balance, to stay afloat. Often, they aren't the right thing to say; the words turn into beliefs about ourselves and one another.

Before the age of ten, I couldn't take a trip without ending up in an emergency room somewhere with fevers and infections. The regular use of antibiotics wore down my already impaired immune system, creating a vicious cycle. I also suffered from anxiety and developed an addiction disorder around the age of thirteen that would be the foundation of troubled behavior for over a decade. This is not uncommon—according to the CDC (Centers for Disease Control and Prevention) one in three teens will experience an anxiety disorder. I lost my grandfather when I was twelve, a childhood sweetheart, and a few friends in my junior high and high school years.

Several other disturbing events helped to destabilize me. Tragedy and trauma turned me into an inconsolable teen who went looking for relief in all the wrong places.

I became a club kid addict by seventeen. It wasn't hard in Manhattan. I had a fake ID for anywhere that asked. But often they didn't ask. At that time, it was easier for me to buy club drugs than alcohol. Ketamine, ecstasy, and cocaine were easily procured in the bathroom of any bar or nightclub. These were the days when the Meatpacking District still sold meat. You'd leave the Tunnel nightclub in the early morning and be greeted by the scent of rotting meat. What a time to be alive.

There's another piece of this story, but it will only get a little airtime here. I have an older brother who is one of my favorite people in the world. I idolized him from day one. I thought he was the coolest person in the world, and I followed him and his friends around for a decade. Sure, at times we fought like cats and dogs like any brother and sister. Well, I'm not sure the games we played with kitchen knives were normal, but our mom was writing about serial killers in the background. However, most of the time we had each other's backs. We ran around Manhattan in the '90s, getting into trouble, but it was so different back then. The trouble we got into didn't end in a fentanyl overdose or crashed cars. It usually ended with a friend throwing up in the kitchen sink and clogging it or a family heirloom getting damaged.

Despite all that, I did shockingly well in high school, graduated from Johns Hopkins University, and received my master's degree from NYU. I worked for A-list companies (including Random House and Sotheby's, well, the Floater Program, which was the entry level training program that sent Sotheby's candidates to every department to learn about all forms of art). Underneath it all I was a mess. I was missing that foundation of healthy self-esteem and even being aware of what I wanted. Addiction had robbed me of the years when most teens and young adults figure out who they are and what they want in life. Because I didn't really know who I was or what I wanted, I did things I thought my parents (particularly my mom) would approve of, such as attending a prestigious university or working for a great publishing house. Of course, nothing worked out well because I wasn't traveling on the right path for me.

A marriage in my twenties didn't make me better. Going to rehab for the second time and getting a divorce soon after didn't make me better. Becoming a screenwriter didn't make me better. I had two decades of messy life before I was desperate enough to do all the work it takes to grow up. That is often how recovery works.

With my mom, there came a time when I blamed her for every unwise decision I had made in my life. Those included the marriage I wasn't ready for, the promotion or destruction of other questionable relationships, work/career issues, emotional issues, financial loss of everything I had, and a few others that will come out along the way. Did my mom play a part in some of those decisions? Turns out, it doesn't matter. But by the time I reached my thirties I was enraged. Like smoke coming out of my ears enraged. We'd had decades of unspoken feelings about each other and family issues before it all boiled over and left us both feeling broken and betrayed.

Truth be told, I had been warned by a sober friend that my mom and I were codependent and a ticking time bomb, but I didn't believe it. Codependent means you lack healthy emotional boundaries with each other. If my mom was upset, I was upset and vice versa. For the record, healthy people don't take on other people's emotions, and they aren't reliant upon the happiness or approval of another person.

We will explore more about codependency later.

At that time, I couldn't see the writing on the wall. Even though I was literally living in my mom's home and working for her, for some reason that did not faze me. It's an odd thing to think back and write about all this, which was by far the toughest time of my life, when my life today is so peaceful and recovery centric. Don't believe for one second that people don't change. We do. Some of us have the painful but necessary task of becoming totally new people. Everything blew up for me. I had a nervous breakdown in my early thirties. A romantic breakup, a family fight, financial mistakes, spinal surgery, a move, and I was done. This was all after I had gotten sober.

The miracle was, as difficult and mildly insane as I was back then, I was willing to listen to mental health professionals. So when things with my mom really took an unpleasant turn when I was thirty-five (yes, we were both adults, but I'll speak for myself in saying in age only), I sought the guidance of professionals and did the work that was recommended. The first advice I got was to leave my home and my mom and cut contact with her. Yeah, take that in. This is what's so important to understand. We had unwittingly hurt each other and couldn't move forward together. To find myself I had to be on my own. For a while.

For us, codependency, enmeshment, resentment, and emotional warfare were quite enough to create a dynamic that we had to break to rebuild. It was hard. No, it was brutal. It's the only time in my recovery I was medicated for suicidal depression. Yet, because I made that difficult decision and endured all the consequences, and there were many, I got better. Like all the way better. The last ten years of my life have been a book in and of itself. I wouldn't trade them for anything, but my thirties were coal-to-diamond years— years of pressure and pain.

For me, being on my own without family support made me a survivor. Against many odds, I could make it on my own. Thousands of people in recovery learn this lesson. They can do it. I don't wish for others to find out they can swim by jumping into the deep end without the benefit of swimming lessons. Not everyone wants to recover from codependency by doing what my mom and I did, and not everyone can. But if you are in a dark place, know this—recovery can solidify you in ways nothing else will. If you are willing to do the work, you can come out shining like a diamond.

So what did my life look like when I left my mom? I had messed up across the board. I found myself a New York City trust-fund kid without a trust fund or a family. I was divorced, alienated from most of my family, and all alone on the other side of the country. I had moved to Los Angeles where my recovery journey began. Suddenly there was no mom to fight with, no one to blame for my situation other than myself, and I had more fear than I could bear at times. In those early years of my "life recovery," I'd wake up at 4 or 5 a.m. with my heart racing, truly worried about my future. I endured a couple of straight-up abusive employers, financial instability, depression, loneliness, dating nightmares, and was helped by many twelve-step programs.

No matter what happened, I always did the work. I attended whatever group to which I was referred. With time, distance, and therapy, I got honest with myself about who I was and what had happened. I could see my part. I may be self-centered, but I'm not a toxic narcissist. After a while, I felt nothing but sadness. The rage dissipated, the resentment was worked away, and I felt something was missing terribly from my life. I didn't have sisters or cousins geographically close. My grandparents were all deceased by my adulthood, I never knew my grandmother Elinor. For me, I needed my mom back.

It's easy to feel lasting hurt at our moms for not giving us whatever it is we think we needed. But, in my experience, none of that matters when deep down inside all you want is her love and approval. Maybe it's there, and you can't see it. Maybe it's there, and you can't hear it. Sometimes losing your way with your mom is no one's fault. What matters is finding your way back if you can. My mom and I are a mother and daughter who adored each other from day one yet struggled for decades to keep the peace between us. That's an understatement. At times, we armed ourselves with nuclear warheads, ready to launch at any moment. I'm sure had we known we were traumatizing each other for life, we would have acted differently, but we didn't know how to reach each other.

When something so fundamental as the mother-daughter relationship is out of whack, many of us will try to compensate in other ways, but it will never be the same. Receiving love and approval from your mother is the core of everything. If you desperately crave that love and don't feel it or can't get it, ultimately all these other things (insert boyfriend, money, career success, being thin enough) will fall flat.

By the time my mom and I got back in touch, almost four years had passed. For four years I lived in Los Angeles, completely disconnected. Mom hadn't known where I was or how to contact me. Looking back, it was way too extreme, and that's why I believe this book is so important. So here I am, sharing this private and painful journey because I believe moms and daughters need a voice for hope. A voice that says, it's okay to be in a bad place and not get along with your mom. It's okay that you screamed at each other and said horrible things. It's okay if you're on opposite ends of the spectrum about style, politics, pets, finances, children, and on and on. We must learn how to treat each other with respect—whether we're selfish, codependents, alcoholics, depressives, control freaks, or impossible in other ways. Now, obviously, if your mom/daughter is dangerous, you need to take care of yourself.

There's another book on what to do if you and your mom should be separated forever, but that's not my book to write. For me, anger was killing me slowly from the inside and the outside. If you have an addiction disorder, eating disorder, or really any other destructive behavioral issue (I'm also looking at you, self-harm), you will not get better if you are angry or holding onto rage. It will come out in all those ways, and you'll be stuck in a cycle of hatred and shame. You don't want that. I didn't want it. I wanted to fix everything that was making me miserable.

My hope is we can give you some insight into this dynamic and the most common issues we fight about so you can find your way in a softer, gentler manner. If you can't, the hard way of detachment and separation works, too. Whatever your choice, there is recovery if you want it. When my mom and I came back together, we had both done so much work that for a while we didn't talk much about what caused the breakup. We had both learned to listen rather than interrupt and insist on being right. Pain had humbled us both, and we only wanted peace.

This time, we would follow new rules and do what was necessary to make peace possible and lasting. One of the greatest triumphs of my recovery is that I went from a deeply unhappy, troubled person who was not reliable, or likable at times, to a mostly happy person who has learned how to manage emotional issues, communication, and relationships. This was a transformative change in every way that turned life from a black-and-white drama to a colorful story filled with love and light. So I want to open this book with the message that if you've found your way here, this most precious relationship is not everything you want it to be. Do you have a spark of hope that things between you and your mom can improve? I'm here to tell you, they can.

Exactly what true harmony will look like in your family may differ from ours because there is no one size that fits all solutions for relationships. If you have a criminal or toxic narcissist in your family, you may never have a happy holiday photo. But do not let that discourage you! You can find peace and understanding even if you have a complicated mom. If you have been, at times, a complicated daughter, you can be loved again. How do I know this? Well, get comfortable and take a deep breath because we're about to travel to places that may be sad to read about. But if you can relate, you'll find some clarity. With clarity comes solutions, and solutions bring recovery.

Think About This

Hearing the story of a mom who didn't feel as good as her mom and then a daughter who also felt less than her mom, you see that insecurity can run as a pattern through generations. When a grandma and a mom are focused on achievement, daughters can feel abandoned and alone. If a mom has lost her own mom and can't talk about her anguish and struggles to anyone, her daughter may not be able to connect with her pain and find common ground or compassion for her. Add shyness and anxiety to the picture, and you have a recipe for conflict and more anguish.

Here we can start thinking about empathy for the first time. Remember how Leslie talked about the release of getting something out on paper and being surprised when reading it later? Sometimes things you didn't know you felt come out and surprise you. Also, when you read what you wrote you may no longer feel the same things months or years from now. That's what we hope for when you start journaling about your mother-daughter relationship here. You may feel angry or hurt now, but let's see if you've changed at the end of your writing journey.

TIME TO JOURNAL

Here's the fun part. So many people we know have told us they have a book in them but don't know how to get it out. Here is your opportunity to start telling your story. Grab the journal of your choice and a pen. We're setting out on an expedition of self-discovery and storytelling. At the end of each chapter, we're going to give you the writing prompts to explore your feelings about your mother/daughter regarding each subject. This is purely for you (whether you are a mother or a daughter). You don't have to share your insights with anybody. If you and your daughter or mother are reading together and journaling separately, only share the positive responses with each other.

You might want to add some thoughts about Grandma or Great-Grandma if you've been fortunate enough to know her. In any case, always try to balance your negative feelings with some positive ones. Force yourself to remember some good things about your mom/daughter, especially if you think you hate her or believe she's wrong or unreasonable right now. The purpose of journaling and exploring your past is not to feel enraged by what your mother/daughter did/does to you but rather to find commonalities to your experiences and bring awareness to the inevitable misunderstandings and misconceptions that arise along life's bumpy road. Remember, your mother was influenced by her mother, and she by the grandmother who came before her.

Four Proven Benefits of Journaling

EASE STRESS

If you're new to journaling, don't worry about getting it right or having something meaningful to say. A few minutes of marshalling your anxious thoughts into sentences takes the annoyance from whatever irks you out of your head and releases it onto the page. For example: "Today it rained, and I lost my keys," is enough to tell a story.

SELF-REFLECTION FOR PERSONAL GROWTH

Following our journal prompts will help you develop greater awareness of who you are, what your values are, how you affect others, and how they affect you. You will see yourself from different perspectives and learn ways to improve your communication skills and behavior.

MANAGE UNCOMFORTABLE EMOTIONS

Many girls and women are taught to bury their emotions and act nice. Journaling about hurt and angry, confusing, or conflicting feelings will help you begin to navigate through pain to healing. Journaling about your emotions gives you a voice for change.

LIVE YOUR BEST LIFE

Writing a few lines every day about the little things that bring you pleasure join mindfulness and gratitude, two essential components of happiness. Your senses of touch, sight, sound, taste, and smell are just one example of things you can notice and write about.

JOURNAL PROMPTS

1. In a paragraph or two tell your mother's story. Who is she; where did she come from? What was her life like? How was she as a mom?

2. In a paragraph or two, tell your story. Who are you? Where did you come from? What was your life like growing up?

3. Can you give a history of your relationship with your mom/daughter?

4. What is your relationship with your mom/daughter now?

5. What about your mom/daughter makes you mad, sad, unhappy?

6. How would you like your relationship with your mom/daughter to be different?

CHAPTER 3

Mother/Daughter Emotional and Personality Styles

Let's look at the collection of personality and emotional styles you and your mother/daughter may not have in common. Who are you really? You may think you're the sweetest, kindest love bunny in the world but act that way only to your pets or grandchildren. To everyone else you may seem mean, opinionated, and demanding. In fact, you can be both without seeing your own other side.

On the other hand, you may think you're a bad mom because your reasonable expectations for family members are met with disdain and rage. For example, no one in the family wants to help with the chores, grow up, or be kind to you. It's the family dynamic. You aren't supported, and family members, including your daughter, may make it appear to be your fault. Unpleasant family members projecting their feelings on you is one of the most painful things on earth. Mothers and daughters (and other family members), as we have said before, are not always a great fit and not always kind and loving.

We don't always see, or hear, ourselves the way others do. The person you project may be off-putting or seem nicer than you really are. You may be copying a tone of voice or taught to act a certain way to be that doesn't reflect your true self. We're complicated beings. That gets us to the question of how we become the way we are. What influences us most? Is it our environment, our mothers and fathers, and where we live? Or is our psychology and behavior genetically based? The question of nature versus nurture has been debated by psychologists for a hundred years, and the answer is complicated. The input of your parents and environment both influence you, and so does your genetic makeup.

Regardless of how your unique package of qualities developed, your personality and emotional styles define and reveal you. They also establish how you're going to relate to your mom/daughter. Let's start with basic qualities. Hippocrates was the first to define human qualities, or personality types, based on his theory of the humors in the body in Classical Greece around 390 BC. In Hippocrates's words there are four temperaments: sanguine, choleric, melancholic, and phlegmatic.

- The "**sanguine** type" represents social usefulness.
- The "**choleric** type" is characterized by extroversion, being outgoing.
- The "**melancholic** type" is characterized by an analytical and detailed-oriented presentation (obsessive compulsive, anyone?).
- The "**phlegmatic** type" is relaxed and easygoing.

How do these descriptions translate to you and your mom/ daughter in today's world? Not that helpful? A new Johns Hopkins study (2018) defines the four personality types in a different way as "average," "reserved," "self-centered," and "role model." These new personality types are based on the traits of open-mindedness, extraversion, neuroticism, agreeableness, and conscientiousness.

- The "**average**" type is defined as people who are high in neuroticism (a tendency toward negative emotions including anxiety, depression, and volatility) as well as being low in open-mindedness. At the same time the average person, while harboring self-doubt, may appear social and outgoing, even self-confident. Most people fall into this category, which is also characterized by being opinionated and closed-minded. Are you surprised to hear that women often fit into this category? Do you recognize the duality of being anxious yet social, full of self-doubt yet appearing self-confident? Keep in mind the close-minded quality you may recognize in yourself or your mom/daughter. It's when you open your mind to new ideas that you also open your heart to love, compassion, and forgiveness.

- The "**reserved**" type is defined as people who are high in agreeableness and low in extraversion and neuroticism. You know the type. Quiet, often polite and thoughtful, but not very outgoing. Reserved people often prefer their own company, and you may not know what they are thinking and feeling.

- The "**self-centered**" type is defined as people who are high in extraversion, yet below average in openness, agreeableness, and conscientiousness. The size of this population typically increases with age. Self-centered people are the ones who dominate conversations, share all their opinions about everything, and want and expect things to go their way. Self-centered people don't see other people's points of view.

- The **"role model"** type is defined as those who are low in neuroticism and high on open-mindedness, extraversion, agreeableness, and conscientiousness. Apparently, this is the group you want to be associated with. They can see other people's perspectives and are empathetic and fair. They often have a high level of emotional self-awareness.

The Hopkins study also reveals that people's personality types often change as they mature. Teenagers tend to be more self-centered, while older people tend to be more conscientious and agreeable. As you can see here, only basic personality types are defined. Each human, however, has a mix of personality traits and characteristics. No one is perfect in every way. For our purposes, we're going to offer some commonly used descriptive terms to which we can all relate. These are just a few characteristics that may help to define your personality and emotional style. You will have several of the traits and characteristics listed here, and they may change depending on who you're interacting with as well as your age.

Your Mothering Style

- **Laissez-faire:** You don't worry about or enforce rules, and your children walk all over you.
- **Just call on me:** Whatever they need, you're there. BFFs (best friends forever; you wish and sometimes are).
- **My way or the highway:** You're the expert on everything. Controller extraordinaire.

- **You follow the six characteristics of a functional family:**
  (1) Honest communication, active listening, and healthy
  exchanges; (2) respect; (3) acceptance; (4) tolerance and love
  for vulnerable members of the family; (5) collaboration and
  involvement; and (6) healthy coping skills.

The happiest and most functional families with the best relationships have the six characteristics listed above in common. Honest communication is at the top of the list. But having honest communication is difficult when different personalities and emotional styles clash. We're going to look at who we really are and how our personality and emotional styles can interfere with healthy relationships. These are not official psychological terms, just a way for you to think about yourself and your loved ones. First, let's look at your mom's emotional style. You have adapted to her emotional makeup in one way or another, or perhaps in many ways.

Your Mom's Personality Style

- **Cool and detached:** She's great in emergencies but can be distant and difficult to reach emotionally. She's busy and maybe a working mom with lots of responsibilities.
- **Roller coaster:** Her disposition is like that of a teenager. She has ten moods a day, led by feelings of the moment rather than thinking things through. She can be fun but also irresponsible. You never know where you are with her.
- **Hysteric and anxious:** Everything's a drama. She's attention-getting, always in crisis mode. She's fearful about everything, worried about all the things that can go wrong, indecisive, and can be paralytic and stifling.
- **Empathic:** She will always feel your moods and will always work to make you feel better, often to your detriment and her

own. Codependents and enablers often fit in this category.

- **Perfectionist, self-righteous know-it-all:** She's hovering and intrusive and will always treat everyone as eight-year-olds making mistakes. She has the answer to every question and won't hear any other point of view; you can never win.
- **Balanced:** She's a real grown-up, rolls with the punches, can analyze situations and make sensible, practical decisions based on the facts, not emotions or bias. She knows when to back off and hold her criticism.

When we look at the basic personality types, naturally we would like to think of ourselves as fitting in the open-minded leader's category. Well, Lindsey and Leslie would, anyway. Looking at the emotional styles above, however, we get a more nuanced picture of our mom, the person who shaped us.

Isn't it also interesting how mothers and daughters can have wildly different personality styles? Our friend Jennifer is extremely reserved. She works hard and is successful, but she's the least flashy and self-promoting person we've ever met. Her hippy mother, Susie, on the other hand, can't walk into a function without making a scene. Between her wild clothes, boisterous personality, and tendency to put Jennifer on the spot, Susie is a constant source of anxiety for Jennifer.

Leslie Shares Her Mother's Parenting Style

My mom was cool and detached. She didn't let on what she was feeling. You couldn't tell if she was angry or pleased. The only way I knew she was mad or disappointed in me was when she gave me the silent treatment. I took my teacher's pen off her desk in first grade and brought it home for lunch break. I think I just meant to borrow it for a few hours. When my mom saw it, however, she knew it wasn't mine. She didn't say a word but put me in the car, drove back to school, and stood there, completely silent, until I returned the pen and apologized. No further discussion of the matter.

In my new school, in third grade, after I had returned from a year in Europe, I removed a yo-yo from someone else's cubby and put it in mine. My own possessions did not include a yo-yo, much less a fancy one that lit up like this one did. Here's an example of a child not being able to ask a mom for a toy because she would refuse. I don't think my mom ever visited a toy store. I've said it before; my mom was a fan of books but not toys. When a class search was initiated for the missing yo-yo, my older brother was summoned from fifth grade. He was asked whether the yo-yo in question was mine. He announced to the teacher and the entire class that I was a thief. This proved that I was a poor liar, worse thief, and that my brother would never in this lifetime have my back.

This time my mom did not participate in my humiliation. The yo-yo was returned to its owner, and I never stole anything again. My brother had ratted me out, and my mom didn't say a thing about it. My mom simply could not discuss stealing with me. The whole issue was too frightening. What if she were raising a thief? She'd neglect it until it went away. Sounds like a good plan? My mom was anxious about everything. Seems a contradiction? Her boldness, her shyness, her determination to make something of herself, her silence in the face of problems, her reserve. Her passion for social justice. We humans are complex creatures.

As we began writing this chapter, I wrote a glowing account of myself as the kind, compassionate, loving, and supportive mom I thought I was. I believed every word. When Lindsey read it, she told me in fact I had been closed-minded, thought I knew everything, and could be cold as ice. What? Sweet, gentle, loving me? Moms, how many of you see yourself the way your daughter sees you? This is the reason journaling is so useful. Writing the book made us look at ourselves in a new way. In any case, my mom was hard to reach and not an oversharer or people pleaser. As a child and young adult, I struggled to get her approval, and it was never forthcoming.

I believed that my mom didn't think I was smart or talented or pretty enough to conquer the world or do much of anything, but she would never dream of saying so. And I don't know if that feeling of mine is true. What I know is that I left all my stories that were rejected by the *New Yorker* (one editor wrote nine long letters to me over the years about the lack of feeling in my work) by my mom's special chair, but she never read any of them. I never knew why.

A few months ago, Fanny, my mom's French dressmaker who taught me to sew when I was twelve and is now ninety-four, revealed to me that my mom had told her just before she died that my work simply wasn't ready yet. It was an eye-opening clue. She didn't consider me a failure, just not ready yet to be published. So here it is almost fifty years later, and I have an endorsement of sorts. See why what moms do and say is so important?

My mom often advised me to be anything but ordinary. But what does ordinary even mean? The Gordons weren't an ordinary family, and no family really is. Every family is struggling to survive and thrive even when wealthy and seemingly perfect. Some families have more difficulties than others. Happy families are connected and caring, but silence doesn't necessarily mean you aren't loved. While my mom let me stumble along acquiring experience and information in my own way, she also let me figure things out for myself. She didn't tell me I was a good or bad writer because frankly she didn't know. Her hands-off emotional style made me hunger for emotional connection. I felt alone—and never good enough to be extraordinary.

Now Let's Look at Some Daughter Personality Styles

Here are just a few characteristics that may help to define your personality as a daughter. You have many of these traits and characteristics, and they may change depending on who you're interacting with as well as your age. Different experiences and healing from adverse experiences can help you change and have better relationships.

- **Rebel:** I am mischievous, rule breaking, often in trouble. No one can tell me what to do. I am stubborn and sometimes the truth teller in the family.
- **Easygoing:** I can adapt to whatever. I have a sunny disposition. I'm not going to lie, and everyone loves me.
- **Peacemaker:** I can't stand confrontation and fighting. I'm a compromiser, always ready to smooth things over when family and friends get hot and bothered.
- **Family clown:** I love to make people laugh. I can get attention anywhere, anytime. I'm a comedian and entertainer. Often, I feel sad and insecure inside.
- **Quiet:** Nobody knows what I'm thinking. I feel invisible and overlooked often. You might even say I'm afraid of my own shadow. I just don't want to be wrong or ridiculed. I don't feel safe at home or at school. I feel alone and too shy to make friends. I'm often the most sensitive one in the family.
- **Loud:** Am I confident or bossy or just trying to survive and get my voice out in a noisy family? You're not going to miss me. I make myself, my wants, and my opinions known.

- **Caretaker:** I'm the selfless, helpful one. I am conscientious and thoughtful. Often caretakers, like me, are the heroes who jump to the rescue when no one else moves. The caretakers are the people who often lose their childhoods caring for siblings or sick parents and care for others during their lifetime.
- **People pleaser:** I am aware of other people's emotions. I might be an empath, someone who cares for the feelings of others more than I care for my own. I will work to make others comfortable while I am miserable myself.
- **Manipulator:** I know exactly what buttons to push to get people around me to do what I want.
- **Sneaky:** I can lie with a straight face. I hide what I'm doing. No one knows what I'm up to. I have my own agenda.

Lindsey Shares Her Daughter Personality Style

I don't remember ever not having the people-pleasing component to my personality. All I wanted to do when I was little was to make my mom happy. In fact, it probably went beyond people-pleasing. I became enmeshed with my mom from a young age and later with friends. What that means is if someone else, mom or others I cared about, was unhappy, I was unhappy, too. It's a lack of boundaries with people. I took on their feelings and even was unsure of the difference between what my mother wanted for me and what I wanted for myself. But it worked perfectly for my mother and me in my childhood. We were incredibly close, and there was little friction between us in those days. Sure, there were bad days, days I didn't want to go to school, and the tantrums flowed, as well as days when my mom would get a book rejection and she would struggle, but our real issues centered on illness.

I felt uncomfortable in general. I was a colicky baby and always had an anxiety disorder. I was shy and had a fundamental lack of self-esteem. It's so easy to look back and be judgmental about how we all were as a family and should have known about brain development and parenting, but much of what we'll discuss about trauma and emotional development wasn't known back then. Because of family dysfunction and lack of healthy communication, I certainly wasn't sharing my feelings or fears. As a result, my personality began to change, and it wasn't clear why.

On the one hand, I became angry and disillusioned about the tragedies happening in my life, and that made me irritable and difficult to deal with. On the other hand, there was another side emerging as well, the one that could adapt to whoever or whatever was happening—the chameleon who could change styles as fast as I could change clothes. I had to be the people pleaser around my family, the rebel at school, the club kid when I was out, and of course the growing addict that would run the whole show for over a decade.

The once sweet, people-pleasing girl turned into a teenage rebel complete with ever-changing hair colors and multiple styles. I became the sneaky manipulator, not because I wanted to cause trouble, but to be able to do what I wanted and avoid my mom's judgmental eyes. Make no mistake, there was still a strong drive in me to do what my mother wanted me to do and make her happy, but rage was building because I felt misunderstood and was beginning to suspect that she was the problem. I believed she cared more about her career and what people thought than how I was doing. Those are the ideas that justified a lot of bad and self-destructive behavior on my part.

This is the reason it's important to ask questions, dig deeper, and look for solutions when you see your daughter changing before your eyes. Sometimes it's normal, but sometimes it's not. The changes were not normal and healthy for me; they symbolized a downfall. You'll read a lot more about that later. Let's say this, my mom's and my personalities clashed constantly at times. Once drugs and alcohol entered the picture, rational thought and behavior went out the window.

I believe two things interfered with the healthy development of my personality. One, when you are an active addict through the teens and twenties, nothing is normal. Your personality is driven by the need to feed a habit just to feel normal. Your goals are not what they should be. Your ambitions slow to almost nothing, and relationships are strained if you have them at all. I wasn't busy nurturing my skills and finding things to be passionate about. I wasn't feeding my creativity and building self-esteem. The result was a very immature, frustrated person. I felt I had something to say but didn't know how to get it out or stay focused. I was so busy trying to manage anxiety, depression, self-loathing, and insecurity that life was a constant chemistry experiment.

The other big problem I had in the personality development department was that I didn't know who I was or what I wanted other than to be a party girl. I didn't aspire to be a lawyer, or anything, really. I don't remember thinking about it very much, so it seemed easiest to do what I thought my mom would want me to do. When you live your life for someone else, it never goes well. I really thought if I could make my outsides look okay with the right school or job or location, then I would feel okay about myself and the world. Building the outside to develop the inside doesn't work. You must have an infrastructure, and I didn't have one. I would rebuild everything, including who I was and wanted to be later, once the drugs and alcohol were out of my system and my life.

Think About This

Have you ever thought about what kind of person you project to the world and your loved ones? It may be surprising to learn that you have turned out to be very similar to the mom you didn't want to emulate. It was fun creating this list so that we could look at different styles, check off the boxes, and think about ourselves in a neutral way for a change. It's not that you're bad or good or healthy or unhealthy but rather what are the components of your personality and where do they come from. When you consider personality and communication styles in a neutral way, you can begin to see how you may be stuck in old feelings and old ways of communicating that never served you well in the first place. You may also see that some of those patterns and personality styles are imprinted from the mothers before you.

TIME TO JOURNAL

Revelations happen when you start sharing your thoughts and feelings with yourself, truthfully. We'll get into honesty in the next chapter because being truthful is the foundation of all healthy and productive human endeavors. You simply can't have satisfying relationships if you're walking on eggshells with someone and just can't or won't tell the truth. But first, are you being open-minded or closed-minded with your mom/daughter? Are you compassionate or judgmental? Of course, telling what you know about yourself honestly takes some doing. Can you honestly say you're moody and not easy to know? And can you tell the truth about your mom without feeling guilty or that you're betraying her? When you answer questions about your mother's personality, you can be honest but not to her. There are ways to say inconvenient and uncomfortable truths in a healthy way—but only when your relationship is on solid enough ground for you both to stay calm and feel loved, not judged.

JOURNAL PROMPTS

1. What personality most fits you from the Hopkins descriptions?

2. What personality style fits your mother?

3. What is your mother's mothering style? What is yours?

4. What was your mother's emotional style? What is your daughter's emotional style?

5. What is your emotional style?

6. Do your styles clash or fit together? Give some examples of ways you're similar and different.

CHAPTER 4

Communication: What You Say and What She Hears

Communication is one of our favorite subjects because it is the key to getting along not only with mom and daughter but also with everyone else. Your personality and emotional styles are just part of the communication picture. Now we're going to dig a little deeper and add how you communicate and the messages you send as well. What are moms saying, what are daughters hearing, and what information have daughters received that they can't forget? No matter where you started on the nurturing scale, the way you communicate and what you say are either the keys to your daughter's empowerment or the greatest hurdles she may face in many areas of her life. The importance of mother-daughter communication cannot be overstated.

Let's take a minute to travel back in time to infancy to explain how the first communications you received from your mom or primary caregiver have affected your emotional growth and development. While you do not actively remember your first thousand days, research shows the first three years set the stage for your mother-daughter relationship and your sense of worth. Just a note about day care and the mother-daughter bond. Recent studies of the impact of day care indicate higher levels of empathy, resilience, and prosocial behavior later in life, which are positive results. The mother-daughter bond is not shown to be negatively affected by day care. It's not about the number of hours a day that moms and daughters are together in the early years but rather how mothers behave when the two are together. Nurturing moms smile, are playful, and communicate their love in the way they touch you, look at you, speak to you, and respond to your needs. This kind of communication is called "mirroring" and provides the warmth and safety infants must have to develop a sense of self. Self-esteem and knowing who you are later in life derive from this kind of maternal nurturing.

Moms who are emotionally unavailable for one reason or another (depression, work, circumstances out of their control; even chronic cell phone preoccupation counts as being absent or unresponsive) deprive babies, toddlers, and later children, teens, and young adults of the opportunity to see themselves reflected and responded to in moms' eyes. It has long been known that babies who lack mirroring from their moms also lose the crucial give-and-take exchanges that create a social environment in which babies can participate in the potential for a relationship. A daughter's feeling of powerlessness and lack of worth can start here, and so can an insatiable longing for mom's love that attachment expert and author Kelly McDaniel outlines in her book *Mother Hunger*.

How are you and mom/daughter communicating with each other right now? Not so well? Let's move to the time when your memories began and consider the tone in which your mom talked to you. What are some things she said that stuck with you your whole life? And what are you saying to your daughter who may be angry with you right now? We're going to ask you about this later. Everyone communicates through words, body language, personality styles, and actions. Each of the ways information is transmitted is important.

Think about this: When you talk, what kind of words do you use? What is the look on your face? What do you want to accomplish? Is what you're saying helping or making things worse? What can you do that's positive? Whether you intend to or not, you send messages with every raised eyebrow, every dismissive gesture, every turn of phrase. Every casual cruelty. The side eye, the sharp intake of breath, the grunt of disapproval. Each is a message sent and received. You don't know what your daughter is hearing or picking up and keeping. The communications that pass between mothers and daughters last forever. We'll give you some examples and ask for yours later.

Communication is a two-way process involving the following elements: a sender, a message, a medium, a channel, a receiver, a response, and feedback. However, it is not enough to have just these elements; there should also be cooperation and understanding between the two parties involved. This is where the standard definition falls short. In fact, there's much more to the exchange of information. You communicate through the things you say, the things you're never allowed to say, your body language, personality, communication, and cultural styles. Here are three physical forms of communication that send messages you receive and note. They define your responses.

Body language: Your mom/daughter's body language around you reveals a lot. Does her body tell you she's engaged with you, or is she always busy and looking somewhere else? Is she warm, approachable, and embraceable, or reserved and hands off? How does it feel when she touches you? Do you feel safe and at home? Or is she stiff and standoffish? Does she push you away?

Facial expressions: What does your mom's face say when she looks at you? Does she light up and smile? Does she have special facial expressions that reveal she's annoyed to have to deal with you? Is she unresponsive? Without saying a word, your mom's face can say it all. If your mom is impatient or annoyed, her face will tell you. Her face alone will also tell you what to do, not do, and when to back off. We take our cues from her, and they can be confusing.

Tone of voice: Tone of voice can also be confusing. We know people who sound harsh but are sweethearts who will do anything for you. A mom's angry voice does not necessarily mean your mom is a destructive meanie. By the same token, a passive aggressive mom can hide behind a gentle voice. Tone of voice may be cultural, too. Many happy family members yell at one another without being hostile.

Communication styles also send messages that affect our behavior. When only one person speaks and the other can't get a word in or gets interrupted, this mom/daughter is saying: *Only my opinion and thoughts matter. You and your thoughts and feelings don't matter. I'm better than you.* What is the response to moms/daughters with the exhausted, defeated voice of martyrs? They are communicating how hard they work, how difficult life is, how inconvenient you and your needs are. The martyr's voice can be a form of guilt-making and manipulation. The mom/daughter with a constantly hurt voice sends another message: *I'm so sensitive, and you're so mean.* This hurt-feeling voice is a form of manipulation, too. Here you're walking on eggshells and know that you can't ever have an honest conversation.

Then there's the advice-giving voice, the mom/daughter who voices her opinions and research on everything and isn't always right.

Does talking without taking a breath or relentlessly interrupting sound like your mom/daughter? We all have friends or family members who dominate the talking space and don't want to hear from anyone else. They're experts on everything. When it's your mom, you either fight with her all the time, and rarely win, or you want to flee as soon as possible so you can make your own decisions and live your own life.

Here Are Some Communication Styles to Consider

Combative: I am quick to react to any perceived slight. I'll defend any position I have, and I hate to think I am ever in the wrong. Aggressive communication involves expressing thoughts and needs in a forceful and confrontational manner, often disregarding the feelings and opinions of others. This style can intimidate and alienate others, damaging relationships and hindering effective communication.

Conflict avoiding, nonconfrontational: I'll do anything to avoid a fight. I don't like to see people fighting and don't want to get involved or take sides. That makes me appear and act passive. Passive communication involves avoiding conflict, keeping opinions to oneself, and prioritizing others' needs over one's own. Moms/daughters with this style often struggle to express their thoughts or assert boundaries, leading to potential frustration and misunderstandings.

Controlling: I want things to go right, be done in the right way, my way. I may be something of a perfectionist or an extreme worrier about what can go wrong if I'm not in control.

Narcissistic: Narcissism is more than just being self-centered or selfish. It means you can only think about yourself in every equation, in a toxic way. There is no one else to consider. You don't really care about other people's feelings. Narcissists lie about you to your friends and loved ones to cause trouble and make themselves look good.

Passive-aggressive: I seem sweet, but underneath my nice exterior, I can be as sharp as a serpent's tooth. I'm the person who purchases donuts for you and then gives your share to someone else. I will open a door for you and then close it on your foot. I confuse people with my niceness. Passive-aggressive communication combines elements of both passive and aggressive styles. It involves indirect expressions of negative feelings, sarcasm, and subtle undermining behaviors. This style can create confusion and erode trust within relationships.

Sensitive/oversensitive: I am sensitive and let everyone know it. I may use my sensitivity as a weapon against you, always claiming to be hurt by something you or someone else has done. I may also be sensitive to slights but not dare show it.

Victim: I feel like a victim. I do everything for everybody else and resent it. I both play the victim and feel the victim. People pleasers, codependents, and enablers often feel victimized by their over-helping.

Patient/impatient: I am patient and loving and willing to hear your side or let you find your way, or I am impatient and grab things out of your hands when you can't do something fast enough to suit me.

Empathic: I am empathic. People who are empathic can also be people pleasers. Being too empathic and people-pleasing can be problematic. If you feel your daughter's pain too much and want to shield her from disappointment, you may prevent her from learning to live with the setbacks and pain that is inevitable in every person's life.

Emotionally intelligent communication: Emotionally intelligent communication emphasizes understanding and empathizing with others' emotions. It involves active listening, observing nonverbal cues, and responding in a sensitive and supportive manner. Emotionally intelligent communicators create a safe and inclusive environment where all voices are heard and valued.

Lindsey was effective at antagonizing Leslie as a way of deflecting investigations into why she looked and acted sick. The pattern started with deflecting, finger-pointing, blaming, and trigger tempers, and a complete lack of self-control ruled. Moms have trouble defending themselves when attacks against them turn vicious. What can start as misguided communication in high school can blow up into verbal warfare in college and escalate into recurring emotional hurricanes thereafter.

Our friend Lisa and her mother are in a constant state of verbal warfare. They love/hate each other, and their complex feelings of frustration over not being able to control each other come out in daily screaming fights. There is not a day when they aren't on the phone fighting over something. You'd think they'd take a break from talking from time to time. When you come from a family where people scream at each other, however, it's practically impossible to stop doing that unless everyone agrees, or you stop talking to them. How your family members treat one another is all you know. You will act the way they do. More families than you think are struggling with basic healthy communication. If healthy communication skills are not something you were taught, you're not going to have them.

These are patterns and behaviors you begin to identify in rehab or therapy and then work to create new reactions, or non-reactions, and different ways of communicating. For many people this is the hardest part of recovery. For Lindsey, putting down the drink was easy compared to learning how to react differently, pause when agitated, not step on other people's toes, be kind, compassionate, find gratitude, basically change an entire way of being and thinking. Some of the following examples will be about the effect of moms' communications on their daughters, and some will be about daughters' on their moms. Communication and its impact go both ways. How and what moms and daughters communicate to each other have profound and lasting effects.

Moms Can Sound Mean

Leslie remembers the first mom who admitted that she hated her daughter. It was Barbara Walters. When Lindsey was three, we delivered the newspapers to Barbara every morning for a month on Martha's Vineyard because Barbara couldn't drive. Every morning we'd have a bit of a gab when she came out to the car to get the papers. Barbara couldn't wait to get back to work in New York because her daughter was being an annoying brat. Nothing to do in that quaint cabin down a two-mile dirt road, and mommy couldn't drive. It was a tough situation for a nine-year-old.

"I hate my daughter," Barbara said right in front of the nine-year-old she cited.

Leslie was shocked because Barbara also defined her daughter as her "adopted" daughter. She was a proponent of adoption and wanted to encourage people in that direction. Combining the words "adopted" and "I hate my daughter," however, created a separation and lasting wound that no mother ever intends.

Your family's communication style is one way fighting between mom and daughter begins. If your family is loud and contentious, your daughter will be loud and contentious, unless she's daunted and shy. In some cultures, arguing is a way of life. Family members can be screaming at one another all day long and not think anything of it. Just discussing, they might say. Everybody can get their views out. If you're not a fighter in this kind of family, however, you may well feel overwhelmed by nosiness and criticism and long for the safety of anonymity and quiet.

In other cultures, moms loudly berate their daughters to get them to perform better: "Are you stupid? Are you crazy?" Moms who berate their daughters can be brutal on self-esteem: "You only got B+? Why not A?" You can scare your daughter into achievement, but she won't love you for it. This also goes for guilt-tripping, telling your children in graphic detail how much you sacrificed for them or spent on them or gifted them. We know moms who are like accountants. Mom Georgina knows to the penny how much she spends on her daughter Elsie and never fails to point out the value of each item she provides. Georgina says things such as: *Do you know how much that thing that I just gave you cost? You're so ungrateful. I wonder why I do so much for you. You don't deserve* ___ [whatever it is]." Why does she do that?

When moms don't feel appreciated, resentment follows, whether silent or verbal, and it lingers. "Look at all the sacrifices we've made for an ungrateful child." Sadness and frustration are natural consequences when a child doesn't return love and generosity and just wants more. A resentful mother can communicate rage or victimhood to her daughter, which may trigger rolling of the eyes, and you're playing the martyr again. Not the compassion or gratitude mom really wants.

Another kind of communication problem can evolve around

conflict over personal freedom versus cultural demands. Girls want to be more free and "modern" in cultures where freedom is not an option. Is your daughter dismissive of what you have to say and treats you and your sacred opinions and traditions with contempt? Who has she learned this from? Belittling is hurtful and may trigger a desire on your part for retaliation. A brilliant internist and painter I know, Suzy, told me her mother defines her as the black sheep of the family. Another doctor, a successful pediatric surgeon, Laura, tells me she is not valued as much as her sisters who married and had children.

Yet another pathway to fighting can be for power and control. This goes back to personality styles and where you and your daughter might fit on the personality charts. Are you in a constant battle of wills in which one of you must conquer the other and be declared the winner? Has this been going on since kindergarten when your daughter had tantrums over absolutely everything? Your personalities might not be a good fit, but you still love each other.

Moms come in many different forms. What are you like? Are you a helicopter mother hovering over your daughter's every move, no matter how old and competent she is? Or are you a doormat, dominated from birth by the spawn of the devil? Leslie can relate to both. When you're triggered by disrespect or downright torment, adrenaline shoots through your system and you need a release. Where are you going to get it? You shouldn't hit back verbally or scream. Your children can be damaged for life and repeat your behavior with their children. But what about you? Are you getting something out of the fighting?

Has fighting become your addiction? Fighting when it's habitual or chronic can be a kind of addiction in which there is brain reward from the drama, the hysteria, the screaming, and adrenaline rush of feeling wronged, insulted, or undermined. And it's hard to stop. When you see and listen to mothers and daughters in hopeless rage and conflict, their communication style reveals a lot. Are they yelling at each other, snapping at each other, sniping, calling each other names? Is one talking while the other is sulking? What's happening? Who wants what and why?

Leslie Shares Messages from Mom She'll Never Forget

I'm going to speak as a daughter and granddaughter for a minute because the words our moms use when they communicate can last a lifetime when they may have meant it to last only through childhood. Here's an example. The only advice I ever received from my grandma was: if you don't have something nice to say, don't say anything. My granny was frightened of speaking out, so my mother was very regal and nice. I never heard my mom raise her voice to get attention or say a mean thing about anybody.

When I was, maybe five, three things happened that would influence my whole life. The first was that I disappeared for a little while one day. When my mom realized I was not in the house, she went into a panic. I was not next door where our neighbor let me explore the treasures in her sewing basket. And I wasn't across the street at the Colemans' house. She finally located me in the laundry room off the garage where I was busy telling the washing machine repairman all about my movie producer daddy who worked with Charlie Chaplin in Cali-forny-a. I was having a grand old time. My mom, on the other hand, was appalled.

"Don't be a teller," she said as she hustled me away. "You're such a blabbermouth." I relished the word. "Blabbermouth." I'm a blabbermouth.

Around the same time, I visited Brenda Coleman across the street. Children were allowed orange cheese puffs and Coca Cola in that house, and I was junk food driven. Brenda's older sister (whose name I don't recall because she is the villain of the story) challenged us to find the hole where our pee pee comes out. She procured her mom's makeup mirror for us to investigate. Brenda and I snuck into the bathroom. The evil sister dared me to go first, so I took off my panties and tried angling that tiny mirror between my legs to get an answer. It was my first ever look, and it was confusing. *Perhaps it was a trick question,* I thought. There didn't seem to be a one-hole answer. I was perplexed and couldn't figure out what to say.

Suddenly, the bathroom door flew open, and Brenda's mother barged in. She'd been tipped off and was furious. My regal mother was duly summoned from across the street, and I was hustled out of the Coleman house never to cross the threshold again.

What just happened? I would never get another Coke or cheese puff in my life again, and Brenda was taboo, too? What? What? It wasn't my fault, I protested.

"It doesn't matter what other people think" was all my mother had to say about the matter. She looked like Princess Margaret. You didn't push with that look on her face. But what did that mean?

It doesn't matter what other people think. That was the message my mom sent. What I received was a global proclamation, and it has stayed with me my whole life. Other people are dangerous. Don't count on friends or evil sisters or other people's moms. Only our family matters. So mafia. My mother also told me on many occasions, "No one will ever love you as much as I do." Boom. My only person was my mom. Soon after, we left the quiet suburb on Lake Michigan and the extended family I loved, never to return.

The statement that no one would ever love me as much as my mom was the tie that bound us even after her death. All the adventures that followed with my mom were about that one line. Those words may have made me feel good as a little girl, but they created an almost paralytic shyness and prevented me from seeking friendships and asking for help when I needed it. My mom got cancer at the age of fifty-four, when I was only twenty-six. I was left alone two years later, feeling that no one would ever love me again. Only family matters. Although I was with her every day in the hospital, she gave me no deathbed blessing to make me feel I'd be all right or assurance that I could find other people to love and to love me. She simply couldn't say goodbye. It felt as if life was over for me. Luckily, Alex and Lindsey were born, and I had other people to love. But what if I hadn't had them?

You see how a child's brain works. It's not logical. Those early messages from my mom are more than sixty years old, yet they are memories I cannot forget no matter how old I get. Messaging is so important. My mom never said I was lovable or that I would be loved and cherished by many people. She said she was my one person, and I believed her. She didn't mean to hurt me, but she didn't use empowering words that set me free to love and be loved by others.

 ## Lindsey Shares What Daughters Hear

Are there things your mother said to you that haunt you to this day? Or are there things she said that formed you, and not for the better? One of the phrases my mother would use that I believe her mother used with her is, "Pull up your bootstraps." It means stop complaining and get with the program. In some instances, a phrase like this works and is appropriate. For an insecure child who already struggled with understanding and owning her feelings, this further proved that pushing them down and being okay with whatever needed to happen was the correct thing to do. There was no way to know that those words would turn into an emotional code, but sometimes that's what happens. We say things and often have no idea how they're heard and whether they've hurt.

How a mom comments about a daughter's looks, weight, intelligence, habits, competence, and personality matters. If you tell your daughter she's chubby, she will internalize that forever. If a daughter is mocked for her smarts, or lack thereof, it can be paralyzing. While it's easy to get into the habit of saying whatever's on our minds to the people closest to us, words have power. What your daughter hears from you will influence her. There is no question that as an adult I can see that my friends who had supportive, loving, kind moms do not have the self-esteem problems that those with critical moms have. The message is: use your words wisely.

Think About This

Communication is tricky because both moms and daughters can use words that hurt. Both can be dismissive and cruel. Both can use angry voices instead of soft ones, and those words and voices can become a pattern that's not easily broken. Worse, as moms, you don't know what words and which messages your daughter will remember, no matter when you say them. You can be a pretty good mom and still say some things your daughter will never forgive you for.

Was Leslie a girl-child and an ugly one as she was often told? She was a girl, all right, but never an ugly one. She did not know it. In some cultures, mothers used spit on their daughters so God would not be tempted to take them. You can always find reasons to explain away hurtful things as not meant to deeply wound. Acknowledging that you said hurtful words and apologizing can go a long way to healing.

There are also the sins of omission, things you don't say that maybe you should. For instance, "You make me mad and frustrated, but I still love you." If no one taught you positive language for love and appreciation, you could begin to communicate better by learning better things to say when a conflict arises, as well as ways to stop an argument cold. Here are some quick tips for ending an argument. You can say: "Let's put a pin in it," "I'll think about it," or "Let's stop for now." You can also walk out of the room for quiet alone time and then do something soothing to calm down. You can nicely end a phone conversation. You can also take a break from speaking for a while.

Awareness of what's really going on is the key here. Lasting communication solutions are possible when both moms and daughters want to do better and can look at themselves honestly. Also, moms and daughters need to be able to back off, to compromise even when they don't agree. If you have a controlling or manipulative mom or a daughter who must win or becomes angry and argues when you express your feelings, communication is not the problem. Clashing personalities and other issues may be the problem.

In healthy relationships, moms and daughters can listen without interrupting or arguing, can validate feelings without telling each other what they should do or feel, and can say "You may be right" to end an argument without needing to win. Healthy relationships always emphasize the positive, not the negative, about each other.

TIME TO JOURNAL

The goal here is to identify the ways you and your mom/daughter communicate. Before you can even think about changing, you need to know what's really happening between the two of you. Your style of communication is one thing to consider. Another thing to consider is what your conflict is really about. In journaling about your communication life with mom/daughter, you can sketch out a specific story around words you can never forget or describe the way your family communicates that's been passed down. You can write a letter. You can make some charts and lists of your own about what you say and how you say it.

JOURNAL PROMPTS

1. Describe your family's communication style. Judgmental, supportive, accepting, combative, teasing are just a few possibilities. Where does it come from? Dad or mom? How do family members get along at the dinner table? How do you feel when you're together?

2. How does your mom/daughter communicate with you? Impatient, patient, supportive, nagging, yelling are a few possibilities. Give some examples of how she sounds.

3. What would you like communication with your mom/daughter to sound like? Give some examples.

4. What do you hear when your mom/daughter talks to you now?

5. Write a letter to your mom/daughter about how her communications make you feel. But don't send it. This is for you.

6. What are some words your mom said that you will never forget? You can write a little story here. And you can tell a positive one, like the day you became a blabbermouth for life. Also add how this made you feel.

CHAPTER 5

Getting Honest About
the Secrets and Lies

L et's explore the lies we tell, the secrets we keep, and the denial we all have about so many things. Everyone has some denial of uncomfortable realities. We need them to maintain a semblance of sanity. For life to go smoothly, we all look the other way sometimes. Some of us, the empaths and people pleasers who fear confrontation and conflict, smother our feelings when we fear the negative consequences of revealing them. Turns out, we can't fight everything we don't like in life. Polite lies keep the peace. Secrets that would harm others are best kept private, and denial is the fuel that keeps many families running for generations.

For us, denial around certain issues was a way of life. That denial was what kept the drama going. And oh, what drama there was between us. Nominations for Academy Awards are in order. Issues of denial, secrecy, and lies are not necessarily toxic, however. They can be seen by mothers as a form of protection against too much pain for a child to bear. For example, if your daughter doesn't know the killing, slavery, and discrimination that happened to her family, she will be spared from the overwhelming pain it caused to her loved ones. Most families do have devastating injustice somewhere in their past. In any case, no family is without its traumas, either recent or from generations ago.

Mothers and daughters keep secrets for many reasons. Mothers who gave up earlier children or were sexually assaulted by a family member are two good examples of secrets that mothers may keep. Abuse of any kind is not something mothers/daughters like to talk about. Other issues mothers may not want to share are their family history of mental illness, addiction, horrific discrimination, forced repatriation, and war. Even emotional challenges they had to endure as single mothers or widows can be kept secret to allow their daughters to grow up without fear.

Silence around trauma is common because of the shame we feel about the devastating things that happened to us. Paternity, for example, is now something that can be established, and DNA makes it possible to learn shocking truths you may only have suspected. Should moms tell daughters they've been raped or that their dad was a lover no one knew anything about? There is no right answer for revealing secrets like these.

Think about your family's secrets; you know you have them. We all grow up believing we must fit into our community's rules, whatever they may be. If there are people (or behaviors) that don't fit, like a sketchy uncle or a hard-core drunk or a philanderer in a religious community, the family may well deny it and keep the secrets. It's the right thing to do, isn't it? Is a family member gay, an addict, unfaithful, a porn enthusiast, debt-ridden? The list of secrets we keep goes on and on in every family and every culture.

Leslie's Family Secrets

We had lots of juicy secrets in our family. We had distant relations who were eccentric at best, people who handled money badly, family feuds over business and wills. Sound familiar? A grandmother had been sexually assaulted at the age of eight, and her mother committed suicide because of it. The eight-year-old heard her mother apologize to her just before she died. One of my aunts developed schizophrenia after her newborn baby died. She was hospitalized on and off her whole adult life. That's just the beginning of our family tree of mental health.

We also have alcoholism, discrimination, hardship caused by migrations, religious confusions, and many traumas that we probably don't know about. So many secrets affect us without our being aware of them. Here's the issue with generational secrets. During times of war and repatriation, certain kinds of lying may well be a requirement for survival. Other kinds of family lies and secrets, however, create distress, shame, and damage over the generations. Only a generation ago, our culture demanded that we hide all inconvenient truths. Here's where your maternal family history comes in. We'll give ours as an example.

My middle-class grandmother was indulgent and sweet to all her grandchildren but not someone you'd run to for advice or solace. Her mother was born in 1848 in France and may not have known how to read or write. All I know about my great-grandmother is that she wouldn't eat tomatoes because she thought they were poisonous, ate bananas every day, and never talked about anything unpleasant. She died the year I was born.

What I was told about my great-grandmother is that she had nine children without a doctor's help, for modesty, but this is probably not true) and was a devout Christian. In a Nebraska census that an aunt showed me to prove my Jewish heritage after my mom died, my great-grandparents are listed as the only Hebrews in the territory. I have my grandmother's book from the *Self and Sex Series, What a Young Girl Ought to Know*, 1897. My grandmother received the book in 1902 from her sister Belle and gave it to me when I was a young girl. The book has a lot about God's intention for girls in the name of purity and truth. I particularly remember the section on how to wash without touching yourself.

What did my grandmother know about her mom's immigration from France or the circumstances of her marriage? She never shared any stories and very little advice. My mother had some trauma related to refusing baptism in the river when she was a teen. I learned this from an uncle, not from her. My mom did not practice Christianity, married a Jew, but never became Jewish. My core secret was a religious confusion unexplained yet powerfully influencing many of my young vulnerabilities. This unexplained confusion about my mother's silent, yet deeply held, beliefs kept me uninformed about everything related to sex and unsafe as a young woman and is an example of secret keeping.

Secret keeping, such as not explaining to your daughter the facts of life or not daring to tell what your religion is or that there is addiction in the family, can cause one kind of damage. A moral code that includes habitual lying to manipulate and control others, or to get away with (or cover up) bad behavior, causes another kind of emotional damage. With habitual liars in your family, you don't know and can't act on what's really happening. One lie, repeated by another and by another creates a reality in which it feels impossible to determine what's true. I call it living on shifting sands, where you don't know what's true or what is going to happen next. Lindsey and I have experienced that.

How can anyone trust what we know or feel if we're not sure what's really going on? The same applies to generational and trauma secret keeping. Family secrets have consequences. Children who aren't allowed to come clean about abuse, sexual orientation, or family traumas are denied the right to tell the truth, to think critically about what's happening to them, and to find safety and relief. They are denied their own reality. Often that denied reality is exactly what leads to shame, lack of self-esteem, and many other kinds of emotional and mental health issues. Depression and anxiety are almost guaranteed. Suicide is also a risk.

Lying is complicated because it can be a habit or a component of a personality disorder such as narcissism or sociopathy. Lying and denial are an integral part of behavior and substance use disorders. In any case, millions of people lie as a way of life for all kinds of reasons. Lying can make life easier and let you off the hook if you get away with it. Parents ask: Did you do your homework? Did you walk the dog (or do your assigned chores)? Are you smoking cigarettes or marijuana, vaping, drinking, taking grandma's pills? Where are you going? Where were you last night?

 Lindsey's Secrets

I've always loved secrets. Love them, love them, love them. I don't remember why I started keeping secrets. It's just something I've done for as long as I can remember. Having something private that only I knew, or shared with someone, was deliciously satisfying to me. Maybe it made me feel important. I was insecure and a people pleaser, so being able to trade in information was helpful.

My mom and I kept a lot of secrets, but at the beginning they were innocent ones. Secrets are part of the mother daughter-bond, right? "Don't tell Dad we bought a dog," Mom said when we couldn't resist buying our first dog. I was maybe eight. We fell in love with a ball of fluff in a pet shop we visited frequently and went for it, knowing Dad was not going to approve. I kept the secret, and my dad was flabbergasted when he got home that night and discovered a tiny shih tzu, Mr. Chow, named for the restaurant across the street. At first, he thought it was a stuffed animal. Then Mr. Chow peed.

It was fun to share our naughtiness about shopping, gossip, or whatever amused us at the time. Secrets also create closeness. Obviously, you can trust someone you share a secret with, right? But when do secrets become trauma bonding? We'll talk about that later. When I was little, I was terrified of my mom. She was fabulous, talented, rich, adored, and could be mean sometimes. Think of my mom like a bear, and me like a bear baiter. If you poked the bear (my mom) too many times, she would erupt. You didn't want that to happen. Not when I was little and definitely not when I got meaner myself in my teen years.

My mom was an author, and she was busy. It's not that I wanted to lie to her; I just wanted to do what I wanted to do and not be bothered about it. Lying created the path of least resistance. Maybe when a culture of lying has already been created, it makes that easier to do. In my teenage years, lying was just a smoke screen so no one would really know what I was up to. It was also easy because no one was checking up. That's how my mom was raised, and she was very busy—way too busy to be calling other parents to confirm what I had told her. My mom had no reason to lie, so she expected me to be honest, too. I wasn't honest because I didn't have to be. Mom wasn't always around when I was up to no good. One day I called when she wasn't at home preparing dinner as usual.

"Where are you, Mom? It's six o'clock."

"I'm in prison. There's a lockdown, and I can't get out," she replied. "Be home by midnight, I hope."

That's my mom. She was in a maximum-security prison for women in Bedford, working on a research project about the impact of education on inmates. Another day, I returned home to discover she was in the Bronx serving as an NYPD Commander for the Day of the 50th Precinct. She came home in a squad car, and the neighbors were concerned.

What is it like being the daughter of a mystery writer? One day when I arrived home from high school, a projector was set up in the living room. A famous forensic odontologist (bite mark expert) was about to start a slideshow for her research. Unfortunately, his projector began to smoke.

"Lindsey, would you run out to rent a projector from the store on 59th Street?" my mom asked. "I'll give you five dollars."

Five dollars wouldn't do it for me. We settled on twenty dollars, and I ran the errand. Bite marks on human flesh? I was allowed to watch the gruesome presentation and then read about bite marks in her next book.

Do we even want to talk about the neighbor's dead body in a bikini on the beach next to our new house in Sarasota on Christmas morning 1990? I was thirteen at the time. Yeah, you're going to get a good look at that when your mom writes about serial killers. She woke me and my friend who was with us for the holiday. Mom was excited to share the news, and together we sneaked up past the police tape to check out the scene.

"This is not a drowning," she announced. Everyone called her Jessica Fletcher, the character from *Murder She Wrote*, which was popular on TV at the time.

Sometimes mom was in Sarasota working on a book for a week at a time, and while my father was technically at home, he, too, was busy. My dad was a banker at the time and worked long hours. My brother was already away in college. There was literally no one home in our midtown Manhattan apartment at a time when my intentions were starting to get worse and worse.

Lying also came naturally to me; I'm a storyteller (guess why), and when no one checks the story, you get more used to doing it, getting more brazen with your lies. As time went on and it became clear I was struggling, my mom would inquire more and more about what might be behind the grungy clothes, rainbow hair, and missing hours; I had a story for everything. In those days, I had little interest in academics, which isn't to say I didn't do well or didn't enjoy quite a bit of it. But nothing really engaged me. I believe I was the first one to have detention reinstated at Riverdale, my high school, because I cut so many classes.

"Where are you going?" Again and again my mom would ask.

"To a friend's house to watch a movie," I would spit back.

Sometimes I didn't return until the next morning with makeup running down my face after having spent the entire night and morning in nightclubs on drugs. When I returned in the morning, I'd be quiet and careful not to interrupt my mom as I knew her morning work schedule. She was working by 5 a.m. If she checked on me later and wanted to feed me a healthy breakfast, I got mean and retreated. This behavior turned into the deny and deflect techniques of my teen and young adult years. I can't say it often enough that even the very best kids lie all the time.

My pattern was to dismiss, deny, and deflect. I'm nonconfrontational. I'll suffer for days if I must have a tough conversation with someone. And while I was angry at my parents in those years, I still wanted their approval. I was never ballsy enough to tell them to seriously go away. So the more they tried to check on me, the more I simply stayed away and retreated into my room where family rarely entered. When I knew I needed help, I called the one person who terrified me the most, my now divorced mom. I was in Baltimore at Johns Hopkins, and my timing was impeccable. It was her birthday. She was out on a date with a psychiatrist at the time.

"Mom, I'm in trouble. I need to go to detox for a couple days," I said. Funny the things we say and believe.

"Detox? What? You don't go to detox for the weekend." Mom answered the phone even on a date, and she was clearly annoyed. "Detox is for addicts. You're not an addict."

A moment later, she said, "Are you in a safe place right now?"

"Yes," I told her. "I am in a safe place."

Then, she got right to solutions. "Do you want me to come and get you? Are you safe to take the train?" She put me on the phone with her date, who took his cell phone outside and asked me exactly what was going on. I'd never met him, but he said, "Don't lie to me. What exactly are you taking?"

After telling someone (an adult) the whole truth for maybe the first time in years, I felt relief. I told him what I'd been using and for how long.

"Don't go back to your apartment," he said. "Go straight to the train station and come home." He knew how serious it was. He knew I wasn't going to last another week living the way I was living. I came home.

The biggest lie I had been keeping since I was thirteen years old, my core secret, was out. I was a drug addict as a teen. I have lots to say about teen addiction and addiction in general. When you see the stats, you will be flabbergasted. I'm saving that for another chapter. For this moment, what's important to know is that the one thing my mother had told me never to do, I had done. And I'd been lying about it for years. This is what millions of teens do. Good kids hide what they're doing from their parents with disastrous results. Every single day. You love your daughter, but she will lie to you like I did.

I hated to tell because I knew I was a crushing disappointment. What came as a shock, however, was that my mom wasn't as angry as I had expected. Finally, there was an answer and confirmation of what she had been seeing with her own eyes. Also, my mom has always been good in crisis. That was just the first step in getting honest. Telling the whole truth on a regular basis took a lot longer. Girls don't always grow up on a regular schedule. I would be messy and confused and snarly for no reason for years before I learned the meaning of restraint.

My prioritizing telling the truth literally has a date on it, a full decade later. I was probably thirty-one years old, newly sober for maybe the third time, visiting New York City from Los Angeles, and I had had a boyfriend in my mom's apartment when she was out of town. The boyfriend in the apartment was not a problem, but I had spilled a red beverage on one of her father's beautiful and pale antique rugs that happened to be in my bedroom. Might have been red wine or Coke. I don't remember now, but I freaked out. I was still emotionally about the age I was when I started using, around fifteen: fearful of mom and wanting to get away with a mistake.

My go-to response was to lie, and I was in a panic. I hurried the boyfriend out and obsessively washed the rug using every product in the house to try to erase the stain. The kicker was I had a flight back to Los Angeles the next day, and the carpet would not dry in time. It was unclear to me how bad the stain would be once I'd bolted. I truly did not know what to do. You notice here that I didn't think of communicating the problem to my mom and working it out with her. It was all about me and my feelings, and I didn't trust her to take it well. How well did I know my mom? Not very.

I flew back to Los Angeles in a complete panic attack about the damaged rug. I called our building trying to find a cleaner to take the rug away to be cleaned, but the doormen would not allow anything to be removed from the apartment without my mom's consent. That, of course, makes perfect sense, but I was super screwed. Not knowing what else to do, I called my sponsor, Olivia, the hard-core twelve-stepper, and recounted this story, telling her I was going to return to New York to make sure the rug wasn't ruined.

"Call your mom and ask her what she wants you to do. It's her rug, she has a right to know," Olivia gently suggested. She always started with the obvious and correct action.

"No," I spat back.

Olivia tried again. "I think you should call your mom, tell her the truth, and ask her what she would like you to do because the rug belongs to her."

"No, that's not going to work," I told her. "She's going to kill me."

Silence. Then, once more from Olivia. "Lindsey, I'm going to need you to hang up the phone and call your mother and tell her what happened."

Now we are having a battle of wills. Olivia, who had some serious problems with her own mom, was telling me what to do. Nobody tells me what to do. I could have killed her. Would I do what Olivia suggested—no, demanded—and take the consequences of my actions? Or was I going to do it my way, which would inevitably cause more damage? The tension was thick in the silence. "Fine," I said eventually and hung up the phone. I was my usual sullen self.

Without waiting I dialed my mom. I led with "I'm so sorry. There was an accident, and I stained grandpa's rug. The white one that's in my room."

There was a pause, and I thought my heart would stop. "I'm so, so sorry. I'll pay for it to be cleaned or buy a new one. Whatever you want." I heard a weird snuffling sound on the line. For a moment no one said anything. "Mom? Are you okay?"

Finally, there was a whimper-y, "I'm fine."

"Are you crying?" From snarly, I'm now devastated. I made my mom cry.

"Yes," she said, "but not about the rug. I'm just glad you told me the truth. I don't care about the rug."

Da Dum! My jaw hit the ground. And just like that, I learned that you get better results from telling the truth than you do from lying. I haven't had a ton of light bulb moments in my life, but that was one of them.

There is a divide in my life from conveniently leaving parts of the story out because I feared how people would react to understanding that it is in those moments of truth saying that we grow and become closer. I learned that the worst that can happen isn't so bad. What I assumed was totally wrong, and reality was far better than I expected.

Now, if your safety is at risk by telling your core secret, then don't do it. I'm certainly not suggesting coming out to a mom who won't understand and might throw you out. What I'm talking about is the kind of insidious lying and secret keeping that will ultimately destroy relationships, hurt people, and ultimately hurt you. That's the kind of lying it's important to watch out for because lying, like addiction or some types of mental illness, can be progressive. That means it'll get worse and worse if you don't address it.

Think About This

You may well wonder why Leslie didn't investigate Lindsey's life more closely than she did. Like drug testing her or calling the parents whose houses Lindsey said she was visiting to make sure she was really where she said she was going. Leslie was a crime writer, after all, and knew how to investigate. Well, let's go back to the personality style chart. Leslie didn't think her daughter would lie to her about pretty much everything, so she was a laissez-faire mom. She assumed that Lindsey was telling the truth and her problems were physical.

In law enforcement, the first thing you learn is: never assume. You can see how the secrets that Lindsey kept meant that her mom couldn't give her the help she needed. But when she came clean and asked for help, then the difficult recovery journey could begin. Moms only know what they know. They can't know what's hidden. If you have a mom who didn't take care of you the way you needed, she may not have known how to ask the right questions or give the support you needed. If you have a daughter who lies left and right, you'll need the tools to come clean to yourself about what's really going on. If you can't help your daughter, you need to develop tools to take care of yourself.

TIME TO JOURNAL

Now that you have some idea of your personality and emotional styles, you can continue telling the story of your life by coming clean on the secrets. This is the time to think about what you know and don't know about family secrets and your own. What have you asked your mother and grandma about the family history of mental health, religion, migration, and discrimination? What won't they tell you? It's okay if you don't know. You can learn these secrets over time. Here you're just going to write what you know about their secrets and about your own.

JOURNAL PROMPTS

1. What secrets has your mother told you never to tell anyone else? How do they affect you?

2. Do you think she's keeping other secrets? Have you asked her?

3. What secrets about abuse or discrimination, bullying, or mental health and addiction are hidden in your family tree of mental health?

4. How many secrets are you keeping? What lies do you tell?

5. How many secrets and lies do you suspect your daughter may be keeping? What are they? Has she experienced rape or abuse, and would she feel she could tell you?

6. What would happen if you came clean to your mother/daughter about your secrets and lies?

STEP 2

Mother-Daughter Areas of Conflict

If you've ever leafed through a cookbook, you may have noticed that many begin with kitchen basics. What we just did in Step 1 was explore some relationship basics. We hope that you learned as much from turning the mirror on yourselves and your mom/daughter as we did. We certainly learned things about ourselves we'd never explored before and shared stories with each other for the first time. Lindsey said the other day that as different as our life experiences have been, it turns out that we're a lot alike. Now, you, too, might have some new ideas about your mother/

daughter relationship: who you are and the way you communicate and connect.

In Step 2, we're going to look at eight areas of common conflict between moms and daughters. Some of these areas may not apply to you, so take what you want, and leave the rest. No matter how well you get along, you're going to find that one or two may be your hot-button topics, and these will be the areas we'll explore in Step 3.

In Chapter 6, food and weight will take center stage. Do you fight about food and diet? We certainly did. In this chapter we'll look at some of the ways that food, diet, and disorders around weight can negatively affect mother-daughter harmony.

Chapter 7 will delve into finances and money. This is an area in which every family has had incidents in its history where money has gotten in the way of healthy family relationships. People fight for it, kill for it, and break up over it. Let's count the ways finances can affect the mother-daughter relationship.

Chapter 8 will take us to appearance and style. Are you alike or different in your style selections? Have appearance changes such as tats, piercings, hair color, and even gender dressing in your mom/daughter created pushback and even disdain? We'll explore.

In Chapter 9, we'll see how moms/daughters fight about boyfriends, girlfriends, and partner choices. We've been there and done that, too.

Chapter 10 takes us to the essential questions of dependence and independence and codependence. Every mother and daughter travel an uncharted journey to independence. For moms it happens twice in a lifetime and can be the most difficult journey of all.

Chapter 11 will explore the boundaries that can keep us sane.

What's our business and what isn't? We all need safe spaces to be ourselves.

In Chapter 12, we'll turn to alcohol and drugs. This is where our mother-daughter story went off the rails. Every other issue we could deal with. We're not alone. This is where even the best educated and kindest moms/daughters lose their competency and cool.

Chapter 13 is about mental illness: what it is and isn't, who has it, and how it affects the mother/daughter relationship. Families coping with untreated or treated mental illness need compassion, faith, hope, and lots of help to heal.

CHAPTER 6

Food and Weight

We cannot live without it, yet food and eating are two of the most difficult human needs to manage. For people living with food insecurity and hunger, having enough to eat means survival, pure and simple. Being fussy about what you eat or getting your favorite delicacies are not an option. When food is available in great quantities, however, habits around getting, preparing, and eating food become more complicated, and so does the mother-daughter relationship. Are you like us in thinking about food all day long?

Food and the next delicious thing we're going to eat is always on our minds. This can be the red flag of a food disorder, an outlet for your creativity, or just a fun activity. Preparing meals may be your job in the family, so you must think about it. The level of your interest in food depends on your history, your culture, your emotional state, your relationships with people around you, and the level of stress you are experiencing. There are other factors, of course, all of which determine your habits and how you think about food and weight.

Do we eat a meal? Do we snack? Do we binge on salty, crunchy crackers, or is it cake time? These are questions that engage and entice this mom and daughter daily. Is ice cream going to tempt us right now, or is today a veggie day? Food is entertainment, comfort, stimulation, love, pleasure. It's also control, shame making, and a constant misery for millions of moms and daughters. To eat or not to eat, as well as what to eat, have become very charged subjects.

As the food and hospitality industries compete to create ever more caloric and addicting foods, the diet industry competes to produce "healthy" snacks as well as expensive remedies for obesity. One industry is making us fat while the other promises to get us thin. Nutritionists and sports trainers have their own philosophies and directions for what we should be eating and when.

All moms/daughters are weight obsessed and constantly influenced by different self-interest groups and people, both social media influencers and the people around us. How many of us can manage healthy food regimes when so many temptations try to derail us? In addition, social media has created a confusing frenzy around body image, which adds another component to the food question. Many of us have body dysmorphia and can be easily influenced. That means we think we're fat when we're thin and vice versa. So, eating or not eating as well as what to eat have become an unhealthy preoccupation for millions of moms and daughters. What goal should we have when it comes to food?

The Eating Evolution

Here is an area where the mother-daughter relationship has many pitfalls beginning at toddler time when daughters first cut their teeth on saying no. By school age, daughters and moms watch and judge each other's habits and beliefs. Research suggests that moms' own eating habits and food choices influence their daughters more than anything else. An authoritarian parenting style can result in the greatest pushback on making healthy diet choices. We've all experienced that. What does your mom eat? Is she a binger or restrictor? Does she indulge in highly caloric eating herself but preach healthy eating to others? Is she consistent or all over the map with diet plans?

We're all quirky when it comes to eating. Secret snacking, bingeing, on-and-off dieting, and restricting all make nutrition a tough subject in many households. By the teen years and beyond, eating can create serious conflict in the mother-daughter relationship. Not surprisingly, relationships with food mirror our relationships with each other. Food and weight can be a black hole of shame, control, and defiance that can lead to food disorders that require treatment and healing.

According to Harvard Health Blog, "Eating disorders are common. In fact, one in seven men and one in five women experience an eating disorder by age forty, and in 95 percent of those cases the disorder begins by age twenty-five. Many kinds of eating disorders may affect children and teens:

- **Anorexia nervosa** is an eating disorder characterized by an extreme fear of gaining weight. People with anorexia nervosa often see themselves as overweight when they are at a healthy weight and even when they are greatly underweight. There are two forms of anorexia nervosa: The restrictive form is when people greatly limit what and how much they eat in order to control their weight. In the binge-purge type, people limit what and how much they eat but also binge and purge—that is, they will eat a large amount at once and try to get rid of the extra calories through vomiting, laxatives, diuretics, or excessive exercise.

- **Bulimia nervosa** involves bingeing and purging but without limiting what and how much a person eats.
- **Binge eating disorder** is when people binge eat but don't purge or restrict. This is the most common eating disorder in the United States.
- **Avoidant restrictive food intake disorder** is most common in childhood. The person limits the amount or type of food they eat, but not because they are worried about their weight. For example, someone with inflammatory bowel disease may associate eating with pain and discomfort and so may avoid eating. Children with sensory issues may find the smell, texture, or taste of certain foods deeply unpleasant and so will refuse to eat them. This is more than just "picky eating" and can lead to malnutrition."

Children can go through periods of not eating for many reasons, and managing eating can become a mother-daughter control issue.

It wasn't always this way. In primitive societies food was sustenance. There wasn't much variety, and humans consumed what they could grow or catch. While preparing food for consumption might have taken time and energy, humans ate to survive, not just for pleasure. Civilization and trade changed all that by introducing new foods and intoxicants such as sugar, tea, chocolate, coffee, alcohol, tobacco, and even cocaine and opium. As the world got smaller, the appetite for intoxicants in foods grew, and so did the variety of foods available. We must add intoxicants into the food picture because mood foods are addictive, so it's not our fault when we crave them.

When we talk about intoxicants, we mean foods and substances that change mood, blood sugar, and even brain function.

If you're wondering why you crave sugar, the simple answer is that sugar stimulates the same part of the brain as cocaine. The brain's reward system, called the mesolimbic dopamine system, gets activated, and you feel good briefly. Your brain lights up and then tells you it wants more later. Sadly, your brain doesn't know what's good for you and what isn't. It reacts to stimulants. Chocolate, tea, and coffee have caffeine that provide an energy boost, and alcohol can be both a stimulant and depressant. There is no judgment about cravings and addictions. They're just facts. This mother and daughter have coffee or tea every day, and chocolate most days. Sugar is a constant challenge. So why do many of us think about food all day long?

Three Compelling Reasons We Obsess About Food

- We have so many food choices. We have access to both healthy and less healthy foods. No foods are seasonal anymore, so nothing is out of reach. If you want it, you can have it. That means we must decide every few hours which way we're going to go. Our self-control becomes a question every time we get hungry.
- We can't turn around without seeing tempting restaurants, food, and snack ads. Advertisers want us to think about highly caloric foods. Even when we don't want to think about it, food triggers are in front of us.
- We have cravings for foods that alter our moods. So, when our blood sugar dips and we get sluggish and "hangry," we crave the foods that will give an instant high. Cravings trigger our willpower and our self-esteem.

To make food and weight issues even more complicated, there are growing industries around wellness, nutrition, food science, and psychology. This growing nutrition industry competes with the diet, hospitality, and food industries. Together they offer conflicting messages that can become toxic eating, dieting, and self-talk habits.

Cultural Influences and Economics

You can't think about food without bringing cultural influences and economics into the picture. Food is not just sustenance for most cultures. Food is love. Food is comfort. Mothers want their daughters to be well fed and happy. Food is a language of love, as we said, when food is available. For many cultures you can see the joy of sharing homemade meals every single day of the year. Mothers throughout the ages have dedicated their lives to preparing food for their families. Cooking according to the seasons has also been part of the enjoyment of food.

What has changed for twenty-first-century moms and daughters is the convenience of fast food and takeout. Mothers in many countries don't have to grow, or bake, or spend all day in the kitchen unless they want to. And many mothers are working and don't have time to focus on shopping and cooking. Frozen or prepared foods in grocery stores and takeout from restaurants provide meals on demand. Takeout can be expensive when it's healthy foods you seek.

Takeout can also be cost-effective but highly caloric. Which do you choose? Again, choosing what you're going to spend to avoid shopping and cooking is another challenge. We haven't seen research on how the convenience factor has changed the mother-daughter dynamic. But we can hazard some guesses from our readers' and our own experience.

Where cooking is a family affair, food is personal. Moms have the power over meal decision-making. The food provided is what the family eats, and children don't get to order something different. That model can be positive role modeling for future generations. Moms' pride in cooking and providing family meals can also create a strong bond when daughters participate in preparation and families take the time to eat together. Mother-daughter cooking, like other shared activities, can provide the most lasting family happy memories and connection. There may also be greater satisfaction and closer relationships when mothers and daughters swap recipes and continue to cook together throughout their lives.

Research does confirm the value of families' eating together and sharing conversation whether food is takeout or homemade. One thing we know is that easy access to prepared foods has increased our daily caloric intake. The ability of moms and daughters to pick their menu at every meal tempts them to choose foods that provide instant gratification and pleasure. The feel-good model of eating also becomes a habit that's passed from one generation to the next. While freedom from preparing foods is a boon to convenience, one unforeseen consequence may be the lack of personal connection to healthy ingredients in food as well as the satisfaction that moms and daughters get from planning meals and cooking together.

Control and Weight

We've talked a little bit about the evolution of food and temptations that have contributed to escalating obesity. Now we'll look at control and weight. Behaviors around food and eating are deeply rooted in control. Here are three areas of control to consider: self-control, mom's control, and daughter's control. It all depends what stage of life you are in. What we eat (when there's enough) is the one thing in life we can control. No one can force us to consume food. Control around eating deeply affects the mother-daughter relationship and the way we feel about ourselves.

Here we would say that family patterns are contagious. In families that don't have much interest in food, weight may not be an issue. People who eat for nutrition, not for delight, generally stop when they're full and don't think too much about it. Not being tempted by sugar helps. Where families have no boundaries in what they will eat or the amount, there may be weight issues and low self-esteem. Remember sugary and fatty foods are addictive, and so are salty crunchy carbohydrates. Eating whatever you want whenever you want can affect your weight and your relationships. It can make you unhappy. You probably already know that.

Family eating is a habit, it's a culture, and it can be a form of control. It's hard to be thin in a big family or to be heavy in a weight-conscious family. There tends to be judgment around eating, no matter what kind of family you have. Moms and daughters are constantly watching each other. A thin mom may have an unhealthy focus on her daughter's weight. That happened to Leslie. While food was celebrated in Leslie's family, there was also a component of restriction, which can become a habit. Where there is restriction in young girls, there is risk of a food disorder in adolescence. A toddler and young daughter may refuse food to exercise her autonomy. She may also refuse food to thwart her mom's authority or to spite her. Getting your daughter to eat at any age can be a control issue in the mother-daughter relationship. That happened to Lindsey.

Leslie's Experience with Food and Weight

On my father's side of the family there was very little interest in food and no controversy surrounding it. Everyone was and still is a "normal" weight. You eat enough and no more. Cake is just a celebration component of life, not an everyday event. No food police or calorie accountants there. On the other hand, food (and drink) is everything on my mother's side of the family.

My mom was the first in her family to start purposefully restricting. She was an early follower of health foods and supplements. I was raised by Mr. Wei, a Chinese chef. My breakfast was fried rice with the leftovers from last night's dinner. Very Chinese. My mom brought a paper napkin with her to dinner every night to quietly dispose of the special desserts Wei made for her. I had no such tricks up my sleeve. I had to eat everything. I was overfed for years and always aware of the caloric cost of my forced feeding. In the entertainment business, my family had an image. It was not acceptable to be too heavy, so I limited my eating as soon as I could. I am to this day a caloric accountant and card-carrying member of the food police.

Food is a subject I love, and weight is a subject I know about. Both cooking and restricting have been my constant companions throughout life. When my kids were little, I made all their meals from scratch and allowed them to choose what they wanted to eat. Bad idea. I often made many dinners to suit different tastes. What was I thinking? It was not how I was raised, but I wanted to be the food diva my mother wasn't. I remember only one occasion when my mother cooked for me. I had an illness on Wei's day off. No takeout in those days. My mom served me Campbell's tomato soup and saltine crackers.

For decades, Campbell's tomato soup was the one thing I always had when I was sick. Wei would make me Chinese penicillin, which is the same as Jewish penicillin (chicken soup) with the addition of fresh grated ginger. Now I wouldn't touch Campbell's soup. "Made from concentrate, too much salt," Wei would say. When I'm sick these days, I make tomato bisque with fresh tomatoes, roasted red peppers, and a dash of half-and-half. Call me a foodie.

So my kids had complete control of me and my happiness. Won't eat this, won't eat that. And later, won't eat anything. Control around food. When someone who will remain nameless had a seriously unhealthy relationship with food, I experimented with fasting to see what it would feel like. I wanted to use what was happening to me as a powerful argument for someone to eat. Not eating shuts down your brain, and I didn't feel good at all.

"No one can function well without food," I would say. "Food fuels your brain."

Try telling that to someone with a food disorder. Then, I started eating for that person in my life who wasn't eating. It didn't help me and didn't help anyone else. You see what was happening here: there was both control and codependency in my behavior around food with my daughter.

If someone in your life has a food disorder of any kind, they don't want interference. If you interfere, trouble will ensue. What happens when someone you love is eating enough sugar and carbs to make them sick on the way to a vacation? You're the food detective. You know how sick your loved one will be. What do you do? You either say something and risk conflict in your relationship or hold your tongue and cope with the consequences. We'll talk about this in the section about boundaries.

 # Lindsey's Experience with Food and Weight

We both wanted to weigh in on this one because food has been a subject of great love and great distress, so it helps to see this one from both points of view. Like my mom, I love food and always have. I've also been disordered with food over the years. When I was little, my mother and I loved everything about food—the shopping, the preparation, the cooking, the eating, and the food coma. I still love all of that, but my relationship with each component of that equation has evolved. In childhood, the focus was on food as pleasure. I wasn't aware of what ingredients cost calorically, so I grabbed whatever I wanted from the aisles, and we cooked with butter, sugar, and oil with reckless abandon.

I have wonderful memories of the cooking and baking we did. Imagine having a mom who could cook literally anything from authentic Chinese food to coq au vin to homemade jams and bread. You don't realize until you're an adult how special these talents are. I'm so grateful that my mom shared cooking with me and taught me enough to be competent in the kitchen. Cooking and the ability to create stunningly beautiful dinners and desserts is one of the many things I love and admire about my mom. In the mother-daughter relationship, appreciating your mother's talents and efforts is important, no matter how much she annoys you. Keep that in mind.

I do believe cooking has been a through line and activity that has brought my mom and me together from the very beginning. Food and cooking are a healing component of many of our stories. My mom instilled in me her love for food, creating meals together, and even the bonding that takes place when we cook. When I was little, we had high tea, and it was the treat I looked forward to every day. My mother used to say I ate up to my elbows, and it was true. Growing up, I had a healthy appetite, and food was a delightful part of life.

Somewhere in middle and high school I became self-conscious about food, and I don't know where that came from. At that time, heroin skinny was chic, and I was not skinny. Perhaps, my self-consciousness was around my weight, but whatever the cause, I didn't feel comfortable eating in front of people in high school. I remember starving my way through the day, munching on candy or something that wouldn't seem like I needed real food while dying to get home so the eating could begin.

On the other hand, if I was eating in private with one of my food buddies, let the games begin! The eating buddies, and my mom could be one of them, were the best because people who love to overeat will come together and do what they love most—eat.

My eating issues became serious with substance abuse. The need for food as a mood lifter decreased as my drug use grew. I was very thin on and off as I struggled, and I'm sure that was disturbing for my mom to watch. As an adult, I know it's frightening to see someone you love not eating enough or overeating to feel better. We all have people in our lives who struggle with food regulation.

This is one example of how food can become a control issue. Moms want their daughters to eat the right things or eat with them, and daughters want whatever they want. Food becomes a charged topic when you're not on the same page. Nobody wants to be told what to do, and it feels awful to have someone watching your every move. As an adult, I can still find it irritating when my mom judges my choices. So, moms, here's what I think. It doesn't matter how good your intentions are, no one likes being told what to do.

Ultimately, I found ways to make healthy eating my friend, but only some of my motivation came from Mom. I had to do my own research. Finding the right diet is a personal choice. When I got into recovery, healthy eating was not my top priority. My goal was to stay sober. Over the years I've become a healthy eater now guided by nutritional needs and health concerns. Finding the right way to support your mom/daughter in this area is helpful to your relationship.

Think About This

As you can see, food is deeply personal, and we all have experiences with family and food that have brought great pleasure and extreme anxiety. You don't have to have a food disorder to have a complicated relationship with food. Regulating what we eat is a challenge for all of us. Having a great relationship with your body image is rare, so we must add a note on how our ambition to be beautiful can bring on food disorders. Now is the time to find some awareness around your habits and culture and see how they affect your mother-daughter relationship.

TIME TO JOURNAL

The goal of this exercise is to get honest about our own relationship with food so that we can have a healthy relationship with our mom/daughter. We also need a healthy relationship with our body image. Not easy, we know. When it comes to you and your mom/daughter, what was your journey like? Did you have enough to eat? Maybe you did but your mom or grandmother didn't. Is food a control issue in your family? Are you happy/unhappy with your or your mom/daughter's eating habits? Are there ways you could work together on the food issues? Improvements that you could make together? Let's remember the good times, like Lindsey did, and then you can touch on whether your mom/daughter supported your diet choices. Are there ways you and your mother can share balance around being healthy?

JOURNAL PROMPTS

1. How did you feel about eating as a child? Describe what kinds of food you ate and your relationship with mom around eating.

2. What was your family's relationship with food like?

3. Did anyone try to change your relationship with food? Explain how.

4. Does food ever make you unhappy and you secretly think your eating is disordered in some way? Explain how eating makes you feel now.

5. Does your mother/daughter support your eating habits? Explain how.

6. Is this an area where you would like to make changes? What kind of changes would you make?

CHAPTER 7

Finances and Money

umans have had strong feelings about money for as long as it's been around, so forever. Society can't function without money; moms can't take care of their daughters without money. Money and how to handle it are of critical importance, yet many women are not properly prepared to earn, manage, or talk about money. For the purposes of this book, we're talking about personal finances here.

Personal finances are all about the way we manage money and assets, and this is another potential snake pit of conflict for moms and daughters. Money makes the world go around. It also affects our self-esteem, our well-being, and even our health. If you lack the finances to cover basic needs such as shelter, food, medical care, transportation, and education, life is stressful and frightening—for both mothers and daughters. You can feel less than around your peers, family, and colleagues. You might become so plagued with worry about making ends meet that your fears make you emotionally or physically unavailable.

If there's a surplus, on the other hand, there may be entitlement, behavioral issues, spending issues, and other kinds of dysfunction that accompany excess. There are plenty of cautionary tales of wealthy mothers and daughters caught up in materialism and superficiality that ultimately erodes good sense and healthy decision-making. Without financial know-how and healthy financial habits, mothers and daughters can get themselves into trouble and conflict over money.

While your possessions may define how you think about yourself, wealth doesn't necessarily make you happy or solve all problems. In fact, great wealth can cause more problems than it solves in an unhealthy family model. That's the reason managing money and creating healthy values around money are so important. A healthy attitude about money and work, as well as having some control over its management, creates a solid foundation for mother-daughter relationships, no matter their financial circumstances.

There are millions of stories about families who have very little in the way of material possessions but who feel rich and happy. For some cultures, having enough is more than sufficient for happiness and contentment. For others, not having enough is a constant stressor and source of shame. Basically, money is fraught whether you have it or not. We all are more than what we have or earn. We all need to know and feel that. A person's value doesn't depend on how much they have materially, but how many people feel this way?

Why Is Money So Fraught?

Money represents everything—freedom, status, love, importance, even where you sit on an airplane. You know who's who based on money. For mothers and daughters, everything from what they eat, what they wear, self-care, pet care, home life, social life, schooling, and more is affected by the amount of money they have, the way they manage it, and their values around it. So, while it's all just money, it can represent how loved you feel, how taken care of you are, whether you look the way you'd like, and whether your dreams are valued. No pressure, right? When you start to break it down, it's obvious that money means so much because it affects so many areas of our lives.

Because finances play such a big role in the mother-daughter relationship, an unhealthy attitude about money and work can do serious and lasting damage. In sustaining unrealistic or disparaging beliefs about money and values, such as "We're rich" or "We're poor," mothers and daughters can make misguided and harmful choices. Simply providing, or not providing, an education sends a million messages to your daughter and the world. We've seen families go into debt over their children's first-class education when their children didn't appreciate or deserve it. We've also seen families that could afford tuition but would not pay for top universities after their children had worked for years to get in.

People who live for money, power, and prestige may pressure their daughters to prioritize values that leave them emotionally empty in important ways. Emotional wellness, satisfied intellect, and happiness are often not considered when mom's focus is on achievement and status. On the other end of the spectrum are moms who spend their income for their own gratification and don't adequately support their daughters' schooling and health care needs. Just because mom refuses to see doctors or invest in health care doesn't mean her daughter doesn't need those services. Moms who are compulsive shoppers or have reckless and dangerous money behavior can throw a family into a deep well of debt and chaos.

If your family has any form of dysfunction, finances will be part of it. In many cultures, women don't have control of the family purse strings and don't know where the money is or how it's being spent. Lack of financial control is anxiety making. How about addiction, overspending, or gambling in the family? Try to find the money or where it goes. You won't be able to because it disappears without a trace. When addictive behavior is in the picture, family members are often left in despair, sometimes without the basics they need to survive. Before diving down into that issue, let's look at why money can become toxic in the family dynamic.

When Money Is Toxic

In the mother-daughter dynamic, fighting about finances is seldom about money itself. It's usually about control. Financial abuse, which is an extreme version of financial control, is common in dysfunctional families. Research indicates that financial abuse is experienced in 98 percent of abusive relationships. The victims indicate that their lack of ability to provide financially for themselves was the main reason for staying in or returning to such a battering relationship.

If mom and dad (or caregivers) are engaged in a deeply unhealthy relationship with money, it's going to trickle down to the mother-daughter relationship. When daughters grow up seeing a toxic/control dynamic around finances between parents, she may copy that behavior with her own daughter down the road. Either way, money is control. If there is not enough money, daughters may have to forget about new clothes, school needs, easy transportation, or money to spend on entertainment or with friends.

Money is always going to be a hot-button subject. The strained issue of toxic finances shades everything it touches. The despair felt by daughters who can't have what they think they need is deep and can leave traumatic scars, especially if they were teased over the lack. At the same time the shame felt by mothers who can't give their daughters what they want or need brings a whole other level of emotional pain and embarrassment. When finances are toxic, angry feelings around money can be active volcanoes.

If there's too much money, bribery and manipulation can be another kind of toxic dynamic between mothers and daughters. Moms can use money to buy their way into or out of trouble with their daughters by focusing on the value of material things rather than emotional development and qualities that make people loving and kind. Daughters can become so used to having their parents' money, they believe the assets are theirs to use as they please. Daughters who have no money boundaries can get their mothers in terrible trouble. Addict/alcoholic daughters can bankrupt their families by stealing and needing decades of recovery services. We believe having boundaries and a healthy understanding of money and finances are necessary for a healthy and satisfying mother-daughter relationship.

Leslie's Experience with Finances

This is another area where Lindsey and I both want to share a few words about our experience. What was most interesting to us was how we both had the same experience with finances. It's important to clearly illustrate where my lack of knowledge was repeated with Lindsey. Had I known I was sending Lindsey out into the world with the same lack of financial savvy I had, I would have done things differently.

The most important part of my story is that no one taught me how to earn or manage money. While my parents lived a lavish lifestyle, I never had any money of my own. I was dependent on what they decided I should have rather than what I wanted or needed. Remember the incident when I wanted but couldn't have a yo-yo? My association with successful parents often felt like a punishment, not a benefit. This lack of control over my finances made me desperate to earn my own living. But how could I do that? These days, the children of wealthy parents can start their own businesses or trade on their position or beauty alone. There was no way for me to do that.

When I visited Walter Cronkite at CBS in 1970 to ask for a job in the newsroom, he told me the Evening News was not a suitable place for a girl like me. He assured me I had the credentials, and he would be happy to hire me. However, he had spoken to my dad, and my parents did not approve of the late hours or the newsroom culture where I would work. In short, they didn't think it would be a safe place for me. I was twenty-four. I made the rounds. When I went to Arthur Ochs Sulzberger, publisher of the *New York Times*, to ask for a job writing an opinion column, Sulzberger told me the *Times* had no interest in publishing women's issues or humor in the Opinion section. At *Vogue*, where the beauty editor was a personal friend of my mom's, I failed the typing test.

Against my parents' wishes, I had worked as an advertising copywriter, then as a copywriter at Bantam Books, a columnist at *New York Magazine*, a freelance magazine writer, and a novelist and playwright. Everywhere I worked my bosses affirmed my writing competency. Because of my family, however, it was often assumed that I did not need money and was consistently paid a lower salary than anyone else. Another note here. Boys from wealthy and successful families have always had entrees to jobs, and perks, and opportunities, that were not as a rule available to girls. Wealthy families wanted and expected their sons to use their connections while girls did not have that freedom in the business world. Sexual favors were one way to get ahead no matter who you were, but that was not something I could do.

Today, the wealthy and privileged are paid more for their connections. In my day, being a girl and having connections was a disability. In an effort not to give me special treatment, I was paid less. My low salary in all my writing jobs made me feel less than and ensured my dependency on my parents. There is some debate now about nepotism and the impact it has on businesses and families. Getting special treatment or being valued because of money or the lack of it can both be hurtful.

Lindsey's story is more meaningful than mine in some ways. As financial education and money management had not been part of my culture or experience, it was not part of my daughter's. Instead of teaching her the value of money, I taught her how to spend and have fun with it. When mothers don't do their financial homework, this is what happens.

 ## Lindsey's Experience with Finances

I have a radically different vantage point from my mom when it comes to money. You're about to see how money and personal finances play a major part in my story of addiction and of recovery. You see, when you spend two decades in and out of recovery, you meet a lot of people along the way. Think rehabs, sober living, support groups (in multiple cities), and on and on.

Most women I've met have a co-occurring diagnosis, which means addiction and mental health. People with mental illness (depression, anxiety, bipolar disorder, food disorders) as well as addiction often need to seek recovery in more than one area.

For me, after I had time in recovery from addiction, it became clear I had a deeply unhealthy relationship with money. I have sought help for my money dysfunction and will need guidance with this issue for the rest of my life. Both having money and lacking money made my life miserable. In short, I am traumatized by money.

Here's where my mom's experience and mine differ. We both come from privilege, but I lost it all. When I got into trouble, I fled. I made the decision to leave family and friends behind and go out on my own. I was not prepared for life without financial help. I had never examined a bill to see if it was correct or opened a bank statement. There were bookkeepers and accountants for that. I had a trust fund from the sale of my grandfather's company in 1988, and I had access to it starting when I graduated from college.

Today, estate planners for wealthy families recommend restricting access to trust funds until young adults reach the age of thirty or forty. There are plenty of examples of how wrong things can go when children grow up knowing they have money and are able to spend it before learning how to create a viable life without it. I wish I could say I did something good with my trust fund. I did not. I was too sick in those years to know better. I had addiction, moved many times, had a lavish lifestyle, a marriage, and a divorce by the age of twenty-nine, all of which depleted my assets. I did not understand that money can run out and that debt could make things much worse.

Numbers are not my forte, and I still get stressed when dealing with them. When I couldn't get through algebra in high school, my teachers switched me to mechanical drawing instead of tutoring me. No one helped me learn math. No one taught me about money or how the stock market works. My ability to manage money was to call a banker and ask for more, which I always got. I didn't know when a money manager failed or stole from my account. I didn't know what it meant when I had 100,000 shares of a tech company, and the value went to zero.

In my messy thirties, as life got real, the money was gone. I found myself in quite a bind. Then came the fight and split from my mother, which created a whole new set of circumstances for me. I had no ten-room family apartment to run to, no houses where I could stay. I was truly on my own. I had to earn a living and hustled to find writing and communications work to keep myself afloat. But this was not the lax "writer/filmmaker" life I'd been living, partly on my mom's dime, for so long. This was me—midthirties, divorced, postspinal surgery, seriously depressed, single, and having to survive on my own.

Have you ever been so angry that you were willing to do something that would have profound consequences for you financially and emotionally? Because I have. At thirty-six, I decided it was time to leave my hometown for good. I was done with the city that left haunted memories on every corner. I could no longer afford the city I had both adored and hated. I wanted a fresh start in the sunshine where I could be invisible for a while. I packed up what I had and put it in storage. I left for Los Angeles with one suitcase and moved into a furnished Airbnb with enough money to pay some bills but not start a full life. It was a mixed time because there were true highs and lows in those early Los Angeles years.

I found myself at the age where my friends from high school were buying their second homes and I was living paycheck to paycheck, in debt, with almost no understanding of how I'd gotten there. Sometimes I felt so furious over everything that happened I thought I'd never get over it. How could I have been so dumb and reckless with my money? How could I have squandered so much on so little? Sometimes I was terrified about the future and my ability to recover everything I had lost. Then, other times I'd be overwhelmed with relief and wildly hopeful about what I was capable of, if only I could reach my potential—I had escaped New York, and I was finally on my own. It was not the lavish life I was used to, but I had always loved Los Angeles, and now I was free to do whatever I wanted whenever I wanted. My mom was out of the picture.

I spent a year waking up at 4 a.m. every morning convinced I would be homeless, but that passed as the months went on, and I always found a way to pay my rent. I also joined a financial recovery program, which changed my life. I hadn't been aware I had money trauma or a dysfunctional relationship with money. Having a sponsor and friends in that program made life exponentially better. There were other people who had the same issues around money that I had; they found solutions and were recovering.

My mom has had her own financial traumas, but she's never had to clean a house to pay an expensive vet bill. As a former trust-fund kid with a BA from Johns Hopkins and MA from NYU, I don't find it easy to share these early mistakes and losses. Many young people screw their lives up and don't know how to fix it. You can fix your life no matter how hard the challenge seems. I had maxed out a few credit cards, not knowing how debt works, I had cards to stores that were in collections I did not know about, and there was that little tax issue.

At twenty-two, I had used credit cards and spent like a forty-year-old. In my thirties, and financially unstable, I had a nervous breakdown. Money owned me in a demonic way. When I had too much, I had a bizarre survivor's guilt. I didn't feel I deserved it, yet it made me feel better than other people. I overspent to feel better, I bought ridiculous things to make me look better. I spent recklessly. Then when there wasn't enough, I lived in complete and utter deprivation and panic. Money consumed me, and I was closer to suicide over money issues than I ever was over addiction. With addiction, I always knew it would end, that I would get through it and feel better eventually. With the money, I wanted to die. The fear of not having enough, the shame at having lost so much, the despair over knowing how far behind my peers I had fallen. It was money that almost destroyed me, and learning how to manage it brought me back to sanity.

Think About This

Every family has a history with money, and the health of your mother-daughter relationship is going to be closely tied with the family's experience with finances. Everyone has some kind of issue around money, how to spend, how to earn it, how to share it. If you and your daughter are fighting over money, it's critical to understand where the feelings come from. What are the real causes of your conflict? Once you have some clarity and understanding about your habits, then comes the learning process and the healing.

Does your family have certain habits around money that you can think of? Is there a feast-or-famine mentality, or does a constant fear of not having enough create anxiety? What was your financial education like? Did you get any financial education from family or at school? If this isn't your core issue, that's great! We applaud you for having fine financial skills. We have journal prompts for you to think about, too.

TIME TO JOURNAL

Screaming at each other over money is absolutely the worst and a recipe for bad feelings. If money is a tough issue, this is a wonderful opportunity to learn how to support each other in healthy ways. In this section, we want you to think about how you feel about money. Does it cause good feelings or bad? Do you feel secure or insecure? Is your mother/daughter a financial support or a financial stressor? The goal here is not to point blame ever, just enlighten and clarify so you can know how to move forward in a better way.

JOURNAL PROMPTS

1. What did you learn about money from your mother?

2. Did your mom learn from her mother?

3. Do you have good financial skills? Does your mother/daughter?

4. Does dealing with money or talking about money make you uncomfortable? If so, why?

5. If you have great financial skills, how did you get them?

6. If you feel challenged by money or earnings, explain why.

Bonus: Do you have financial skills you'd like to learn? If so, what are they?

CHAPTER 8

Appearance and Style

D o you and your mom/daughter fight over clothes, personal expression, and style? You would not be alone here. The expectations of culture, values, religion, gender, and personal beliefs can all affect the mother-daughter relationship when it comes to appearance and looks. Daughters have many more options for personal expression than their moms did only a generation ago, but freedom to go overboard and even make permanent changes can have negative consequences. Stigma and personal safety may result from attention-getting dressing. Attracting hordes of men can be dangerous, and extreme styles can be stigmatizing. It can be a real problem for the mother-daughter relationship.

Not every mom and daughter have conflicts in this area, of course, but appearance can become a power struggle that makes mother-daughter harmony challenging. Moms' wishes and expectations may conflict with messages daughters receive from the wider world as well as the messages they want to send about themselves.

Who should decide the appropriateness of a daughter's appearance? When social media encourages fifteen-year-olds to have millions of TikTok followers just by showing off their body, does this make skimpy dressing and getting likes from strangers right for your daughter? Girls are showing off their physical selves and changing them with surgery. Even expression of gender itself can be controversial. Moms are trying to look younger; daughters are trying to look sexier. Looks can drive you crazy, for sure. Let's get to it.

Moms and Image

A mom's style can boost her daughter's self-esteem and give her confidence for life. A mom's style can also cause acute embarrassment. Mom's quirky taste in clothes can cause a lifetime of tough moments even for the most confident daughter, especially if she exposes herself on social media. And the same goes for a daughter whose style is extreme, who is active on social media and who opens herself to the judgment of others.

What do mothers want for their daughters? In the simplest terms, moms want their offspring to mirror themselves and look the part defined for them. Moms want their daughters to be safe, to form healthy relationships, and potentially to achieve more than they did. It gets more complicated when moms use their daughters to fulfill their own dreams and ambitions, especially when it comes to their looks. If a daughter is conventionally pretty, her mom may want her to use her beauty to get a rich husband or rise on the social ladder. A good outcome might reflect well on her and be the model for what she thinks will be a happy life. Is that selfish? Maybe.

Ever since Jane Austen wrote about women as social commerce, we have enjoyed reading about beauty and the jockeying for status. It is not just fiction. Status and looks defined Leslie's first marriage and set her up for confusion and profound self-esteem issues. Beauty and status are commodities still. If a mom focuses on outward attractiveness for her daughter to achieve success, however, it sends a message that looks are everything.

Here's where good looks have a dark side. Any woman who believes her appearance is her greatest asset is going to be insecure about how she looks every day. Every pimple becomes a threat. After all, beauty is difficult to maintain. No one is attractive all the time, or forever. Your attractiveness is only one aspect of you, and not the most lasting quality. On the other hand, if a daughter is not considered pretty by her family, culture, or schoolmates, her mom may want to fix or hide her, or encourage her to develop herself in other ways. This can be conflict making or esteem building.

And what happens if a beloved child starts to alter her looks in permanent ways that hurt and disturb her mom? How does that affect the mother-daughter relationship? What should a mom do if her daughter is walking around half naked, putting herself and her friends in danger? What if she is covered with tattoos and piercings, and mom is conservative, embarrassed, or worried? Let's see how our lasting views of ourselves and our attractiveness develop. But first a note on social media.

Social media has had a powerful impact on moms and image. Being a mommy influencer, for example, can mean documenting your child's every move to get attention and build an audience. While some moms may have the best intentions, making your child's life and growing pains public on the Internet leaves both of you exposed to unintended harm and dangers. The potential perils of promoting yourself and your daughter include stalking, predators, trolls, and giving access to other unsavory people through comments. Furthermore, infants and children are not able to decide for themselves whether they want their lives to be documented for other people's entertainment. Even worse, the images will last forever. In Leslie's experience family privacy was everything, the very opposite of the way it is now.

Leslie's Appearance Experience

In my case, my mother never once told me I was pretty. As a designated "girl-child and an ugly one," how could I feel confident? I had chubby cheeks and was sometimes nicknamed chipmunk or chippy. My freckles and curly hair were dominant features. I had a pot belly, which resembled that of my grandmother, who urged me to overeat for starving Armenians.

Like all children, however, I was cute. And quite by accident I became an influencer. As a five-year-old I was dressed to help a business level up. I had my own personal stylist. When Stanley Marcus became the chairman of Neiman Marcus in 1950, the store was looking to brand itself as "Continental Chic" in Dallas.

My dad was a movie producer and friend of Marcus. In those days everybody who was anybody was a crony or friend. I became an inadvertent influencer for Neiman Marcus children's wear. The boxes of gorgeous clothes arrived seasonally. And I modeled and wore them on our family travels in Chicago, Paris, Rome, New York, and London with the greatest pride. I did not know I was a model. I just knew that being well dressed was fun.

In London, when I was seven, I wore a Neiman Marcus dress on the set of *Moulin Rouge* and fit right into the Belle Epoch mood of the United Artists "picture," as movies were called back then. At

Pinewood Studios, John Huston stopped filming to carry me around on his shoulders and show me the costumes and makeup. No wonder I became fascinated with textiles and style. "Pictures" and fashion were real life to me. They are also real to Lindsey. When I grew out of my Neiman Marcus dresses and coats, my cousins in Chicago wore them. There was no downside to being stunning as a child because it did not go to my head. People looked at me, admiring my clothes, as fans look at the children of celebrities today. But no one ever took my picture in Cannes or Nice, or anywhere.

There are no records of me, very few photos. It was not permitted to photograph me or my beautiful mother. And I never once thought the attention I had received as a child had anything to do with the actual me. I was a movie industry accessory. When I was thirteen, however, the body fix began. Moving into seventh grade and upper school, I was heading for the trauma of losing my girlfriends and the boy I adored to much better-looking people.

In one year, I fell emotionally and academically from the top of the class to the bottom. Suddenly I was not one of the beautiful people, and I was alone. This was when the words "girl-child and an ugly one" had catastrophic meaning to me. What happens in middle and high school when girls are not as cute as they once were? What if they lose their friends? What if they are not doing well academically?

My sudden inferior performance in school worried my mom, but instead of exploring my emotional condition, she sent me to Columbia University for intelligence testing to see if I was getting less smart as well as less pretty. Unfortunately, she forgot to send someone to pick me up. Don't ask how I found my way back to the Bronx after many hours of grueling testing. In any case, no one ever told me the results of that important IQ test, which makes me feel to this day that the results were not good. Was my intelligence a dark secret that could hurt me if it were known? How important is smart anyway?

The reason I tell this story is that when I was not thriving at school, and after the results of my IQ test came in, my mom chose to fix my appearance, not my grades. When a twelve- or thirteen-year-old girl enters middle school, she may not be prepared with the life skills she needs to navigate the transition between a loving environment and a socially and academically demanding one. For example, I missed some important schooling when we were traveling in Europe, and no one taught me how to study. Education gets serious in middle school, and I did not know how to learn hard things. But my mom decided that a physical overhaul was the solution to the problem. If not smart, I had to get better-looking.

Mr. Wei drove me to Manhattan and waited downstairs on 8th Avenue while I got my next assessment. I climbed the stairs to Joe Pilates's famous studio by myself to learn what could be done to fix me. Joe was an old German bodybuilder who had once worked in a circus and later designed the bodies of movie stars. I was his youngest victim and about to be designed on the model of Marilyn Monroe.

"Your mother is a thoroughbred," he told me; "You, a Shetland pony. Lot of work to do."

Joe, who had worked on a few bodies for Dad's TV shows, had a plan. Joe's philosophy was to open the chest, define the waist, develop the core muscles, and build strength, balance, and stamina. He designed my pudgy body to have 32" 22" 32" measurements. It took a few years, but I did not turn out to be alone on this project. Both my mother and father went to Pilates. It was a family thing we all did.

I was the first "Pilates baby" and loved every minute of it, even the cold showers at the end of every session. I worked out for years in the original Pilates studio with dancers and musicians trained by Joe and his wife, Clara, and then Hannah, the third Pilates musketeer. What was great about my Pilates training was that it started early, and it set me on a path of self-regulation and exercise. I was in control of my body if nothing else. And my parents were part of it. Pilates training gave me physical confidence and a Hollywood body. Of course, I did not know that it was a commodity. I just knew it made me feel better, and the clothes looked good. Now I had to dress like my mom did.

Here are the rules I had to follow. Do not wear blue jeans. Your butt is too big. Do not wear prints. Flashy is tacky. Jackie Kennedy did not wear prints. Do not show too much chest, and no breast at all. Do not pierce your ears or mutilate your body. Do not wear clothes that cling. Always wear a girdle and hose. Your bottom shouldn't be seen and mustn't wiggle when you walk. Ladies don't wiggle. Always wear a jacket to cover any part of your body that might potentially wiggle. Your hair shouldn't move, either. Important accessories are scarves, gloves, and designer purses. Never go without at least two defining accessories. Your accessories are your passport. Always have a clean hanky up your sleeve to wipe your nose. And never, ever take your girdle off.

What is the message that this kind of appearance sends? Well, for one thing, ladies are not girly and fun. Ladies do not have butts or breasts. They simply cannot tease. Teasing is tacky. Girls are solemn affairs, not humans. Better be good, or else. Don't laugh or talk too loudly. And speak intelligently, or don't speak at all.

Not surprisingly, I was a preppy dresser as a teen and young woman, and I still am. At every party, I will be the one wearing a silk blouse, a blazer, and flashy shoes with heels when everyone else is sleeveless and flip-flopped. I wear heels to the grocery store. While I longed to wear prints (until the age of Pucci and Gucci), I did not argue with my mom's style. You can safely say I am still her clone stylistically. Like every mom, I have ideas about how a girl and a professional should look. But my ideas are only right for me. This is true for pretty much everything. I had to learn that, ironically, from my daughter. Recovery is about learning where your lane is, and how to stay in it.

Did I want Lindsey to be a little Leslie clone? Maybe. We can laugh all the way around the block on how silly it is for moms to want their daughters to be just like them. I sewed Lindsey's clothes when she was a child and cut her hair short, like mine had been. She was adorbs.

"You're gorgeous," I'd say. "What a beauty." Lindsey didn't believe me, of course, and she never wanted to emulate my little lady style.

One note I must add about my mom. She did finally get me the academic help I needed and moved me to a different high school where I thrived and graduated second in my class. An all-girls school was the right choice for me. Moms' timing may not be perfect, so it is important not to hold grudges for what they did not do but rather be grateful for whatever they were able to do.

Lindsey's Experience with Appearance and Style

Simply put, your appearance is the way you look. But it's so much more than that, isn't it? Your view of yourself and your appearance affects absolutely everything in your life. From how you dress to how you carry yourself to who you attract and how you let people treat you. It all has everything to do with the way you feel about your appearance. What was I thinking until adulthood? That I was an ugly duckling. That my mom was beautiful, and I had not inherited her looks. In my younger years, I lived in this constant, uncomfortable state of self-consciousness, but I was also a people pleaser, which made having choices and speaking out impossible. My confusion was difficult for everyone else, too. If you're wondering what that looks like and feels like, it's like this: If someone was upset, I had to fix it. To the point where other people's feelings were what I was aware of, not my own.

If someone wasn't happy with what I was wearing, I'd immediately change. I did and wore what my mom, or whoever was watching me at the time, told me to. I was enmeshed with other people's wants and needs. I also learned incredibly early to keep my own feelings and needs to myself most of the time, so the disease of emotional isolation began early for me. Just like secret keeping. I don't know how or where these behaviors started, but it has always seemed safer for me to keep feelings hidden. If few people know the true you, the chances of being made fun of or hurt decrease.

When I was little, I would sit on the floor of my mom's closet and wrap myself in her fur coats and scarves. I'd clomp around in her heels and watch her, rapt, as she put on her makeup and jewelry. I thought she was the most beautiful woman in the world. My mom didn't have bad skin or trouble knowing what to wear. She made it look easy. She did not seem to understand why I felt so different and ugly. Of course, now I look at pictures and see why she didn't understand. I was not the deformed person I thought I was. Mom didn't understand because there was no way she could have imagined that the lack of self-esteem she had experienced as a child and teen were the same feelings I had a generation later. Why does that happen? My mom never told me to feel bad about myself.

On the contrary, she told me I was beautiful and her precious angel. So why did I inherit feelings from generations past that didn't apply to my reality? This brings me to an important point about your family's culture and how it affects you. Culture doesn't change with the times. My family was unusually old-fashioned. My grandfather wore a blazer on his own beach. My father was a prepster, too. My great-grandmother wore a corset every single day, and my grand-mother raised my mom with rigid rules she still follows today.

Mom would regularly buy me the clothes she wanted me to wear. We'd look at them approvingly in stores as I tried them on, and then they'd sit in my closet with their tags still on never to be worn even once. In real life, I was showing how I felt on the inside with my clothes messy, torn, and in need of repairs. My hair wasn't spared from the rapidly changing styles of the nineties. My hair color went from platinum blond to Manic Panic wine color to black and on and on. I do remember being quite scared after I had gone to Patricia Field's, in the days when there was a salon run by drag queens in the back. I had my hair stripped white. It didn't come out as planned, and I was left with a head of yellow and white striped hair.

Worse, I had to fly to Florida the next day to show up for a huge party my parents were hosting in Sarasota. I remember arriving at the airport wearing a hoodie with the hood up. "What's up with the hood?" my mom asked, frowning.

"Nothing. I never look good when I travel."

"Let me see."

"No." I was a charmer.

"Okay then." Mom ripped the hood down and gasped. "What the ____?"

My long hair was in stripes from the bottom up. Deep yellow to mid yellow to blond to colorless at the roots.

"Yeah," we're going to have to do something about that," she said.

The surprising part of this story is mom wasn't mad that I had colored my hair before her party; she was furious that I'd gotten such a bad job down in Greenwich Village, instead of a more professional salon uptown. She was going to cut those yellow stripes out. She lured me into her bathroom and proceeded to cut my hair back into that weird bob/bowl-shaped haircut I'd managed to avoid for years. It's the only haircut she knows how to do. The problem this time was, I was a junior in high school, not a toddler, and it was embarrassing for months. I did dye it black. I have a picture of the black bob.

Think About This

Our appearance may play the biggest role in revealing how we feel about ourselves. We all tell a story in the way we look. This includes the expression on our faces. Does your daughter/mother smile and enjoy banter or hide behind a sullen look? How is her hygiene? Does she bathe, wash her hair, and brush her teeth? Everything about her appearance tells you how she feels about herself.

Does she have friends? How do they dress? How do dad and her brothers treat her? Fashion is self-expression. Girls want the freedom to follow the fashions of the times, or their own. These days that may mean tattoos, piercings, a lot of makeup, skimpy and revealing clothes, rainbow hair. It may mean grunge or Goth or androgynous. It may be everything you detest, or it may be just like you.

If you are fighting about your daughter's/mom's appearance, think about what she is telling you. What does she want? Is she trying to get your attention, negative or positive? Is she depressed? Are you open to hearing about what is happening to her inside? No matter where they are in the world, daughters want to be seen as individuals. They want to be understood, accepted, and loved for who they are and the way they look. All daughters want their feelings to be acknowledged and heard, but not all moms are open to listening without offering a rebuttal.

TIME TO JOURNAL

Validating your daughter's feelings may threaten a closely held belief system or challenge the health of your family dynamics. What are the demands of your culture or community? Are you taking sides against your daughter when she becomes too independent in her attire or style? Do you call her names or shame her? Listening without arguing doesn't mean you have to agree with her style or appearance. You do not have to offer solutions that only work for you.

Mothers may tell their daughters things that are not true about their daughters' appearance, either that they're not good-looking or that they are especially good-looking when they're not. Either way, girls can get confusing and destructive messages that stick with them and make life and relationships difficult down the road.

JOURNAL PROMPTS

1. What did your mother teach you about appearance?

2. How comfortable are you with your looks?

3. Can you listen to your daughter's feelings about her appearance without being a fixer?

4. How can you help your daughter feel good about herself?

5. If you're a mother who is critical or a faultfinder, learning acceptance of others will help your daughter's self-esteem and acceptance of you.

6. Is there anything you'd like to do to improve your style?

CHAPTER 9

Friends and Boyfriends/Girlfriends and Romantic Partners

*A*re your mom's/daughter's friendships and romantic partners a source of conflict in your relationship? Having friends, boyfriends/girlfriends, and a romantic partner provide not only support but also many opportunities for growth. Who can you talk to? Who helps you when you need answers and new ideas to inspire? We all need mentors, guides, teachers, and friends. Our moms are great but can't be our whole world. Moms provide one perspective. To be whole and balanced, however, we need connections outside our family circle. Expanding our world beyond each other has saved this mother-daughter relationship. We couldn't reach our potential without help from outside sources.

We know many daughters who have been profoundly hurt by their moms, but even those who deeply love and appreciate their excellent moms need to go out in the world and find other influences. Growing up and acquiring new friends can cause conflict between moms and daughters in so many ways. Friendship itself can feel like a threat, especially when daughters are not making the healthiest choices.

For both moms and daughters, friends, boyfriends/girlfriends, and romantic partners can be a source of jealousy, control, and codependency. Has this area caused drama and lasting wounds for you? The way moms and daughters manage their friend relationships can have a positive impact that improves their lives or negative and destructive consequences that tear them apart. Some moms want complete control over their daughter's choices in friends and boyfriends/girlfriends. Others stand by helplessly as their daughters choose inappropriate or even abusive companions to share their lives.

Daughters can have the same dilemma. Mom's friends and boyfriends can be a source of embarrassment, unhealthy behavior, and even danger. A teen daughter's attempts to be safe in a home where there's drinking or drug use can cause conflict and verbal abuse. When mom is a drinker or substance user, she may not consider that bringing her buddies home can cause problems. While being high may seem funny at times, or easy to excuse, drinking and drugging around children and teens is always unsafe. Those who are high on drugs are reckless and can behave in frightening ways. This goes for both moms and daughters. Who is at home, and what are they doing?

Why Healthy Friendships Matter

The motivational speaker Jim Rohn has said, "We are the average of the five people we spend the most time with." When we heard that expression, it really made us stop and think. Think about that for a moment and consider what the five people you're closest to reveal about you.

The most common way we make friends is through our interests and geography: people who live in the same neighborhood or who go to the same schools, churches, music groups, or other shared activities. Self-esteem also affects how moms and daughters choose their friends and love relationships. If your self-esteem is well developed and solid, the chances of your being attracted to people who have the same robust characteristics increase exponentially. Healthy friendships and relationships foster trust, loyalty, dependability, encouragement, and other equally supportive traits. They also provide a great model for your daughters.

Insecure moms/daughters, on the other hand, who have jealousy issues, or a mean streak, may attract friends who accept their behavior and feed into the drama. Do you know friends who constantly fight, talk behind each other's back, steal each other's boyfriends, girlfriends, possessions, and repeat personal information? They are untrustworthy, undependable, competitive, demanding, and possessive. Their romantic relationships will also be tumultuous, possibly even abusive.

Who Are Your Friends?

Who have been your best friends over the years? Who were you drawn to, the sweet girls who can do no harm, the pushovers, the bullies, the wild girls who get you into trouble? Where do you fit into the healthy friendship equation? Being aware of who you are is important when it comes to understanding who you've chosen as your friends and boyfriends. If all your friends are pushovers, maybe you're the bully. If you're doing everything for everyone you know, maybe you're the pushover. The goal here, as with everything in this book, is not to judge but to achieve awareness so you can make changes. Finding friendships that are equally supportive and compassionate is a great goal.

Creating and maintaining healthy friendships takes hard work and an ongoing commitment. We've heard many women over the years say that they have a broken picker, meaning they choose unhealthy friends and partners again and again. This usually stems from having dysfunctional parents and role models. You may have been raised to believe that emotional and even physical abuse are normal, and happiness in friendship is not a realistic goal. What do healthy friendships look like?

Characteristics of Healthy Friendships

- They are supportive of your needs and wishes.
- They listen and hear what you say.
- There is a healthy give-and-take.
- They bolster your self-esteem with positive feedback.
- They don't criticize you or your family.
- They are constant. They don't run hot and cold.
- Good friends don't ghost you or make you feel bad.
- Good friends don't bully you.
- They make you feel safe and good.

Healthy Friendship Challenges

Is jealousy a problem for you? Some moms see nothing but green when it comes to their daughters' friends and love interests. Here, conflict can arise when moms' jealousy interferes with their daughters' appropriate social growth and independence. Other moms consider their daughters' friends and boyfriends a reflection of themselves. Do you or your mom encourage friendships only in your own social circle? That narrows your opportunities for broader life experiences and creates anxiety and stress when mother/daughter tastes in people don't match.

We've heard moms say, "It's just as easy to have wealthy friends and husbands as poor ones." Is it? Daughters may make choices to please mom that don't suit or make them happy. The status basis for establishing friendships is not genuine or satisfying as a strategy for happiness.

Moms can also play a big role in the lives of their daughters and their daughter's friends. There are the sports moms, or dance moms, who devote their lives to driving their daughters and the team around and act like a member of the gang, as well as the moms who go all out to have the gang live at their home. These devoted moms may feel the most letdown and lonely when daughters grow up and establish lives of their own. Moms come in all forms when it comes to their daughters' friends.

Conflicts over Romance

How often do your love stories go smoothly? Compound moms' experiences with those of their teen and young adult daughters, and it can get very messy. Moms can inadvertently see themselves in their daughters' relationships, or even want to be part of them and share in the excitement and drama. Or they can try to break it up. Moms can encourage unlikely matches, like Leslie's mom, but the reverse happens, too. Our friend Mary Ann's mom believes her choice of partner is unworthy and does everything she can to undermine the relationship, often torturing Mary Ann with everything that's wrong with him. And cheating can create problems with moms, too. When Carol decided to forgive her boyfriend after he cheated on her, Carol's mom wouldn't let it go, raging about his bad behavior at every opportunity. Both the case of a mom being too involved with the progress of a relationship or a mom shunning a partner to halt progress are boundary issues.

Romantic love is magical, overwhelming, intense, and sometimes goes terribly wrong. For moms, dealing with daughters in love can be complex and destructive. Young romantic partners can open a Pandora's box of problems for the mother-daughter relationship. If a mom/daughter doesn't approve of the boyfriend, or girlfriend, holy war can erupt. Race, class, education, politics, sexual orientation, these are big issues for many moms. Having a daughter insist on a partner who doesn't fit mom's expectations and traditions is terribly upsetting.

To avoid conflict, many daughters go to extremes to hide relationships their moms won't approve of, and even leave home forever to escape the fighting. Daughters also choose relationships that will drive their moms crazy on purpose. Are you addicted to drama? Do you have a matchmaker mom with a picker that's the opposite of yours? While both moms and daughters experience pressure when it comes to their romantic relationships, and we could go on about this forever, finding a way to be safe and have peace is the very best thing we can do for each other. Fighting over who should do what is a conflict no one can win. How can we be true to ourselves, honest about why we make the choices we make, and lower the temperature so that we can enjoy what's positive about each other?

Predators and Abusers

Predators come in all forms, and they all pretend to be your friend. There are dangerous and violent predators who meet moms and young daughters online, in game rooms, chat rooms, and dating sites. Moms/daughters should be able to discuss the Internet and its dangers without inciting a war. A conflict can arise with boundaries here. We also run into more subtle predators. These are narcissists and sociopaths. Many wonderful moms/daughters are caught in a web of manipulation from toxic people who pretend to be the opposite. When entangled with a predator, we can be left wondering, *Where did the charming, interested person I met go, and how did I get into a relationship that's destroying me and my family?* We've been there.

Red Flags of Predatory and Abusive Behavior

- They come on strong with charming behavior and love bombing.
- They are excellent liars.
- They create a false sense of intimacy they will use against you later.
- They have no boundaries and say and do whatever they want.
- They criticize your friends and/or family.
- They have control issues (control what you eat, wear, where you go).
- They control the finances.
- They aren't supportive of your needs and wishes.

As someone who has sponsored many women in recovery, Lindsey has seen the wreckage caused by male predators who worked their way into a vulnerable family, preyed on the mom, and then preyed on the daughter. Even worse, Lindsey has seen moms not believing their daughters about abuse and taking the boyfriend's side.

The reverse happens, too—where a daughter ends up in a romantic entanglement with mom's romantic partner. As mothers and daughters, we have natural instincts to protect each other, so if your mom/daughter is concerned that you have an abuser in your life, take that seriously. It's important to look out for each other's safety, and dangerous situations can escalate quickly into domestic violence or worse. The people we allow into our lives and families can have wonderful or tragic consequences.

Imagine the drama and fear when the romantic partner of a mother/daughter comes from a troubled, abusive, or criminal background. It would be impossible not to worry about her safety and security, knowing she could be in danger at any moment. Here's where good intentions can erupt into war. While the mother-daughter bond is powerful, so is the drive to protect a new love.

 Lindsey Talks Friends and Mom

Friendship is very important to me. At times people have come between my mom and me. We certainly fought over some friends more than others, but this wasn't a serious issue for us. I had total freedom with my friends and boyfriends. My mom never pushed me to be friends with anyone, never disapproved of friends or boyfriends until there was a reason to, and she always included whomever I wanted in our family activities and home. She was incredibly generous when it came to my friends and boyfriends, but my friendships made my mom lonely.

When you're young, you just want your parents to go away and leave you and your friends alone. That's what I wanted anyway. I have always had close friends and adored them. I never had trouble making friends or finding boyfriends, but when I was younger, I kept my circle small. All the discomfort, anxiety, and other issues I've talked about before prevented me from being inclusive or kind to everyone around me. I feel badly about that, and I do believe karma is real, so be careful about how you treat people—your girlfriends and boyfriends and mothers. You may judge someone or treat someone badly only to find yourself in the same spot at a different time in your life.

When I was in middle and high school, I suddenly wanted to hang out with my friends all the time. Looking back, I can imagine how sad and disappointing it would be to see your little mini-me growing up and not wanting to be with you anymore. In high school I spent all my time with best friends. Some of my favorite memories throughout my life are with my friends. Even the friends I've lost touch with are all meaningful to me, and I think of them fondly. Sure, there were fights with girlfriends and crushes who didn't return my affections. Friendships created the appropriate amount of heartache and angst for my teen self, but it was all in the realm of normal. Throughout those years my mom was busy with her writing career and often out of town. I remember her constantly asking why I had to go out at night.

"Nothing good happens after ten p.m.," she'd say. At that time in my life, everything good happened after ten p.m., so I disagreed, and off I went.

I didn't have a real boyfriend until I was eighteen. My mom told me not to have sex in high school, and I followed her advice. While I had lots of male friends, romance was not in my life until the end of my senior year of high school. As an adult, I've joked to my mom that she remembered the "don't have sex talk" but missed a beat on some other important talks.

Later as a young adult in New York, I returned to the dynamic of trying to live my life and be with friends and boyfriends and leaving

my mom behind. Back then, it always felt as if I had to choose between one or the other. Today, we understand that we can have time
together and time with others without leaving the other behind.

Remember earlier when we wrote about how daughters often im-
itate whatever their mothers do? I've turned out to be a carbon copy
of my mom in many ways, including relationships. My starter marriage was an exact copy of mom's starter marriage. I've followed her
path in many ways when it comes to my romantic patterns.

My mom often did too much for others only to be disappointed
when the effort wasn't returned. That's me to a tee. My mom could
be wonderfully accepting and inclusive but also have a sharp tongue.
I'm the same. I followed her patterns without realizing it. When I was
younger, I felt I had to be submissive even though mom never told
me to be that way, never. When I got older, some of the rage I saw
her display, I copied as well. We do what we know. We marry what
we know. It's easier to replay the dysfunction we know than go into
uncharted waters. What's important is to become aware of what went
wrong, learn how to repair the damage, and do better next time.

Think About This

Part of growing up is bonding with friends and spending time
with them outside of home. This separation between mother and
daughter can be seen as natural or become a constant source of conflict. Moms are models for friendship and romantic partners just like
everything else, and daughters follow in their footsteps or choose
friends and lovers who are the opposite of what their moms want for
them. Here, personality and communication habits play a role in the
severity of your conflict.

Moms can be intrusive, jealous, and controlling. They may be
right; they may be wrong. But only you can determine whether your

friends are helping or preventing you from being your best self. Moms, are your friends and romantic relationships causing problems for your daughters? Having healthy friendships is not something we can manage for each other. There is a learning curve in any relationship, but it becomes clear in time whether friends and boyfriends are safe for us and our family, whether they lift us up or hold us down, and whether they truly have our best interests at heart.

TIME TO JOURNAL

This is a good time to think through your relationships and see who has the most influence on you and what that looks like. If this is a fighting issue for you and your mother/daughter, think about all the ways her opinion and influences differ from yours. What's going on? Awareness and understanding are the first steps to fixing both your heart and behavior.

JOURNAL PROMPTS

1. Do you have friends that make you feel bad or cause trouble for you? Who are they?

2. Does your mother/daughter have friends that cause concern? Explain why.

3. Can you see any patterns with your mother's /daughter's friends and boyfriends/marriages and yours?

4. Are there any boyfriends/girlfriends (romantic relationships) that are unhealthy in the family? Describe them.

5. Have you ever talked to anyone about it if you have concerns?

6. If you fight with your mother/daughter, what do you think the biggest issue is?

CHAPTER 10

Dependence and Independence

Is control your mother-daughter issue? Join the club. From the moment daughters emerge from the womb, their perilous journey from dependence to independence begins. Every mother-daughter pair travels its own path into the unchartered territory of separation. Growing up and separating can seem natural and easy but also agonizingly difficult. Moms may be different in a hundred ways, but most moms have these three things in common. Moms are fearful for their daughters' safety, want them to succeed in life, and are highly motivated to protect and guide them.

At the same time, daughters struggling for autonomy may feel impatient rage at every attempt to manage them. Here's a fact. No one wants to be told what to do or bossed around. Complicating the dynamic of holding on and letting go is the fact that moms must work very hard at controlling their emotions and behavior while daughters melt down and tantrum away—sometimes clinging to their terrible two's behavior for a lifetime. If drama (sulking, throwing tantrums, silent treatments, screaming) is an effective strategy for control, why lose it? If mom melts down or is a drama queen, on the other hand, she loses respect and authority. Daughters hold their moms' unfettered emotionality against them.

"You're the adult" is an accusation moms risk hearing from cheeky daughters.

Here is something we don't talk about much. Children have no idea of how difficult it is to be a mom and a grown-up, with all that entails. Compassion for moms in childhood, teen years, and young adulthood may be absent altogether. Here's a fact. We live in a patriarchy. Men are in control of our government and societal laws. Here's a generalization. We're raised to respect and fear our dads and often take our moms for granted. In cases where dad is the financial provider, the emotional life and needs of moms may be ignored or overlooked.

Moms overwhelmed by responsibilities often suffer anxiety about how they will be able to survive work, marriage, divorce, economic difficulties, and the added stress of inevitable battles with even the best and kindest of daughters—sadly, for moms. Daughters are the ones who grow up and leave. If that departure has been full of bitterness, the pain is lasting for both moms and daughters.

The Delicate Dance of Holding on and Letting Go

From the very beginning the only constants in the mother-daughter relationship are the eternal conflict between dependence, independence, and change. How well moms manage the evolution of shifting roles and needs from babyhood to womanhood and beyond will determine the emotional growth of their daughters and lasting satisfaction in their relationship. Moms can find these transitions as difficult as their daughters.

For example, if moms are impaired by a mental illness such as depression, a narcissistic personality disorder, or addiction to mention a few, daughters will need to heal from their emotional wounds before effectively mothering their own daughters. We tend to become like our models in unexpected ways.

Growing up is all about change, but so is motherhood. Cutting the umbilical cord launches the very first step to independence that a baby makes. Baby has a long road ahead and marches steadily toward autonomy. One of the hardest things for a mom to accept is that the daughter she created and carried so long is no longer hers. The minute the baby is born, she is herself, with a name and personality and path all her own.

Emotionally you may feel your daughter is always yours, but her sole job is to grow up, be independent, and function effectively with a life of her own. In short, she must steal your thunder and your power. Why do you think all Disney movies have dead mothers? To remove this awkward step from the storyline. If your mom is out of the picture, you can grieve her loss, and you never have to leave her behind. Daughters experience profound changes as they mature, but the same thing goes for moms.

While daughters are developing, moms are also experiencing countless personal life changes that motivate and influence their behavior. Physical changes and aging, illnesses, family relationships, spousal upheavals, divorce, economic ups and downs all impact the emotional development of moms. Moms may be seen as the moral compass of the family, the breadwinner, the hedge against chaos, perpetual support, or any number of other noble roles, but even the most educated moms are learning as they go along. Martyr moms may take on all the tasks and let everyone know it. Society traditionally has put the burden of responsibility and maturity on women. But frankly, few moms really understand the emotional impact our behavior has on our daughters.

The delicate balance of holding on and letting go is where the mother-daughter relationship faces challenges at each stage of development. Every mom-daughter couple has their own personalities, patterns of behavior, influences, and level of emotional intelligence. Some moms are great with babies and toddlers but keep that dynamic going long after their daughters no longer need constant surveillance and help.

Helicopter moms stay involved with every single facet of their daughters' lives. Being too hands-on can prevent daughters from making their own choices without feeling guilt or shame at wanting to do something different. By the same token, moms who are preoccupied and busy with their own lives may let go too soon. The good thing is that no matter how badly astray the relationship goes at one stage, it can be restored later. There is no deadline for healing.

Signs of Controlling Moms

- Won't let her daughter question or discuss mom's decisions.
- Is demanding and insists on her daughter's obedience.
- Won't let her daughter make any of her own decisions.
- Won't allow her daughter to have her own choices about anything.
- Won't let her daughter have any independence at home or outside of home.
- Mom has to be right in all conversations and disputes.

- Dictates all aspects of her daughter's life.
- Helps without being asked.
- Has high standards and rigid rules that are impossible to live up to.
- Tells her daughter how to do things she already knows how to do.
- Doesn't respect her daughter's privacy.
- Doesn't allow critical thinking or her daughter's own opinions.
- Makes her daughter feel guilty and stupid.
- Manipulates by withdrawing love.
- Frequently uses the reason "Because I said so."
- Disparages and puts down.
- Uses punishment as coercion.
- Lacks empathy and behaves in uncaring ways.

Parenting with Blinders

Who am I and what does my daughter mean to me are questions moms may not ask themselves as they move through the parenting stages. Ego and self-esteem play a big part in all our relationships, and here, too, ego is a driving force. In the mother-daughter relationship a mom with too much or too little ego can be deadly. Daughters are influenced by everything their moms do, and ego is the I/me component of mom's personality. When the relationship is all about mom's wants and needs, her parenting will be motivated by her ego.

In this scenario, a daughter's looks, achievement, and behavior reflect on mom and gild or tarnish her perceived image. All-about-me moms also might become jealous and compete when their daughters begin to outshine them. They may compete for the admiration of friends and boyfriends. By the same token, moms with low sense of self and self-esteem can easily become doormats for strong-willed or demanding daughters.

When it comes to parenting, there is no such thing as "mom knows best" because moms only know what they know. There's more to being a good parent than following your own inclinations. Instead of assuming that you're well-enough intentioned and informed, you can learn more and do better. How do we learn more? We can examine the part our egos, personality styles, and behavior play in the conflict or harmony of our mother-daughter relationship. If we don't know where our influences come from or why we react the way we do, we risk parenting with blinders. That means taking the path of least resistance or making the motions without thoughtful introspection, compassion, and empathy.

When Codependence Is Your Issue

Codependence is learned, and once you become codependent in one relationship, this pattern may repeat itself in other relationships. Leslie has been a victim of codependence more than once. Leslie remembers an employee, Judy, who was so enmeshed with her daughter's, Angie's, needs that codependence ruled her life. Daughter Angie got into one scrape after another daily, constantly demanding money or her mother's help during work hours. We'll get to boundaries in another chapter, but here's where boundaries were needed both at home and in the office. Judy regularly used work time to bail Angie out. She was constantly stressed by her daughter's needs and drew Leslie into the black hole of her codependency. When Angie reneged on a rental in another city that Judy had cosigned for, Judy demanded a raise from Leslie to cover her loss. Codependence with her daughter made Judy repeat that pattern of codependence with her boss. When her boss's patience ran out, Judy had to go.

Codependence is often the culprit in difficult mother-daughter relationships. As either a daughter or a mother, you may be terrified every time the phone rings because the phone rings way too often. You may be enmeshed with a mother's/daughter's emotional moods. Some moms are only as happy as their unhappiest child. You may care too much about things in your daughter's/mom's life that you can't control. What is your daughter/mother doing now? What does she need? What does she want you to do?

How difficult is it for you to comply? You might ask how many things a mother/daughter could possibly want in a single day? The answer is there is no limit. Codependence may begin as wanting to be helpful or caring for someone who needs you. Helping makes you feel good. You help because you can. Codependence becomes toxic when you can't separate yourself from the other person, and you can't be happy if your child/mom isn't doing well. You can't let your child fail even if letting the child fail is the only way for her to ultimately succeed. You can't let your mom make her own decisions when you think she should be doing something else. You just can't let go.

Leslie's Experience with Dependence and Independence

My mom had important work to do and was busy trying to make a better world for those in need. She believed that life was golden for me and I had no excuse to complain about anything. Anxiety and insecurity, which all children have about something, were not permissible in my world. This may be a common theme in families in which there is wealth and privilege. Your job is to be nice and carry on.

Stiff upper lip, cheerful countenance, and no arguments were the major rules I had to follow. Emotional support was not forthcoming, and hands-on childcare was performed by a Chinese couple who did not speak English. My nanny, Mr. Wei, taught me to cook, gamble, drink whisky, and smoke by the time I was ten. For this reason, I am culturally at least 50 percent Chinese.

In terms of personality, my mom was laissez-faire, nonconfrontational, and reserved. I've never said this before, but these traits might well qualify her as being an emotionally absent parent. Mom's personality style and secret concerns about my attractiveness and intelligence meant I was on my own. Her lack of interference had both positive and negative results. On the negative side, I felt I didn't matter. I wasn't very good.

Left to my own devices, I could have gone either way. On the positive side, freedom meant I could read anything, learn anything, go anywhere, and develop any interest. I danced at the American School of Ballet, the name I remember, until the teachers said I had to come every day. My mom determined that I was too short to be a dancer and therefore no more ballet lessons were forthcoming. I moved on to music and studied voice and classical guitar. No one stopped me there. My mom refused to give me a sewing machine but did approve the purchase of a guitar. Because I didn't feel good enough, I became a chronic self-improver. Poor health when Lindsey was a baby and her addiction in the high school years made me codependent with Lindsey, but Lindsey found her way to lasting recovery on her own.

Think About This

We've read a lot of books about good and bad moms, and codependence, which tend to focus on behavioral characteristics.

Mental health is much more than the way you're acting. It's what's happening inside. Mental health is emotional health, too. How are you feeling? And both moms and daughters cope with challenges to their emotional health at every stage of their lives.

Every family is different, but some things are the same. Moms have tougher behavioral and emotional challenges than their daughters. It's the truth. Moms are often juggling the needs of their daughters and moms at the same time. Moms are growing up, too. As they raise their daughters, they have a wide range of responsibilities and problems to manage along with childcare. Did you ever think about how difficult it is for both moms and daughters to go through their own life changes at the same time? Moms have the extra task of keeping both their behavior and emotions together no matter how difficult their own lives may get. Moms' challenges are something for you to think about.

TIME TO JOURNAL

Here's your chance to think about what your mom may have been going through when she was raising you. Did she have to take care of her own parents? Was she supporting the family? Was someone ill who needed her attention? Leslie's mom was busy. Lindsey's mom was busy. How did that affect their parenting and daughters' dependence and independence? Moms have serious adult tasks and may be suffering from anguish and pain their daughters don't even know about. Daughters grow up and leave. Can you find new understanding and compassion for your mom now that you are older and have the same tasks and challenges that she did?

JOURNAL PROMPTS

1. What kind of responsibilities did your mom have? Was she overwhelmed with activities, volunteer work, family, a job? List them.

2. Which of her struggles and challenges were you aware of? Which weren't you aware of?

3. How much independence did you have?

4. Does your mom/daughter have control issues? Around what?

5. What are your conversations or fights like around these issues?

6. Codependence is emotional reliance on someone else. Have you noticed you and your mother are too closely connected? What does that look like?

CHAPTER 11

Boundaries and Detachment

Boundaries are both a prevention and solution for healthy and difficult relationships. That's the reason there are borders between countries, fences between properties, as well as laws about what we can and can't do to one another. There are no laws and punishment for emotional infringement and pain inflicted by others, however. So we all must decide how to manage our relationships with a maximum of emotional freedom and a minimum of emotional pain. The way we do this is to create invisible boundaries to keep us safe and detachment from pain when our relationships become impossible to bear.

If codependency and detachment are your mother-daughter issues, you might examine whether lack of boundaries is causing your conflict and stress. Boundaries are something everyone touched by addiction needs to address at one point or another. How far do we go for a mother/daughter? How much do we allow our daughter's/ mother's hurtful or unhealthy behavior to rule our lives? What can we do to save her? What can't we do? How do we save ourselves? What are we doing that we don't want to do?

Boundaries Are Spaces Between

Creating space between you and your mom/daughter, even when your relationship is pretty good, can turn out to be the most challenging thing you ever have to do. Boundaries create the safe spaces we all need for emotional survival. When there are no boundaries, moms/daughters can deplete finances and interfere with friendships, love relationships, marriages, work, self-esteem, you name it.

What's a safe space? Maybe it's your bathroom. Maybe it's your sleep time. Maybe it's just being able to get to work on time without the interference of someone's daily meltdown. Maybe it's the freedom to have a vacay from helping. It could also be your home itself. Boundaries give you autonomy to establish emotional and physical safety, whatever that looks like for you.

Seems simple enough, but implementing any kind of safe space for yourself can have tremendous pushback and painful consequences. Even innocent, simple boundaries can trigger breakups and breakdowns. We can't say it often enough. No one likes being told what to do and what not to do. What we communicate and think is fair may seem horrendously cruel to someone else. That's why boundaries are so tricky.

A mom telling a chronically peace-disturbing daughter, "Don't call me after nine p.m. or before eight a.m.," can be perceived as a cruel and unfair restriction. A mom/daughter with a habit of demanding attention and time at all hours of the day and night can be enraged by any limitation.

"How dare she tell me not to call? I'm never speaking to her again." It happens.

As we described in the section about codependency, sometimes crucial emotional and behavioral boundaries have not been established. Have you ever asked yourself where you end and a loved one begins? What does attachment look like for you and your mom/daughter? Is there healthy space and privacy between you? Mental illness is one factor that creates attachment problems, but all mothers and daughters must create their own spaces and tools to detach when one person's behavior infringes on another's peace and serenity.

Mothers and daughters need freedom to be individuals: eat what we want, paint our walls any color, dye our hair without comment, be economical or reckless, have the friends and boyfriends/girlfriends we want, make mistakes that only we can correct, and think for ourselves. Boundaries allow you to be you and me to be me.

Space to Be You

We like to think of boundaries as spaces as opposed to fences. Yes, we all want our privacy, but fences say Keep Out. They are hard nos. Spaces between you and others are expandable. They are freeing. When there are spaces between mothers and daughters, you can both grow with the changes and challenges you face. Expanding space can provide the opportunity to work together to resolve, or ignore, your differences. When you have space, you are free from being consumed by each other's needs and feelings. You are not controlled by your mother's/daughter's standards, habits, moods, or demands. You can fully be yourself and ask for help when you need it but not constantly receive unwelcome advice. Your consciousness broadens. Both of you can be as quirky as you want without shame, guilt, or fear.

Space doesn't happen naturally. It is the opposite of being confined and should be appreciated and nurtured. Giving someone space is a gift that creates trust and self-esteem. With space we can feel confident that we are accepted and valued with all our quirks and imperfections. Our struggles are respected, and we are loved. Setting boundaries is letting your mom/daughter know the behaviors that are okay with you and those that need adjustment.

Types of Boundaries

Types of boundaries vary according to the relationship. With mother-daughter relationships, we're going to stick to the basics: physical, intellectual, emotional, financial, and time. Everyone has conflicts around some of these areas and boundaries can make the difference between having a relationship and losing one.

Physical boundaries relate to your body and personal space, which may include your home. Too much touching or hugging may make you uncomfortable and anxious. Leslie remembers her mom forcing her to kiss and hug distant relations she didn't know. Ugh. Too much advice may set you on edge. Don't eat this. Don't eat that. Your body is yours. It's important to take care of your body, but only you are in control of what you want and what you should do. These days there is a lot of controversy around gender identity, reproductive rights, and tattooing and piercing among others. Who owns your body and should decide what you do with it? These are physical boundaries issues, and they may be something you need to work out with professional help.

Control over addiction is another area where boundaries should exist. For example, it's okay to have a nonnegotiable boundary around not drinking or using in your home. Also, if you're a mom with a teen daughter, you can't physically stop her from having sex or drinking, but you can set a boundary about it occurring on your watch in your home. As long as someone is in your home, you can say no to things they do that make you uncomfortable or frightened.

Boundaries around eating are useful when interference around eating causes anxiety and stress. That's one reason people binge and purge and snack in secret. Is someone watching your every mouthful? Is someone always telling you what and when to eat?

Personal Boundary Questions

- Is your room open to everyone, or is it just for you?
- Can you take a nap without interruption?
- Can you take a bath in private?
- Does your mother/daughter (who doesn't live with you) invade your house at any time without asking, stay too long, eat food you'd planned for yourself or other guests?
- Does she go through your medicine cabinet?
- Does she examine the contents of your purse or backpack or refrigerator or suitcase?
- Your personal space includes your desk and checkbook. And your credit cards.
- Do drugs and alcohol arrive when your mom/daughter comes to visit?
- Does she "borrow" your possessions without asking?

Intellectual boundaries are all about your ideas, thoughts, beliefs, and spiritual life. Our family has Jews, Christians, Buddhists, Democrats, and Republicans. Some family members are big charity donors, and some don't know what the word "philanthropy" means. Are the gun lovers friendly with the gun control advocates? Do the

AA members get along with the heavy drinkers? We'd hazard a guess that you have a wide variety of nonmatching ideas, traditions, and practices in your family, like we do.

Boundaries around what you should say to those who don't agree with you are important. Do you want to promote healthy self-esteem and goodwill? Then don't go on about hot-button subjects and get abusive when your mom/daughter doesn't agree with you. Things people say can have a lasting impact. You never forget the names your loved ones call you when you have your own opinions.

Moms and daughters have strong feelings about most things. Some moms think they have all the answers and are opinionated about everything. That can be hard to endure. No one is right all the time, yet some moms want to get the last word and need to be right. When politics or practices get in the way of healthy relationships, boundaries are needed, or daughters will go away. Mad. Here's where minding your own business and staying on your own side of the fence will create harmony, if not agreement. The fence in this instance is the boundary that keeps you kind when you'd rather start a war.

Financial and material boundaries are about what's mine and what's yours when it comes to possessions and money. We all should be able to agree about this but rarely do. If I earned it or inherited it, it's mine. If you earned or inherited, or won the lottery or a lawsuit, it's yours. Items in your home are yours. Your clothes and bank accounts are yours. Finances are so emotional, however, that you can stay furious forever if boundaries are not set about who is in control of the finances and the possessions as well as the future of the possessions.

If your mother/daughter expects financial aid, your clothes, jewelry, credit cards, trips to Tahiti, education, and weddings for her and her children and so much more, you can set the boundaries. What can I afford to give you? What am I comfortable giving you? What don't I want you to have? No, you don't have the right to my safety deposit box or the deed on my house. So, here's where you sit down and ask yourself the questions about what you want so you can be clear about your wants and needs.

Emotional boundaries are about how to manage your emotional space. How a person makes you feel with demands for your attention and emotional support. Do you have a mom/daughter who calls you day and night and wants you to listen to every mood and struggle she has? Also, every snippet of gossip and happiness? Is problem dumping the bane of your mother-daughter relationship? Listening too much will sap your energy. Especially if you are expected to respond. Even long text chains can be challenging to your patience. How much can you listen? How much support can you give? How much do you want to share about your own life and struggles? This is where emotional boundaries come in.

Time boundaries are closely related to emotional boundaries because someone you love to the moon and back may be taking too much of your time. Time and emotional space are your most precious possessions. Time may, in fact, be everything. Say you don't argue about food or finances or beliefs, but there is a constant stream of requests for your help to run out and pick up groceries or babysit or get that resume polished, or (God forbid) do the laundry.

Do the requests for your time include work-related tasks where you help with fulfillment but don't receive financial remuneration for your contribution? Everything you do for someone else takes up your time. Boundaries in the time category can be an agreement to provide a certain number of hours a week or a day. Only a specified number of phone calls. And you split proceeds when you do a work project together. Here is where both mom and daughter are working together to make the relationship fair for everyone.

Detachment

Detachment is our healthiest tool for letting go of emotional pain. Forgiveness is one form of detachment that provides comfort. Faith is another. Here are two of the hardest kinds of detachment we know and have personally experienced: detachment from constant worry and grief about someone who has an incurable disability or terminal physical illness, and detachment from someone who is in active addiction. We can also worry about relatives in war zones or other types of danger. Being philosophical and having faith can help provide that space for achieving feelings of acceptance, peace, and serenity. Everyone will die. We don't have control over when or how we die, so letting go of our desire to control the end game can be freeing. It's not your fault if your mom/daughter is sick or far away and in danger. Detaching with faith and philosophy is letting yourself accept being part of the life-and-death cycle with an open heart and less fear.

Leslie recently heard from Greta, who was panicked about her seventy-five-year-old mother's terminal illnesses and alcoholism. Her mom's doctor told Greta that mom's drinking would shorten her life, and Greta was frantic to save her. Not for the first time, by the way. Greta had hidden the vodka, threatened the nurses, patrolled the liquor stores for decades, and even now in a wheelchair her mom found ways to drink. Greta had been agonizing about this all her life. Why did mom fight her? Why did mom choose alcohol over her? These questions had been eating away at her for fifty years. Her mom did not want to stop drinking. What Greta needed most was to let go of both the need to save her mother and her anger about not being able to.

Detachment doesn't mean you stop loving someone, but you can love someone so much you only hurt yourself. Humans are resilient and often need space (there's that word again) to manage their own life journey. Helping can be love without taking any action. Here's the difference. Say a daughter is overweight and has diabetes. Changing the family diet and everyone losing weight together as a family is helpful and supportive.

If your mom/daughter is in recovery, not drinking in front of her, or not drinking at all, is awesome support that can make the difference between successful recovery and relapse. When mom/daughter is in active addiction and doesn't want assistance, however, detachment means creating that space between you and her to save the one person you can save—yourself. As a mom/daughter, knowing you have no control over a preventable and manageable disease is the hardest thing to accept. Greta finally found that acceptance. She focused on her daughter's wedding and new grandchild, moved out of state, and allowed her mom to live the rest of her life on her own terms.

Are you a catastrophizer, meaning you always expect and visualize the worst to happen? For moms/daughters who are chronic helpers to their own detriment, detaching means letting go of the dreaded what-if scenario that terrifies them and prevents them from saying no. Whatever terrible, awful, scary thing will happen if you don't do whatever the other person wants you to do. Devote time, give money, take care of the kids. Pay the mortgage. For those who are superstitious catastrophizers, letting go means not doing something to prevent the worst thing that could possibly happen from happening. It's not a good reason to do something.

Here Are Some Proven Ways to Detach with Love

- Don't offer unsolicited advice.
- Be clear about your boundaries.
- Let your daughter/mom experience the consequences of her actions without interfering, except when she is a child or a minor and parental guidance is needed.
- Do yourself a favor and recognize that your feelings are real and valid.
- Express your feelings without arguing, and then walk away when things don't go well.
- Take a time-out. This can last a few minutes or a lifetime depending on the injury.

Three Steps for Creating Boundaries

The first step is to become aware of what's happening. Who's doing what to whom? Does your problem stem from mental illness or a personality disorder? Is lack of maturity driving you crazy? Is your issue that of kindness and caring gone wrong? Where does your conflict fit on the types of boundaries list?

The second step is to understand who you are and what you need. You may simply want peace and quiet from perpetual nagging. You may want your finances protected. You may want someone to stop coming to you with every minor crisis. Do you want that person out of your house, your life? Clarify what's wrong and what you want.

The third step is to plan to implement the change you want to see. Here's where you take baby steps and find resources to help when you need support. You can't make huge changes in relationships without help from family members, professionals, or groups. We will talk about conversations around boundaries in the next section.

Think About This

Boundaries and detachment are very difficult to explain and describe without exploring the way your mom/daughter makes you feel. You don't need formal boundaries when you respect each other's needs and space and time and moods. Do you feel good around each other? Have you noticed that whenever there is an ick factor in your feelings, there is a red flag that something is wrong? That's what you need to be aware of. Can you identify what makes you feel mad, sad, exhausted, exasperated? What's your business, and what isn't? Your feelings (and they matter) should be the determinant of the kinds of boundaries and detachment you need to put into place for your self-esteem and safety.

Becoming safe means you are aware of your rights and can say no when your mom/daughter asks for, or does, something that's unreasonable or makes you uncomfortable. In healthy mother-daughter relationships, you can exchange ideas and ask for help. You can get support and have fun together. You're not obligated to be a constant caretaker or fixer. One person doesn't own or dominate the other. You feel good about giving your time or providing financial support in moderation but don't feel mangled and pressured into something you don't think is right or don't want to do.

TIME TO JOURNAL

If we could relive our mother-daughter relationship from childhood on, we would establish better communication and rules for mutual respect in all the boundary areas that we have defined. Moms/daughters all know when we have bad, hurt, raging feelings, but we don't always have stop signs and red flags to stop expressing them inappropriately. Impulse control and self-regulation come into the picture here as well as empathy and compassion.

JOURNAL PROMPTS

1. Do you think your time and feelings are important? Please explain.

2. Is there anything you get stuck doing that you don't want to do? What is it?

3. With whom do you discuss your needs? Tell us about your support team.

4. After reading this chapter, what kinds of boundaries do you think you need?

5. What boundaries do you have in place?

6. In what areas do you need to put boundaries in place? Be honest.

CHAPTER 12

Alcohol and Drugs

What part does alcohol play in your family's life? For moms/daughters in dry communities, drinking probably won't be your mother-daughter relationship issue. For teens who have drinking moms and moms who have school-age daughters, however, conflicts and consequences around drinking can be devastating. Alcohol and drinking are coming-of-age experiences in many cultures; what does that mean for our daughters?

Here are some biology and social insights about the impact of alcohol on our daughters. While girls look fully developed and grown up by fourteen or fifteen, they are not yet adults. According to the NIH, it is well established that the brain undergoes a rewiring process that is not complete until approximately twenty-five years of age. That's ten years after many girls think they're old enough for sex and alcohol. In fact, the prefrontal cortex, the rational part of the brain just behind the forehead, is the last to mature. In addition, teens and their emotions are all over the place, which means teens don't always make healthy lifestyle choices. While the teen brain is still maturing, alcohol and drug use pose extra risks in three ways.

First, alcohol can affect brain function in teens by damaging both cognitive and emotional development. Second, because of the powerful flooding of dopamine (the feel-good chemical) that drugs and alcohol release in the teen brain, teens are more likely to become addicted than adults over the age of twenty-six. In addition, we all know that impulsivity and risky behavior are two hallmarks of adolescence. The third risk that alcohol poses is that it lowers inhibitions and increases impulsivity in teens who are already prone to taking risks. In fact, teens do things while drunk that they wouldn't do sober. The same is true for moms.

And there's a gender component, too. Few mothers know that girls absorb alcohol into their system and brain at twice the rate of boys, which means girls get drunk quicker and stay drunk longer, according to Harvard Women's Health. More research from Harvard Health suggests that women are more susceptible than men to alcohol-related organ damage and to trauma resulting from traffic crashes and interpersonal violence. In the alcohol-gender picture, we also see a stronger social stigma for girls who get drunk than for boys who are rarely held accountable for alcohol-related criminal behavior. It is heartbreaking to us that girls and young women who experience rape have often had too much to drink and are more likely to be blamed for their behavior than the young men who have assaulted them.

Alcohol is ancient and everywhere and affects us all. Drinking has been an American pastime since the colonial days. In fact, beer is still the fifth most popular beverage in the world after water, tea, coffee, and orange juice. For thousands of years when water was not potable, beer was the one safe beverage for human consumption. In short, alcohol has always been with us, and few families have no history with it.

What Is Alcoholism?

Alcoholism is a chronic, progressive disease characterized by uncontrolled drinking and preoccupation with alcohol. That's the definition, but alcoholism can manifest in a multitude of ways. Some people who can't stop drinking are highly functioning alcoholics, and their drinking doesn't damage their life or career for a long time, if ever. Some alcoholics drink in a periodic fashion and can stop for weeks or months but always find themselves drinking again. Then, there are the daily drinkers, the black-out drinkers, the social drinkers, the holiday drinkers—they come in all forms. There are many stages of alcoholism.

What Is Addiction?

According to the National Institute of Drug Abuse (NIDA), "Addiction is defined as a chronic, relapsing disorder characterized by compulsive drug seeking and use despite adverse consequences. It is considered a brain disorder, because it involves functional changes to brain circuits involved in reward, stress, and self-control. Those changes may last a long time after a person has stopped taking drugs."

How Does Addiction Start?

How do you make yourself feel better when things are tough? How do you and your friends socialize? How do you celebrate? What do you do on dates or after bad days at work?

At the beginning, alcohol or any substance use is a solution. A way to feel better from stress, anxiety, depression, heartbreak, relationship stress, family, work, or anything else that troubles you. It makes us more sociable and confident; it creates fake but seemingly close bonds with other people, which can be fantastic for someone who struggles to relate or connect. It's a way to fit in or a way to feel not so lonely while being alone.

Alcohol can be a vessel for creative energy or keep you up and able to work or socialize longer. It's a way to celebrate and is used to celebrate everything. It can be part of your work culture or family culture. It may even start out with a young mother who is depressed or overwhelmed. She hasn't had a drink for nine months, and suddenly she's overwhelmed with baby care. Alcohol can easily become a stress reliever for anyone in any situation.

What most people don't know is that alcohol is a depressant and can be addictive for a significant portion of the population. While drinking starts to help you feel better, as you continue to use it and your tolerance goes up, alcohol ends up making you feel worse. You can feel much more depressed and confused from drinking. Alcohol can disturb your sleep, your mental health, your eating habits, and your ability to have a clear perspective about what's going on in your life. In fact, alcohol is poison. Drink enough of it, and it will kill you. Heavy drinking over time kills brain cells and affects your ability to think and process emotions.

Ideally, before a woman becomes a mother, she'd have a healthy relationship and understanding of the effects of alcohol and drugs and would teach her daughter how to have the same. That is the best hope. However, that is not the norm. As reported by Substance Abuse and Mental Health Services Administration (SAMHSA), one in every eight children lives with a parent who has a substance abuse disorder. The number is probably much higher. Add to that, some 27 million Americans are adult children of alcoholics, and you can see that a huge percent of daughters come into this world with someone in their family who has a history of drug or alcohol abuse. This is not something that only affects some families. Alcohol and drug abuse affect almost every family in America.

Mothers who abuse alcohol and drugs have atypical parenting behaviors. They're focused on getting and using drugs and alcohol, which is what addiction and alcoholism do. Daughters don't get the attention, connection, care, and love they need to develop properly. This can be anywhere on the curve from seeing mom come home a little too tipsy from nights out to blackout drinking in the home. Same with drug use. It can be as small but insidious as a Xanax habit, doctor prescribed of course, all the way to an illicit drug addiction that takes mom to dangerous places and puts the daughter at risk. Whether a daughter is in physical danger or not, she's coping with her mom's unstable moods related to drinking and/or drug use and all the other issues that accompany alcoholism.

The damage goes beyond that because what daughters see, daughters do. Even daughters who swear up and down they will never be like their drunk mom often find themselves using alcohol in the same way their mother did. Our culture promotes alcohol and pill taking, and those messages are reinforced everywhere. Most TV shows and movies promote drinking and glorify drug use. It's hard to find a show where alcohol and sometimes heavy drinking are not promoted. Girlfriends sit around the table with a giant pitcher of margaritas, characters take their miseries out at the bar, alcohol fuels good and bad decisions. It's not just the media that's the problem. Many societies normalize drinking. If you're Russian, English, Irish,

Scandinavian, or American, heavy drinking is part of your culture. Being sober is still more taboo than drinking too much.

Holidays promote drinking, tragedies promote drinking, and having feelings of any kind seem to promote drinking in our culture. The problem is, while some people are fine having a relaxing drink and moving on with their evening, a certain percentage of people will not be able to put that bottle down. For mothers and daughters, high school and college drinking are going to be issues of conflict.

How Alcoholism Affects the Mother-Daughter Relationship

Here are a few of the issues that can arise from having an alcoholic mother: anxiety, fears of abandonment, difficulty forming attachments in adult relationships, emotional dysregulation. And here are a few issues that can arise from having an alcoholic child: becoming an enabler, trying to fix or control, extreme obsession over the alcoholic, losing the ability to care for yourself.

Signs and Symptoms of Alcoholism and Addiction

Increased tolerance; trouble stopping; harmed relationships; unreliable, dangerous behavior (driving drunk, reckless sexual behavior); spending lots of time drinking or recovering from drinking; inability to stop drinking despite efforts to regulate or cut down; cravings; obsession over the next high; change in behavior/eating habits/friends; losing interest in school or work; trouble with family, friends, or partner; legal consequences; regular DUIs.

Lindsey's Story

When I share this piece of my story, it's to show you how addiction can happen, it is not to point fingers at anyone. I have made peace with my addiction disorder. I have found peace and understanding with all the factors that contributed to my disease. No one did anything wrong other than try to manage and cope with a difficult, often painful situation with the information, or lack of information, we had at the time.

I used to describe my addiction as the perfect storm—I had the genetic makeup, I had family dysfunction, I had childhood trauma, and I have an anxiety disorder. Imagine feeling nervous and unsettled all the time. This is one recipe for alcoholism and addiction. The final piece, which really drove it all home, was that I was physically sick all the time growing up. I had roseola and high fevers as a baby. I had chronic ear, nose, and throat infections as a kid. I can still feel how badly my throat would hurt and how I could barely speak for days.

My tonsils were removed when I was seven. I had a rare flu that paralyzed me from the waist down for several days when I was five or six. I was put on antibiotics and different medications all the time. I also started seeing a psychiatrist when I was twelve or thirteen—I'm guessing for social anxiety because I took Paxil in those years. Pills were the answer to everything. That's what we knew in the eighties and early nineties. If you don't feel well, take a pill. Emotionally unwell? Take a pill. Taking drugs is what we did to feel better. Few families were focused on health and emotional wellness then; we were focused on a quick fix with the least work. Again, it was a different time. I'm grateful for today's recovery and mental health awareness, but it is a new movement. Remember when Prozac came on the scene? American culture is as ripe with drug trends for mental health and illness as it is with any other cultural trend.

In addition, alcohol and drugs were part of our national teen culture, and for many families it still is. Drinking seemed to be what all the adults did. In fact, alcohol was one more way to show off. The fine wines, the apple martinis, the champagne flowed in the eighties and nineties, and we enjoyed it. My parents threw marvelous parties. Everyone was glamorous, and they drank. They drank a lot. The famous writers I'd see at my grandfather's house on Martha's Vineyard were heavy drinkers, and everyone loved them. Drinking is what grown-ups and fabulous people do, and that's what I wanted to be. Grown-up and fabulous.

I discovered drugs and alcohol for myself at thirteen. It began innocently with strawberry wine coolers with friends in a parent-less apartment or smoking weed in the park. It wasn't a big deal, and it's what everyone seemed to be doing. But alcoholics are wired differently. Drugs and alcohol affected me in a profound way from the beginning. I can't remember much about that time, and I don't remember my first drink, but I do remember vividly the first time I got high on weed.

I was sitting in my friend's kitchen in her parent's Park Avenue apartment. I think they were home, but we're Gen X, and our parents were a different breed. We were hanging out with a guy from the grade above us, and when he pulled a joint out of his North Face coat pocket, it never occurred to me not to try it. Alcoholics and addicts will talk about chasing the dragon, which means nothing is ever as good as the first high, and we will use over and over and over to chase that feeling we had the first time.

The only way I can describe it is this: All those feelings of discomfort that I had been living with went away once the drugs kicked in. The anxiety that had tortured me since birth was gone. The constant worry about other people and what they thought or were going to do vanished. The chatter stopped, and it was quiet in my head. I felt hazy and giggly and free. It's funny that something that can make you feel free at first will later become a hellish prison from which you can't escape.

In that sense, you can see how creatives get lost in the idea that drugs or alcohol will allow them to create in a different or better way. For me, once I was free from the worry about other people and all the nonsense in my head, I could connect to something else. It was easier to be creative, easier to be myself. That felt good at the beginning. But you can't use drugs to be creative and be yourself. It doesn't work for long.

But that night in my friend's apartment, I was instantly hooked by this new feeling of euphoria and relief and convinced that this is how I wanted to feel for the rest of my life. Finally, at thirteen I had found my solution for living, and it was to alter the way I felt chemically. This made perfect sense considering how medications had been working in my life since birth and was reinforced by what I saw grown-ups doing, as well as what I saw on TV and in movies. Drugs and alcohol were going to be my solution for how to cope with life, no matter what life threw at me. This also went in line with the "pull your bootstraps up" mentality. If I could always control how I felt, then I could always do what needed to be done. This is addict thinking.

When it comes to my addiction and alcoholism, I wanted to know how it happened and why it happened, and I know that today. Remember I talked about being shy earlier? I was, but there was more to it. Alcoholics often describe themselves as irritable, restless, and discontented. Sounds fun, right? There's truth to it. Life doesn't naturally feel comfortable for some of us. For example, I had many friends growing up and belonged to friend groups, but I never felt on the inside that I fit in. I wasn't unattractive, but I thought I was, and that made me terribly self-conscious in public. I felt different and weird and misunderstood. It was very difficult for me to be myself in front of anyone I wasn't close to in those days. There was always this sense of impending doom. Then people I loved started dying.

There were three significant deaths in my life between the ages of thirteen and fifteen. My maternal grandfather, Milton, died when I was thirteen, and that marked the end of an era for everyone in our family. My grandfather was the patriarch of the family, and he actually paid attention to me. He'd take me to lunch in the private dining room at the Metropolitan Museum of Art, or we'd pop over to Helen Gurley Brown's townhouse to say hi. He once sent me a teddy bear that was bigger than I was for a birthday. I loved that Benneton Bear. I loved Milton. He was the only family member outside my immediate family that I felt close to when I was growing up, and he made me feel special. Treasure the people who make you feel special. It was a brutal hit when he passed. For me and for my mom.

When I decided at thirteen that I was going to be a pothead, I naturally gravitated to the kids who were into the same thing. This is the time I met two boys who, by no fault of their own, would change my life forever. I became best friends with an adorable boy my age from another school. I've always had close bonds with friends and boyfriends, and this boy, let's call him Dave, was no different. We talked on the phone for hours and hung out smoking pot in the back stairwells of our parents' apartment buildings. We went to a tennis camp together in Florida.

Dave was my first boy obsession, and I loved him with everything my little teen heart had to give. Dave had a group of best friends, and they did everything together. There was one friend in particular, Jeff (not his real name), who had the same kind of behavior as I did. Jeff introduced me to cocaine when I was fifteen. Again, we partied in a friend's apartment with the parents home and having no clue that a trio of fifteen-year-olds were doing cocaine in the bedroom. But those were the early nineties in Manhattan, and they were fun until something terrible happened.

The only way to write this is quickly and in overview. I don't remember exactly what happened at every turn, so it would be irresponsible for me to give any details I am unsure of, especially out of respect for all the families involved in this story. At the age of fifteen, in ninth grade, Dave was in a terrible accident at the home of a friend. I was not there, and I don't remember who called to tell me. What happened was unbelievably awful, but it was an accident.

The problem with accidents is that not everyone gets to walk away from them. I guess Dave had massive trauma to the brain. A week later, when it was clear that he was brain dead, his family let him go. I haven't spoken of this in decades, but this was a defining event in my young life. When six months later, his friend Jeff jumped out the window of his parents' high-rise apartment, both friends were dead; something changed in me. Those three deaths broke my heart in ways I wasn't going to be able to fix until adulthood. I was dark and misunderstood and listening to The Cure before all that happened. After that, life became about getting away and getting high.

I got into the crazy club scene of New York City in the nineties. I was hanging out at the Tunnel, the Limelight, and Club USA as a teenager and started using club drugs in a serious way. It's odd to think about now, but there were high school students acting like club promoters helping to throw these parties. I knew a few of them and don't remember ever having to provide ID or anything other than the twenty-dollar cover to get in.

By the time I got to college, the wheels had come off. Drug use had become a lifestyle, and it took two and a half years for me to completely disintegrate. An overdose incident in my junior year of college helped me see that there was no future in this life. At that time, I was combining club drugs with Rx drugs and alcohol and weed. At any given time, I had four or five different substances in my body. At twenty-one, I had my first moment of enlightenment. I will die if I keep living this way. I finally called home. Hours later, I walked into my mother's apartment ready to do whatever I had to do to make the horror stop. I'm five feet four and 120 pounds in a healthy state. I weighed 95 pounds, my hair was falling out, I had a pre-ulcerous condition, and I was anemic.

As my mom assessed the pitiful creature that I had become, I felt I was a crushing disappointment. What came as a shock, however, was that my mom wasn't as angry as I had expected. Finally, there was a reason for why I looked so sick and for all my awful behavior. My mom has also always been good in crisis. We wouldn't start screaming at each other about my drinking and using drugs for a while.

In the few days before I took a plane to rehab in Arizona, my mom put her mom hat on, and we did everything we were told to. I was going to rehab and required a "proper uniform." We took a shopping trip to the Gap to find some appropriate clothes. Everything I owned at that time was inappropriate.

As we walked the racks, I had no idea what my mom was thinking.

Calmly, she picked out clothes that were right for rehab as if this were just another kind of camp. In some ways, it was. Her mission was to get me into treatment and not screw it up, and she accomplished her goal. Not until this very moment did I ever wonder how awful that week must have been for my mom. Did she wonder where she went wrong? Did she wonder where I went wrong? Did she think I would make it? Either way, a week later I was at Sierra Tucson and on the first stop in my recovery journey, which is still ongoing.

Sierra Tucson was an incredible experience, and I'd recommend rehab for anyone who can't stop using drugs and/or alcohol. If finances or health insurance is a problem, there are nonprofit recovery centers that can waive or discount the admission fee. Sober living is also helpful, and cheaper, if you have no experience living a safe sober life or have limited finances. I really liked sober living, and I should have stayed longer. I really wish I could report that that's where my troubles ended, but I was only focused on getting back to college and graduating on time. I didn't then understand what a recovery lifestyle was or that I'd need to create one to achieve long-term recovery.

I went on to struggle for another eight years. What does that look like? Read the *Big Book of Alcoholics Anonymous*. The funny thing is even with rehabs and therapy, it wasn't until I read that book that I was like *Oh, I'm an alcoholic!* Our types may vary as alcoholics, but we all do much of the same stuff. I left jobs I shouldn't have, and I made "geographics," meaning I moved whenever I wasn't happy. Sometimes to a new apartment, sometimes to a new state. I knew I had problems, but I was always looking for another answer. Will Yoga fix me? Will the right job fix me? Will LA fix me? Will a guy fix me? The answer is no.

After moving across the country, having a progressive relapse, and getting married, I finally ended up in treatment again at twenty-nine as a newlywed. I thought marriage would fix me. I honestly thought settling down would be the answer. That doesn't work either. It's funny the people and things that get through to you over the years. It was a divorce lawyer who looked at me seriously and said, "You need to stay sober or you're going to lose everything." I heard her. I called someone I met from rehab that day. She led me to Alcoholics Anonymous (AA). AA led me to real recovery and a spiritual solution.

Think About This

Think about all the ways alcohol comes into your life and what alcohol culture is with your family and friends. Consider your family history to see if there is anyone in the family tree who has had problems with drugs or alcohol. What we're really trying to determine in this chapter is whether you have a healthy and informed relationship with alcohol and drugs. It's helpful to look at friends, partners, jobs, and social life and think about how alcohol and/or drugs fit into all of that.

TIME TO JOURNAL

This can be hard to write. Imagine this mom and daughter who have not gotten this honest about our lives until right now. So we know how difficult and painful it is to explore your experiences with drugs and alcohol. Here we want you to explore the place that alcohol and drugs have had in your life. How have they affected both your mother-daughter relationship and your own emotional well-being? We can bet that you have some scars that you don't even know about or know about and pretend they didn't happen.

It's okay to think and write about them here. This is your story, and you can tell it now.

JOURNAL PROMPTS

. . . .

1. How do you use alcohol and/or drugs? (Socially, to feel better, etc.) Describe your use.

2. Do you worry about your drug or alcohol use? Please explain.

3. Do you worry about your mother's /daughter's drug or alcohol use? Please explain.

4. What changes do you want to make around your drinking?

5. If you worry about your drinking or substance abuse, have you ever tried to stop? What happened?

6. If you worry about your mother's/daughter's drinking, have you ever tried to talk to her? How did that go?

CHAPTER 13

Mental Illness

Most people suffer from one form of mental illness or another at some point in their lives. It is part of being human. Mental illness affects the mother-daughter relationship on many levels because we are connected and experience each other's pain. Think about all the women you've known—your mom, grandmother, sisters, aunts, nieces, friends, mentors, in-laws, teachers, colleagues, employers, teammates, you get the idea. How many of them have struggled with anxiety, depression, food disorders, alcohol, or substance abuse? How many friends or loved ones have you seen suffer at the hands of an abusive or toxic partner and ultimately end up with mental health issues themselves? How many moms do you know who have had at least one point in their life when they struggled with their mental health or wellness? Or maybe it's you who has had experience with one or more than one of these.

For those who don't have much experience with mental illness, we'll clarify. Mental illness refers to a variety of mental health conditions that affect thinking, mood, and behavior. The most common forms of mental illness are depression, anxiety, ADHD (attention deficit hyperactivity disorder), OCD (obsessive-compulsive disorder), addiction disorders, food disorders, bipolar disorder, and schizophrenia.

Ironically, mental illnesses are the only illnesses in which the people afflicted often do not think they have a problem. This lack of awareness (or denial) causes emotional problems for those around them. Treatment for people with mental illness is not an exact science, and many people affected do not want treatment. Untreated mental illnesses are partly responsible for addiction and homelessness. Modern realities such as climate catastrophe, pandemics, social unrest, financial instability, and political strife lead to high levels of anxiety and depression for every age.

Mothers who have a mental illness face a complicated set of issues. In a position of trust and responsibility, they don't want to fall apart. When they can't care for their families, profound depression and shame can shake their sense of self-esteem and have a lasting impact, even after they recover. Postpartum depression is an example of a common mental illness that can devastate a new mom trying to adjust to new responsibilities. When moms with alcoholism are in active use, they can exhibit a roller coaster of unhinged behavior that comes back to haunt them when they get sober. They may face both stigma and lack of trust even years after they have become stable and responsible. Even moms who treat their mental illness responsibly can plunge into despair at times. Depression affects everyone on many levels.

As moms affect daughters with their mental health problems, the same goes for daughters who change their moms' lives forever when despair leads them to addiction, overdose, and suicide. Mental illness is complicated, and the way it affects each of us individually and as a mother-daughter couple can cripple us with anxiety, stress, and despair. Add the worry about school shootings and other sociopolitical and environmental events, and it's easy to lose hope or feel discouraged.

Mother-Daughter Mental Health Connection

Poor mental health in mothers leads to poor mental health in daughters. Mothers who are struggling with mental health challenges tend to struggle with taking care of themselves and their daughters. The risks to daughters living with a mother with untreated mental illness go beyond neglect. These daughters are exposed to instability, frightening events, and a complete lack of emotional and physical support. Their basic needs aren't met; if there is abuse in the home, the chances of these daughters growing up to struggle with self-esteem issues, substance abuse issues, or untreated mental illness skyrocket.

On the other side of this coin are the mothers living with a daughter with mental illness. This can be an equally devastating situation. Mothers trying to manage a troubled daughter who resists treatment can find themselves traumatized and end up emotionally disturbed themselves. We've seen mothers watch with horror as daughters starve themselves to death and mothers seek treatment themselves over the untreated addiction of a beloved daughter. When someone in the family has a mental illness, it affects everyone.

If you are wondering about what mental illness looks like, here are the signs and symptoms.

- Feeling sadness more than usual.
- Excessive fears or worries or extreme feelings of guilt.
- Extreme mood changes of highs and lows.
- Withdrawal from friends and activities.
- Feeling more confused.
- Significant tiredness, low energy.
- Problems sleeping.
- Change in eating habits.
- Detachment from reality (delusions), paranoia, or hallucinations.
- Inability to cope with daily problems or stress.
- Trouble relating to situations and to people.
- Alcohol and drug use increase.
- Sex drive changes.
- Excessive anger, hostility, or violence.
- Suicidal thinking.

Mental Health in Today's World

Daughters in today's world are faced with many risks to their mental health. Social media has created an environment of bullying and trolling. Many girls and women gain huge popularity from promoting superficial and materialistic content that leaves a host of well-meaning and healthy girls feeling left out and less than. Social media also creates totally unrealistic physical and lifestyle expectations. It can promote the facade that all is perfect in someone's world when no one really knows what's going on behind the scenes. Phone and gaming addictions are also rising in girls. We tend to agree with those who believe that increased phone and social media use is adding to our attention-deficit culture, meaning short attention spans and the need for constant entertainment. The focus on physical appearance and fitness has also been an issue for girls since the beginning of time.

How many women or girls do you know who have some kind of disordered eating? Whether it's overeating, undereating, binge eating, or bulimia, women are no strangers to eating disorders. Dealing with a daughter's eating disorder has forced many desperate moms into recovery groups and therapy for themselves. When Lindsey was in middle school, her friend Adele was hospitalized with anorexia, and Lindsey visited her in the locked psych ward.

According to NAMI (National Association of Mental Illness), one in five girls has had a depressive episode, and 38 percent of adolescent females struggle with an anxiety disorder. Mental illness is not a niche issue anymore. Mental illness is everywhere, and moms need to know how to support their daughters. Helping a loved one with mental illness doesn't always look the way you think it does. Dealing with a mother/daughter with an active mental illness requires knowledge and a support system for everyone. The days of codependency and enabling surrounding these disorders should be over.

It's important to note here that while we are firm believers in therapy and recovery practices, not all therapists are a good fit for you. When you are searching for help, make sure to read reviews on doctors, therapists, all recovery facilities, and treatment programs. Make sure that the providers to whom you entrust your mental health are qualified and are aligned with your values. Most recovery providers follow the rules, but some are better than others. No one wants a suffering loved one in a facility that is unsafe or shady. That brings us to another crucial note. If you are working with a mental health professional who makes you uncomfortable, talk about it with someone who has experience or get a second opinion.

As in any industry, not everyone is competent or has the same opinions, values, or ability to treat effectively. We have a beloved friend we'll call Kim. Kim was working with a trauma therapist who told her many irresponsible and untrue things about herself and her willingness to get better. After some investigation, Kim discovered the therapist had many bad reviews and had behaved inappropriately with other clients. So do your research, and trust your instincts if you feel someone is making you worse, not better.

 Lindsey's Story

Life is different for those who struggle with mental health issues. We don't always see the world clearly; we have negative voices in our heads that we must work hard to quiet. Quite frankly, some days are bad no matter what we do. I've been diagnosed and misdiagnosed and diagnosed again. Because I was diagnosed with a mental illness I didn't have, I believe rehabs and doctors should not diagnose addicts and alcoholics upon admission. Giving someone a major mental illness diagnosis when beginning to detox after long-term drug use can be counterproductive. Brain function has been severely affected and doesn't work in a normal way. Judgment, character, and basic thinking need time to heal and recover.

I know what it's like to receive drugs for a condition I didn't have, so I believe patients should be diagnosed and prescribed appropriate medication after they have been sober for some time. In sobriety, it is easier to make a more accurate diagnosis. After my first rehab stint, and an incorrect mental illness diagnosis, I was prescribed six different psychotropic drugs that ranged from mood stabilizers to antidepressants, and I took them for almost two years. I don't believe

I needed any of them. After college, back in New York City, I'd be out at restaurants for dinner with my mother and would fall asleep at the table because I was so overmedicated. Maybe being that drugged kept me safe for a while, but it didn't keep me sober. Within a year I was no longer sober and mixing those medications with alcohol and pills.

As my brain function began to recover after a decade plus of abuse, I had an onslaught of feelings about everyone and everything that had transpired. All those feelings that had been hidden for years were exploding out of me, and I had no tools or coping skills to manage them. I had trouble understanding and managing my feelings. I was angry at everyone.

One of the things they tell you in rehab is that when you return to normal life, you can't control other people's drinking and have to accept it. When I returned home from rehab, my mom was still having her daily martinis. Suddenly I saw her drinking differently. I had learned something about alcoholism and family dynamics, and I now felt qualified to identify and point out our dysfunction and her drinking as part of it. This is not a good idea ever.

It certainly wasn't a good idea with my mom, who hadn't done any of her own recovery yet. We were speaking different languages, angry at each other, and neither of us yet knew how to stop the blame game. I had enough recovery to understand a little about what had happened to me and in our family but not enough to be what they call "emotionally sober." I wanted my mom to take some responsibility for what had happened to us and was infuriated when she wouldn't.

My twenties were a mix of emotional issues and relapse issues. Most of the time, it felt like a roller coaster that I desperately wanted to get off but didn't know how. My friendships and personal relationships were rife with drama. All the unhealthy relationship dynamics I learned had become fully formed and blossomed into life chaos. I regularly found myself in codependent and tumultuous relationships with friends and boyfriends. I had unprocessed trauma, untreated anxiety, and depression, and I was emotionally unstable. These were the hurricane years. I blew through cities, romantic relationships, friendships, and jobs. I married and divorced and had a lot of friendships that had been important to me break up as I muddled my way through life.

My mom and I fought bitterly over the planning, or my lack of planning, of my wedding. On one of her book tours I was in a relapse, and she was enraged by my bizarre behavior, which I would not admit was due to a relapse. I'm sure I was awful, but I can't remember that one in detail. I have vivid memories of us getting on airplanes to escape each other, furious and sure we'd never speak again. It was an angry and dramatic time. High drama and outrage are sometimes part of the recovery process. For anyone who is in that place and dealing with recovery rage right now, keep your head up. Alcoholics and addicts do crazy and hurtful things to each other, and it can be horrific. Sadly, the mother-daughter relationship is not immune to alcoholism and addiction; it's one of the relationships that's hardest hit.

Once committed to sobriety, I moved back to New York City and back to my mom. She had gotten sober by this time as well, and at the beginning it was fantastic. I've said it many times: in some ways my mom and I have always been best friends, absolutely the closest, and had the most fun. Coming back to New York, where my roots were, with my mom and I both sober, was incredible—as if my dreams had come true. There was absolutely a pink cloud for us for a while. But a lifetime of complicated issues doesn't just disappear because you're sober. The demons would come out soon.

At that time, in my early thirties, my mom and I decided to start a recovery website to share the knowledge we were learning and that was changing our lives. We were frustrated with the way addiction was portrayed in the media and wanted to show what recovery was really like. In 2011, we launched Reach Out Recovery. For five years, we wrote articles, attended recovery events, acted as advocates, spoke about recovery, and produced two documentaries, the 2016 ASAM Media Award–winning, *The Secret World of Recovery*, and the WEDU PBS special *The Silent Majority*. But personally, I still struggled in life. It's not as simple to say the anxiety returned or that I was depressed. I found that my relationships were complicated, my emotional health wouldn't fully stabilize, and my mom and I were still enmeshed. We had a lot of unresolved feelings about each other. The ups and downs for me in those early years of recovery were extreme.

In my midthirties, I had to face the tough reality that I was not living up to my potential. I had problematic relationships, problematic views about myself, and an inability to stop repeating patterns no matter how badly I wanted to change. I had no idea that the trauma I had endured as a child was preventing me from growing in important ways. I had behaviors and attachments to things that didn't serve me, and they came out in every area of my life. It's an odd thing to accept that because you were treated one way in your childhood years, you may be replaying that with bosses and partners twenty years later. It is only in identifying these behaviors and cycles that we can ultimately figure out the real issues and begin to heal.

After one particularly unpleasant partner, a therapist suggested inner-child work. Weekly, we would introduce ten-year-old Lindsey into the room and ask her how she felt about the decisions I was making. Would I let ten-year-old Lindsey go out with that guy? "No!" I replied. Eyes wide with horror. Something was shifting inside me, seeing myself this way, innocent, not deserving of bad treatment or pain.

Psychodrama and inner-child work led to cognitive behavioral therapy (CBT), which helped enormously with impulse control and emotional stability. I learned techniques like how to draw an "invisible bubble" around myself and not let anyone's energy, or rage, get in. All that sent me down the path, but it did not prevent another relapse, another traumatic breakup, and another lousy boss. Something was blocking me from real, lasting change, and for the life of me, I didn't know how to fix it.

The final blow was when my mom and I got into a terrible fight. In a rage, I left the company we had formed together and cut contact. We would not speak again for four years. I made this break on the advice of a mental health professional who believed that we were enmeshed and had gotten into a cycle of fighting that was destructive and nasty at best. I left the company without notice, suddenly abandoning my business partner, my mom, and our work.

We did not have a referee in the family to cool us down. We both had mental health professionals pushing us apart. I was fragile from a breakup and spinal surgery. I wanted to escape from my mom and didn't care if she never forgave me. Today I understand that when things get out of control, and you don't know what to do, the best thing to do is nothing.

Then, I wanted to make the fighting stop, the fighting with mom, with other people in my life, and with myself. I was finally ready to surrender and do whatever it took to get better and thought another geographic back to California was in order. An addiction specialist gave me a list of rules for my move. No dating for six months, get a sponsor, get a sponsee, get commitments, and get a job.

In the summer of 2014, I left New York and moved to California to find myself. I didn't leave my mother a forwarding address or number. Cutting contact with my mother was the most painful decision I've ever made. I cried every single day the first year, sure that we'd never speak again, and I was still enraged. But, as the months passed, something was changing. If you have a fighting habit, you must get calm within yourself, and that's what I worked on. With time and distance, I lost the fighting spirit. You can get used to calm and serenity just like you can get used to being crazy.

Life was getting easier, but there were still a few red flags in me that needed to be addressed. Luckily, the universe stepped in and by total chance I found myself in line next to Dr. Deborah Sweet, a trauma expert I will interview in Chapter 15. Dr. Sweet was the first person I ever heard talk about somatic work. Somatic work connects mind and body using breathing techniques, meditation, yoga, and other physical activities to affect mood and brain function. More about that in Step 4.

At the time, I felt I lacked the ability to maintain proactive choices and move forward. Dr. Sweet suggested that my condition sounded like the result of unprocessed trauma. I needed one more kind of treatment. So I went back to therapy, this time focusing on achieving goals. I wanted a healthy relationship and a healthy work life. I had learned how to feel good about myself. I had learned about self-care. I had tools for recovery, and I knew what I wanted.

I began EMDR (eye movement desensitization and reprocessing) to finally cleanse the demons still haunting me from the past and to reinforce my progress and new thinking. EMDR is a treatment commonly used for PTSD and trauma that incorporates eye movements with therapy to help process trauma, and it works.

Over the next year and a half, I mixed EMDR with focused talk therapy, and the changes I wanted to see began to take hold. Sometimes it felt like an out-of-body experience watching myself get a good job or make considerable strides in emotional stability and personal development. Finally, after many years of addiction recovery, therapy, and self-help, I was able to feel secure. I don't minimize all the recovery work that came before somatic work. Recovery programs built a powerful foundation that would allow EMDR to help complete the job.

As I understand my story, trauma didn't cause my addiction disorder, but it helped create the vulnerability and space for addiction to settle. Sobriety gave me the gift of being able to see what the real problems were. Time, twelve-step programs, and therapy helped heal the wounds and behaviors. A total recovery lifestyle today is what keeps me healthy, and I've spent the last ten years developing that lifestyle.

A Few Thoughts from Leslie

When we started this book, there was much that Lindsey and I didn't know about each other. We're telling our story for the first time, and boy, it's even messier than I had thought. Remember, we talked about honesty in Chapter 5, "Getting Honest About the Secrets and Lies." Secrecy is something that accompanies both mental illness and addiction. You just don't want to tell. You want to appear normal and okay. You want to keep the facade of being in control and looking good.

As recovery advocates, Lindsey and I have always been warned not to reveal the dark and treacherous side of the recovery journey. It's okay to talk about cancer, but the extremely bumpy, and often costly, road to emotional wellness leads people to think that recovery is not possible. And that might stifle hope. Our wish is to rekindle hope. Keeping secrets only reinforces the stigma faced by moms and daughters coping with addiction. So from me to you, it's okay to look and sound crazy and to ask for help when you do.

All mental health challenges are messy, and yours may look like ours. As moms, we try to fix things and can't. We offer solutions and try to work together. We get angry and resentful when our beloved offspring are unreasonable or worse. We stumble along and toddle toward health when we can. In our case, we had started a new chapter in our relationship and our lives when we saw an article in *The Atlantic* that revealed some 37 percent of young adults are not speaking to one or both of their parents. That article and the sad fact that moms and daughters get separated forever inspired this book.

I could add mom's side to the alcohol and mental health chapters, and moms everywhere would relate to the feelings of betrayal, heartbreak, and rage I felt by Lindsey's choices. But I'm not going to do that because those feelings are in my rearview mirror, and the book is heading into solution. We're going to talk about trauma and the way the brain works in the next section. There's a reason people get stuck in unhealthy relationship habits, and it's not necessarily what you think.

Think About This

Mental illness can affect us and our families in ways we don't necessarily think about. Learning the family mental health history can be helpful in this journey of self-discovery and relationship make-over. Realizing who in the family may have struggled with a mental health issue and whether your mother/daughter may be battling something you didn't realize is enlightening. For many, accepting a mental health issue and seeking treatment is the beginning of a much happier, less dramatic life.

TIME TO JOURNAL

Here we want you to think about how mental health has affected your family and you. Is it a topic you feel comfortable talking about at home? Does your family have shame around this issue, and how has that affected you? The goal here is to find understanding and compassion so we can support each other.

JOURNAL PROMPTS

1. Are you aware of any mental illness in your family? Please explain.

2. What mental health issues did you see growing up with mom or yourself?

3. Did she receive treatment? If not, why not?

4. Was mental health discussed in your family? If not, why not?

5. Have you ever experienced a mental health issue? What happened?

6. Are you and your mother on the same page about mental health? Do you support each other around this issue?

STEP 3

Triggers, Trauma, and Conflict Resolution

In Step 2 we explored a sampling of common mother-daughter issues that invoke frustration and rage on a regular basis. In Step 3 we will dig deeper to explore the way our brains block reason and retain powerful emotions of rage from long ago that no longer serve us now. We will offer tools to take the passion and heat out of disagreements and help identify when the mother-daughter relationship is so toxic you both need to take a break.

Chapter 14 shows how triggers routinely hijack your brain, turning a pleasant outing, exchange, meal into a rage-filled rant. What is a trigger, and why does it take control? Here you will identify your triggers.

Chapter 15 delves into the complex effect of trauma. One incident, or many repeated incidents, of trauma can have long-lasting effects on mom's/daughter's entire life and change the way they interact with the world and each other.

Chapter 16 moves into conflict resolution and ways to take the heat off when your feelings are out of control.

Chapter 17 explores what makes some relationships impossible to maintain. What's to blame and what steps you need to take when breaking up is the safest thing you can do.

CHAPTER 14

Triggers

little biology may help here. Where do your emotions come from? You probably haven't read up on the limbic system recently, if ever. It's a group of interconnected structures deep in the brain that are responsible for your emotional responses and your behavior. Bad feelings? You will always have bad and angry feelings. Bad behavior? That can end. You can experience angry feelings without acting on them.

First, let's consider your limbic cortex. There are two parts of the limbic cortex in the brain that affect your mood, motivation, and judgment. Twenty-seven interconnected categories of emotion have been identified from the basic six: sadness, happiness, fear, anger, surprise, and disgust. You may have noticed that emotions and moods are most intense in the teen years, when the limbic system is not yet fully developed. Self-regulation and appropriate responses can be especially challenging for teens who may not learn these crucial components of healthy relationships either at school or at home.

Not all moms/daughters emerge from their teen years as mature, responsible, and rational adults.

The limbic system is also composed of the hypothalamus, which helps control emotional responses and regulates body temperature; the hippocampus, which regulates motivation, emotion, learning, and memory; and the small but all-powerful amygdala. If you wonder what the culprit is when you feel like you're losing your mind, it's the amygdala. It does cause you to lose your perspective and thus, one could say, your mind.

The amygdala coordinates responses to anger and fear, and it doesn't know the difference between a real threat and an imagined or remembered threat from the past. This is the part of your brain that turns up the heat literally. You can't help the feelings, but you can begin to understand them and learn how to calm down. Toddlers having major tantrums can turn around in a nanosecond, and so can you. Hormones related to PMS and menopause exacerbate the issue, too.

Now let's look at some scenarios and triggers that turn up the heat. You may get along with your mom/daughter well until she says something or does something that launches the two of you into a heated exchange. You may have many areas of conflict with your mom/daughter, and you may have only a few that push your buttons and ignite your amygdala. Anger is one of the most dangerous and powerful emotions humans have. It's a feeling that demands action without assessment or consideration; in short, it's the destroyer emotion.

"I need to react immediately and do something about this," anger seems to demand. You may feel that your head is about to explode. You're a volcano about to erupt. Your mom/daughter whom you love so much can do this to you, often without intending for chaos to ensue.

"My mom/daughter is driving me crazy, and I have to say something or do something to stop it right now!" You know the feeling. It's real because it's chemical.

It's not only moms/daughters that make us mad, though. Anger is everywhere right now, and we all know how difficult it is to hold back when we feel the need to strike out and claim a victory. We want to stop our opponent and sometimes even cause real harm. Here are some of the reasons for an angry response:

- We feel we have been treated unfairly and are powerless to do anything about it.
- We feel accused, threatened, or attacked.
- We feel we're not listened to, not heard, or not respected.

These are powerful emotions moms/daughters make each other feel. Feelings are just feelings, though. Sometimes they are accurate, and sometimes they arise from miscommunications and misunderstandings. Now imagine your mom-daughter conflicts as a minefield of trigger bombs that can go off at any time, taking you from calm to apoplectic in a nanosecond.

These hair-trigger reactions take a long time to develop. Your anger may have begun so long ago you have no idea what started it. You may have said something or done something you don't remember and doesn't make you angry anymore, but your mom/daughter is still internally raging about it, causing you to scratch your head over the violence of her feelings. "Get over it already," you may think and even say. Remember we talked about getting stuck by words or events that were not meant to wound but created havoc on our self-esteem and became the mantra that we live by? That's what we're talking about. That's what we want to identify here and learn to diffuse.

What Is a Trigger?

In terms of mental health, a trigger may be defined as a stimulus that launches a negative emotional reaction. The reaction may be the wish to drink again or have a breakdown or resume unhealthy behaviors. In this case the trigger is mom-daughter conflict. While triggers, or "being triggered," is commonly associated with people who have a history of trauma, addiction, alcoholism, self-harm, disordered eating, child abuse, sexual abuse, or mental illness, it also applies to perfectly normal mother-daughter relationships.

Yes, we trigger each other all the time. We worsen symptoms of resentment/anger and cause chronic recurring drama that make us feel horrible, guilty, furious. You name it. Do you feel as if you're walking on eggshells with your mom/daughter all the time? An expression we love is "My family knows how to push my buttons because they installed them."

Types of Triggers

Moms/daughters with PTSD, trauma, history of addiction, or mental illness know exactly how it feels to be triggered. Many people, however, don't know why they react with such passion about seemingly unimportant things and how that passion erupts and drives them. You'll recognize your triggers when you know the signs and symptoms. There are many kinds of triggers, but we'll just talk about internal triggers and external triggers in the mom-daughter relationship context.

Internal and emotional triggers come from inside, like a dream that freaks you out or an upsetting memory. Emotions can

be extremely triggering for some people. Lindsey has always struggled with having very intense feelings, and many kinds of stimuli
can be triggering for her. Even now, extreme feelings can make her
want to pick up a drink, or food, or shop, and she has to manage
her moods accordingly. As we said, a memory can launch rage at
a mom/daughter who doesn't remember the incident that caused
it. "Me, controlling or mean? Impossible." That was Leslie's pre-
recovery stance.

Emotional triggers are real and not to be underestimated. Many
moms/daughters struggle with issues of abandonment they don't
even know they have until it plays out in their adult lives. For example, we have a friend named Lizzy whose mother was not able
to care for her and put her up for adoption at the age of four. As
an adult, Lizzy still struggles in her romantic partnerships with a
profound fear of abandonment because of this lingering, unresolved
childhood trauma.

Another friend, Eloise, is the mom of an adopted daughter who
has made Eloise part of her trauma and grief every day. Eloise is
drawn into her daughter's emotional sea of discontent and often
feels as if she's drowning in it. Eloise is triggered into feeling like the
bad guy for adopting and then not being able to make her daughter
happy.

Other internal or emotional triggers that create conflict in the
mother-daughter relationship include:

- Feeling lonely.
- Feeling sad.
- Stress.
- Anxiety.
- Depression.

- Experiencing extreme emotions you want to avoid.
- Feeling bored (especially for people new to addiction recovery).

Why would feeling lonely or stressed be a trigger for mom-daughter conflict? Just being in that place of emotional distress, whichever one it is, brings up old, unresolved hurt feelings. Pressure builds around the pain, and when mom/daughter says the wrong thing, resentment and angry feelings erupt like that volcano we mentioned. It's chemical. Even when you've been looking forward to seeing each other, a trigger can ruin the get-together. This has happened to us many times.

Not all moms have directly experienced the trauma associated with mental illness or alcoholism/addiction. But we have all grown up with a variety of neuroses and sensitivities. We have all experienced badly hurt feelings before we were old enough to understand or manage emotions around the incidents. Tumultuous or confusing childhoods tend to live on and wreak havoc in our adult lives. Understanding what happened and that it wasn't your fault can weaken the triggers and provide opportunity for amends when possible.

Allen Berger, PhD, a nationally recognized expert on the science of recovery, in his book on emotional sobriety, *12 Smart Things to Do When the Booze Is Gone*, asks readers to consider the idea that any time you get upset, it's your Mr. Hyde raging. When someone is not doing what you want them to, your unhealthy emotional dependency on them is what's really driving your rage. Emotional sobriety, which we will explore later, means you are independent, not dependent or codependent.

In a nutshell, lonely moms/daughters learn not to make old feelings a reason for current conflict and not to take every word personally. It isn't easy. But understanding and healing triggers, being able to stay calm and centered, and having true emotional sobriety—this is what we are working toward. Emotional sobriety is about growing up.

External triggers are just as dangerous as internal triggers. Those who quit smoking, cut down on sugar, quit drugs and alcohol, got divorced, or lost a child or parent to an overdose or gun violence are easily triggered. A TV show, the smell of smoke or alcohol, passing a pastry shop, or hearing fireworks—anything that produces a strong negative reaction—can be a trigger. War, losing your home, fire, and natural disasters are also examples of external emotional triggers.

Leslie talked about how seeing mothers and daughters having fun together after her mom passed away triggered overwhelming grief and reminded her that she was now alone. Lindsey talked about the emotional impact of losing a first love.

A close friend, Jane, was sexually abused as a child by a friend of the family. Her parents decided not to prosecute. Twenty-five years later, Jane passed her unpunished abuser on the street. Instant PTSD. She raced home, crawled into a ball, and cried so hard she shook all over. That is what we call an extreme external trigger. Other external triggers can include:

- Seeing someone who traumatized you in any way.
- Watching any abuse or addiction you experienced on TV or in a show.
- Walking by bars, nightclubs, or any institutions where something bad happened or you behaved badly.
- Smells, sounds, songs, anything that reminds you of a traumatic event, person, or time.
- Social events or other stressful situations.
- Financial problems.

- Anniversaries, death dates, and other upsetting dates of significance.
- A divorce, breakup, or rejection.
- Feeling ignored or left out.
- Natural disasters.
- Betrayal by a friend or loved one.

You can't avoid bad things happening in your life. Sadly, people you love will pass away. Relationships you care about may end before you want them to. Financial instability or trouble at work can cause severe distress. You've seen how Leslie's lack of knowledge about finances helped turn money into a confusing and stressful issue for Lindsey and a mom-daughter area of conflict. You read about how tragedies in Lindsey's young life helped set the stage for addiction issues and conflicts with mom.

Symptoms of Being Triggered

Feeling triggered causes a few telltale signs to look out for if you're not sure when you're feeling triggered. These physical symptoms are similar to those experienced in menopause and panic attacks. They include the following:

- Shaking.
- Hot flashes.
- Panic or feeling overwhelmed.
- Reacting defensively.
- Racing heart.
- Feeling instantly angry, sad, or out of control.

Some Universal Mom Triggers

When it comes to moms there are quite a few universal triggers. A trigger does not necessarily have to result from a traumatic event.

Having to ask a messy daughter to clean up after herself again and
again can make you intensely frustrated. Moms have so much responsibility that it is easy to pick up triggers when year after year
daughters aren't listening or helping. In fact, some of these triggers
are less about the daughter's behavior and more about mom feeling
she's a bad parent. You'll recognize a few of the biggest stressors from
our hot-button topics in Step 2. Notice how all these issues and behaviors tie together.

- Financial stress.
- Being overextended.
- Not enough alone time.
- Not enough sleep.
- Whining or tantrums.
- Messy house.
- No food in the house/food waste.
- Not being listened to.
- Being talked back to.
- Being lied to.
- Betrayal.

There is a difference between these triggers and those that derive
from trauma. Many of these universal mom triggers are uninten-
tional. A child not wanting to clean her room or eat her vegetables
may feel like a war of wills, but it's not emotional warfare, it's normal
kid testing behavior. Part of separation and independence. We've all
resisted mom requests and commands. It's the reactions moms develop when thwarted that require our attention. Most of the time, we
get into habits and patterns of acting and reacting with no idea how
triggering and hurtful they might feel.

Patterns of Conflict

We all have patterns of behavior. Moms/daughters who don't learn to manage their triggers will continue to repeat their turbulent battles in every stage of their lives. In fact, arguing itself can have an addictive component. There is some brain reward in the rush of adrenaline that accompanies fighting, even when both parties think they want peace.

For example, our friend Kelly had health problems as a child. For years she did not take care of herself, and this caused Kelly's mom to over-worry. Was Kelly getting enough food, enough rest, seeing the doctor, doing what she should? Kelly's mom nagged endlessly and continues to nag to this day, even though Kelly is now a responsible adult and taking good care of herself. This can be a cultural behavior, too.

Because Kelly and her mom have been fighting about personal care for decades, anything about health is a trigger for an adrenaline rush and a fight. Kelly can't help losing her temper because she's not being listened to or respected. Here's where the volcano of rage and resentment builds up. Kelly and her mom need boundaries.

A different example is Casey, an overworked and stressed single mom. She is doing everything in her power to make ends meet and can't be late for school or work. So when her young daughter refuses to eat or is slow to get dressed, Casey's frustration bubbles up, and sometimes she loses her temper. It's not that Casey's daughter is being a brat; it's that being late is a trigger for Casey, who is struggling to stay on schedule.

Resentments can be lasting and morph into rage. Memories of "lazy" daughters who wouldn't help in the past but now want help with their kids: trigger. A picky eater who gave mom grief over food for years but now wants mom's cooking for their family when she doesn't want to cook anymore: trigger. How about irresponsible daughters who get into scrapes or lose things and still expect mom to fix and replace them at forty-two? Trigger. Daughters who only call or visit when they want money: trigger. We could go on with the triggers. Daughters who blame you for anything and everything: triggers galore. Anything that once got your goat will carry forward.

Daughter/Mom Triggers

Nagging is right up there as a major trigger. Moms who nag about the same issues every time you get together, or every day, will always get you. When are you going to get married, give me grand-children, get your nails done, lose weight? When are you going to break up with that rotten boyfriend/husband of yours? Why can't you visit more often, get a handle on your finances, grow up? Can't you fix yourself up a little more? Your boss should give you a raise, why aren't you asking? Just go down the areas of conflict list.

Nagging moms are often the judgmental ones who can't stand their daughters doing things differently from them. They will nag you about your independence and whatever they think is wrong with you: your parenting, the cleanliness of your house, the behavior of your children, you're working too much, or not enough. Nagging is noise pollution, and yes, it can be toxic. It invades your personal space and makes you feel bad about yourself.

Tone of voice is a trigger for everyone. Sometimes just the tone of a mom's/daughter's voice is enough to set you off. Is it a whine that means a complaint is coming? Is it super cheery, so you know an unwelcome request or piece of information is coming? Is it sad and needy so that you're alerted to a coming invasion of the peace snatcher? Tone can set you on edge. You know it when you hear it. It's the fingernail on the blackboard that signals the arrival of something that hurts, irritates, or challenges you. Will you flee or fight?

Criticism is also a trigger for everyone. We just hate it when someone we love and want to love and accept us finds fault. Our reaction can be instant rage. Here are some criticisms that moms may not think are triggering: You're so tired, thin, fat, overworked. You're so grumpy all the time. What's the matter with you? You're lazy, reckless, a spendthrift. This is name-calling. You drive too fast. You're mean to your mom, kids, relatives. You're late. You don't show up. Your husband should earn more so you don't have to work. These are both attacks and criticisms of yourself and your lifestyle that make you feel bad, incompetent, or stupid.

Oversharing is a trigger that often comes up in families when there is a divorce and a wounded or angry mom can't stop talking about it. Moms sharing divorce woes or financial woes or just bad-mouthing dads puts daughters in an impossible position. We have a friend whose estranged wife persuaded his daughter and grandchildren to cut him off when, after twenty-six unhappy years of marriage, he finally filed for divorce. Moms can force their daughters to choose sides, so divorce itself can be a trigger. Oversharing by daughters who need constant emotional and other kinds of support can also be triggers for moms. Personal boundaries are needed to ease the oversharing burden.

Shaming makes you feel hot all over. Have you ever farted loudly in an exercise or yoga class? Shame. Shaming can be public or private and hurt just as much either way. Shaming can be about looks, behavior, past behavior, your intelligence. You name it. You're so stupid to do that. That dress looks terrible on you. You look ugly in that color. Who do you think you are, talking to me like that? You dress (look) like a slut. Do you know what people think about you when you act like that? Everybody knows you're . . . whatever.

A daughter in recovery might be shame triggered and defensive when mom innocently checks up on her. A mom who is new to sobriety might be shame triggered when her daughter questions her about her recovery plan. Oh, the agony of a shaming mom/daughter. Hey, we both do it. Anybody with a gossipy mouth does it. We just want it to stop and to feel that we're okay.

Blaming is another kind of shaming, and a terrible trigger. Moms/daughters (or anybody) who hurt your feelings or punish you and then say you made them do it are toxic. Blaming is one of those triggers you often can't do anything about. You can't talk to or reason with anyone who says you're the cause of their treating you badly. Here again, it depends on the circumstances. It's another story if you're blamed for missing a plane to a family vacation and causing problems for everyone, when in fact you did and it's not the first time. Or you're blamed for ruining a family party because you were drunk when in fact you were drunk, passed out, and vomited on the new sofa. Feelings of blame may be justified, but how can we express our feelings in a nonconfrontational way? Finding new ways to stop or communicate without nagging, blaming, shaming, or criticizing tones of voice is the goal.

Think About This

We didn't add self-righteousness or having to be right on our trigger list, but they certainly could be there. If you have a mom/ daughter who believes she has the moral high ground or feels she's always right, those are triggers, too. We all have insecurities that moms/daughters can use to wind us up. If you've always argued about food or weight, then food has become a topic of great sensitivity, making it even more difficult to talk about. Here, too, culture and personality play important roles in why we fight, and how we fight. If you want peace, but every exchange triggers an explosive reaction, you're always going to be on edge around each other. Does one of you fight dirty?

What are your areas of sensitivity that trigger instant irritation, and even rage, when your mom/daughter touches them? Can you identify the times when you feel the heat rise and suddenly find yourself unable to control your emotions? If you have specific areas of conflict, here's where learning to identify them can make all the difference before you take the next step to manage them.

TIME TO JOURNAL

The good thing about triggers is that the slightest bit of clarity and understanding can make a remarkable difference almost instantly. When we began writing, we had many misunderstandings that made talking about some of our conflicts impossible. When some subjects came up, we overreacted, wanted to get our own point across, and be the one who was right. Righteousness was our enemy. When we were able to identify the triggers and explain them, we often found that both of us were right. We could provide appreciation of each other's excellent qualities and reassurance instead of saying critical or insensitive things that make the situation worse. Now when Leslie is upset, it's Lindsey who has the perspective to see the situation clearly and can help Leslie see that she was triggered, or vice versa. This is a real and positive change that can be achieved by perspective alone.

JOURNAL PROMPTS

1. What are your areas of sensitivity?

2. Can you remember when and where they started? Please explain.

3. What does being triggered feel like to you?

4. How does your mom/daughter trigger you? Name a few ways.

5. What happens when you try to talk to your mom/daughter about your feelings?

6. What would you like to change? Do you want peace, an apology, reassurance?

CHAPTER 15

Trauma

Very simply, trauma is a distressing or disturbing experience. When we are under intense stress our brains cope by releasing adrenaline and cortisol. These hormones signal the fight-or-flight response either to do something to stop a threat or get away. When we can't control a terrifying incident happening to us or people we love, the impact is more profound. We feel powerless and helpless, and that can lead to rage. Upsetting events can literally change the way our brain works. A prime example of brain change is PTSD, which is having the same terrified reactions and feelings long after the danger is over. Rage can take over at any moment. With trauma, as with some other emotions, our brain doesn't distinguish between a trigger and a real danger and will respond to protect us, even when no response is warranted.

We can't talk about trauma without explaining why the brain retains horrific memories that torment and change us forever. According to trauma pioneer Bessel A. van der Kolk, MD, author of

The Body Keeps the Score: Brain, Mind, and Body in the Healing of Trauma, "No matter how much insight and understanding we develop, the rational brain is basically impotent to talk the emotional brain out of its reality." Independent of our wants and desires, the brain has lasting emotional realities that we need to understand and address before we can heal.

While we always knew that it is very difficult to argue with our own fixed feelings about events and people, we were surprised to learn there is a chemical reason for it. We had always thought of the left and right brain as the math and science side versus the verbal and creative side. One side made you an artist, and the other side made you a lawyer, and you're one kind of brain person or another. That's far from the truth. In fact, we need and use both sides of our brain for growth and development, and they both must function together to keep us safe and healthy. But they don't always function together.

The left side of the brain oversees order and reason. It's the side that can debate, learn, and plan. The left side of the brain will organize survival on a desert island. The right side of the brain is the emotional side. It holds the memories and stores the intuition and feelings. During a traumatic event, adrenaline causes the heart to race and ignites the fight-or-flight response. During times of acute stress and horror something else happens. According to Dr. Kolk, the left side of the brain shuts down to allow the right side to do its job without thinking and reasoning.

You've heard of people jumping into flaming cars to save a baby. Recently in our neighborhood, a young mother stopped her car on a busy street to help a family of ducks get safely across. Turning back to her car, she was struck by an oncoming car. Her left brain was not working. Her emotional right brain told her to save the ducks, not to worry about the cars. As with other people who said they just did something heroic without thinking, it was the adrenaline that caused the heroic action.

In the aftermath of trauma, the left brain may have been permanently disconnected from its crucial thinking job. Reason wasn't working during the trauma, so the right brain (the emotional side) took over. Later, the right side of the brain retains the memories and feelings out of proportion to what is happening now. There is no auto-restore of reason and rational thinking for past traumas, no left-brain voice that assures us that was then, this is now. Our right brain has no reality filter, and that's how traumas stay alive. This explains why sometimes moms/daughters see and feel events differently. If a daughter was helpless and hurt and mom was in control at the time of the incident, mom might not remember the event as traumatic whereas daughter will never be the same.

In short, trauma, and repeated traumas, have a lasting impact and can alter everything about the way we feel and interact with the world. Here's a simple example. Leslie's car was T-boned and totaled a few years ago just blocks from home. The police sirens, fire engine, smoking car, coping with insurance, and needing to get a new car were all traumas. Driving was traumatic for months after the accident, and Leslie still gets that panicky feeling on the highway sometimes. All right, she admits it. She won't drive on major highways; she no longer trusts other drivers to stay in their lane.

Before we get into other kinds of traumas, let's think for a moment about the traumas all of us face just being female. Women's reproductive health couldn't be more traumatic. From the age of eleven or twelve, menstruating every month or missing periods are both fraught as we gain and lose weight and have mood changes every ten days. Who hasn't had a gusher without warning in the most inconvenient places? Bleeding itself is traumatic. Remember your first period? Menstruation can be a painful reminder that being a girl has its disadvantages. Have you ever felt a vacation or weekend was ruined because you had your period and just didn't feel, look, or act your best? Thirty or forty years of periods is no picnic. Dare you count how many you've had?

Heading toward menopause is traumatic, too, because it becomes a rage time of life for many women. Why rage? It's the time of physical change when gravity takes over, we don't look or feel the same, estrogen decreases, and testosterone increases. Testosterone is the male hormone that lowers inhibition, and for us that might mean resentment feels stronger. There's no science to support the impact of testosterone on women's mood; it's an observation.

It is a fact of life, though, that moms/daughters are fearful and traumatized at every stage of our lives about what's happening to our hormones, vaginas, and breasts. We have no control over our bodies, and further we're confused about sexuality itself. The mythology of love and romance is based on looking beautiful, attracting men, getting married, and having babies.

In real life our sexuality is trauma at every turn. There's nothing feminine about being a female. Women are prey. Virginity is admired but not protected. Pregnancy when you aren't ready for it is punished, not treated with dignity and support. Violence against women and rape are often treated with indifference or suspicion. It's not easy for many women to get pregnant, and pregnancy itself has many dangers. Some 20 percent of pregnancies end in miscarriage. Leslie nearly bled to death in a hospital hallway. So, while reproduction is natural, there is nothing simple and nothing romantic about it.

How do we communicate healthy values and physical relationships to our daughters when we ourselves are traumatized around one aspect or another of our sexuality? Everywhere on the planet girls are sexually assaulted, but how many girls know their mothers were assaulted, too? How many girls can tell their mothers, and how many mothers tell their daughters? It's part of the lies we tell and secrets we keep.

There is also the reality of postpartum depression, and the trauma of not being able to immediately bond with a baby. The changes in a new mom's life can feel overwhelming at best, and she may lose the ability to care for herself in the process. The traumas of being a mom are extensive and not really talked about openly. We know that even when a mother-daughter relationship is wonderful, there is still trauma in the background that can create problematic behaviors and beliefs. Living in a patriarchy, Kelly McDaniels, author of *Mother Hunger*, points out that this is another trauma of the female experience.

Types of Traumas

These are three common types of traumas:

Acute: This may be the result of a single disturbing incident. Car accidents, natural disasters, and violent assaults are some examples.

Chronic: This is repeated trauma. Bullying at school or work, domestic violence, alcoholic/addict in the house, sexual harassment are a few examples.

Complex: This comes from ongoing and multiple exposure to different kinds of trauma. For our purposes, we'll use women's biology, workplace, and social injustice as examples of complex trauma. The way women are treated in a patriarchy is a form of complex trauma.

Mother-Daughter Relationship Trauma

While it's comforting to think that all mothers love their daughters and treat them with compassion, love, and care, not all mothers have the capacity to show love and affection. Moms who are ill-equipped for motherhood develop harmful behaviors that range from basic disinterest to extreme narcissism. These moms traumatize their daughters with abusive or toxic patterns and set the stage for low self-esteem, abuse from others, addiction, anxiety, and depression. Daughters can grow up feeling unwanted and unloved. In recovery, we've heard dozens of stories from daughters who have spent decades working on trauma recovery to gain a healthy sense of self and the ability to have and maintain healthy adult relationships.

It's not just moms wrecking emotional damage and causing trauma. Selfish, addicted, and mentally ill daughters can also leave a trail of devastated moms scarred by verbal, emotional, and even physical abuse. Mothers and daughters with unhealthy, enmeshed, or toxic dynamics unleash a special kind of traumatizing warfare on each other. For mothers and daughters who are trying to support each other and get along, understanding how trauma has affected you will be one of the greatest challenges and greatest rewards of the healing process.

Common Problems Reported by Trauma Survivors

- Trouble regulating emotions.
- Inability to form close personal relationships.
- Issues of impulsivity.
- Nightmares.
- Anxiety.

- Intrusive thoughts.
- Loss of memory.
- Isolating.
- Changing routines to feel safe.

Generational Trauma

As you reflect on your mother, her mother, and the history of females in your family, you may now notice something called intergenerational trauma. What that means is that unhealthy or toxic behaviors have been passed down both because of unhealed trauma in previous generations and because those past traumas have affected a mom's ability to parent.

Many girls exhibit symptoms of anxiety, mood instability, hypervigilance, and other PTSD responses as babies and grow up with them simply because their mom has experienced abuse or trauma. It's also common in refugees and survivors of war/Holocaust, those who have experienced poverty, food insecurity, homelessness, and drug and alcohol addictions. They have inherited challenges that require patience, new life skills, and compassion to heal. In some daughters, these traumas might manifest as physical health problems. Constant stomachaches, headaches, back pain, and other kinds of physical symptoms have been reported as a result of trauma in the body.

Other Mother-Daughter Traumas

Here are some other common sources of trauma for moms/daughters. You can see that some of these also appear on the common mother/daughter Conflicts and Triggers lists. So now you're seeing how profoundly interconnected our emotional lives, history, and experiences are and how each issue affects the mother-daughter relationship in different ways. The goal of enumerating the traumas is to reveal the challenges of being women that are rarely discussed. The goal is to build community and compassion around shared experiences that have the potential to bring us together instead of tearing us apart.

How Many Traumas Have You Experienced?

- Childbirth.
- Death.
- Divorce.
- Abusive or mentally ill father/husband/partner/brother/ co-caregiver.
- Active alcoholic/addict in the family.
- Constant moving of residence.
- Financial instability.
- Job instability.
- Grandparent alienation (when moms don't allow grandparents access to their grandchildren).

How have these experiences affected you and your mother-daughter relationship? We'll start with biology. As touched on earlier, everything about female reproductive health has the potential for complex trauma: getting pregnant, not being able to get pregnant, carrying a baby you aren't ready for, having an abortion when your family or state forbids it, miscarriage, difficult childbirth, initial mothering, vaginal diseases, breast diseases, menopause. Even a daughter's decision not to marry and have children can be traumatic for some moms and grandmoms. In any case, grandmothers and mothers have experienced many of the traumas we've listed above by the time their daughters reach maturity. So at least three generations (grandmother, mother, daughter) have many traumas in common but may not share common, positive, empowering, supportive feelings with each other about them.

Divorce or multiple divorces can be destructive and damaging when separating partners don't behave well. Long, drawn-out divorces in which daughters become pawns in a game of legal and emotional warfare cause suffering for everyone. Maybe you have seen an ugly divorce play out and watched as hurting parents have not been able to provide adequate support for children stuck in the middle. Moms marrying partners their daughters don't like can cause breakups and painful grandparent alienation when daughters have children of their own.

Losing a member of the family to death by any cause could be a mother-daughter shared trauma. However, a death of despair (suicide, overdose, alcohol-related organ failure) adds another layer of grief and confusion. Constantly moving around because of jobs or other issues may have created problems around making friends and maintaining a community of any kind. That can lead to loneliness, isolation, and worse.

Financial instability is another area that you may not immediately think of as traumatic. But money trauma is real. If you don't have enough money, you may struggle with a feeling of deprivation or fear of losing your money even after you have a flush savings account. Everything from having enough money at the grocery store to your ability to get health care and the material things you need such as clothes, school supplies, and other necessities will be stressful. Mothers and daughters who have money in excess, on the other hand, may traumatize each other with exorbitant spending habits or withholding funds when angry, without regard to consequences. Money is one of our triggers.

Trauma Responses

Trauma is now widely recognized by experts as the potential source of some kinds of mental illness and even addiction. As you can see from the common problems that trauma can cause in the list above, it's a subject with wide-ranging consequences for mental health. For the purposes of mother-daughter relationship recovery, we will focus on hard trauma responses, red flags, and the three A's of recovery.

First the hard traumas, which include death, suicide, war, disaster, assault, sexual assault, child abuse (sexual, physical, neglect), domestic violence, toxic narcissist in the family, and divorce. If you have suffered any of these, you may feel relief at first or once the event has permanently ended. The stress responses you developed to survive your ordeal, however, will still be with you long after the threat is gone.

To feel safe, you may develop new stress responses to cope with what happened. Obsessively thinking about the event or being preoccupied with safety as a result are very common responses. Often, after the feelings of fear or shame lessen, anger may become a constant companion. Intense anger, even rage, is a normal reaction to having experienced a traumatic event. Other responses may include having trouble concentrating, losing hope, and not caring about people or things any longer. You may feel uneasy or jumpy and startle at the slightest sound. Insomnia may plague you along with increased anxiety. You may harbor intense shame and other overwhelming feelings. Safety for those you love may become another obsession. This overconcern, even becoming a helicopter mom, makes you seem crazy and unreasonable to your daughter.

How do you know if your daughter has experienced a trauma? When it comes to young daughters, any kind of behavior change is a red flag. If you have a happy, confident daughter, and suddenly she is hiding in her room, is moody, and has strong emotions of anger or shame, or she now overreacts to minor inconveniences, is she just a moody teen? Maybe something else is going on. Withdrawing from family and friends and wanting to be alone could be clues that something is wrong. A preteen or teenager who does not want to upset her mother may hide the fact that something traumatic has happened to her or she's about to do something risky and dangerous. While your daughter may not immediately be able to talk to you about what's happening, she may need to or want to down the line.

Signs of trouble include suddenly not eating, not being able to sleep, wearing different kinds of clothes, losing interest in things she loved before, and not taking care of herself. Your daughter will leave clues for you that all is not well. You just need to pay attention and learn how to respond.

This is where opening the door to safe sharing is crucial. We can't tell you how many moms are shocked to learn that their daughters kept secrets about something terrible that happened to them. Moms often think daughters know they won't be angry, but daughters don't know that. They may not know their moms are stronger and braver than they seem. Moms must tell them. It's okay to tell daughters that bad things can happen and you'll still be all right. In fact, it's imperative that you routinely tell your daughters that you will love them no matter what.

Most important, your daughters need to know that you won't fall apart if they tell you about upsetting incidents they know you won't want to hear. Daughters, if you don't tell your mom what's going on, she can't help you. Leslie and Lindsey learned the hard way that we have each other's backs, no matter what. You can do better than we did by building the support system before anything happens.

When it comes to the traumas that happen without destructive intent, such as a fall, a car accident, a fire, or a flood, you might have many of the same trauma reactions, and these may need to be addressed, too. Take the car accident for example. Leslie was alone when it happened to her. But what if she'd had a child in the car and it had been a bad crash? Say someone was hurt. She might not trust herself to get in a car again. But avoiding cars because one hit her once is impractical. To get over the trauma, she might need some help from a mental health professional to feel comfortable driving again.

The Three A's of Recovery

Awareness

It's impossible to fix a problem if you don't know what the problem is. Here's what we've been through: all the stages of grief, anger, resentment, sadness, confusion, despair, losing hope, gaining hope, finding gratitude, feeling better, learning coping techniques, and recovery tools. You may be feeling hopeless or helpless right now, but you can change that by taking the first step to understanding your traumas and what caused them, your triggers, and the issues that keep igniting your conflict. We hope that at this point you have some awareness about yourself, your daughter, your mother, your family history, what issues make you the craziest, and if you've experienced trauma. That information alone should shed some light on what's happened to you and your mom/daughter.

It was eye-opening for us to understand how culture and family history had played into our mother-daughter dynamic. It was freeing and enlightening to accept that our traumas were real and the pain we experienced was valid. Now that we know what our triggers are, all one of us has to say is "This conversation about boyfriends or money is triggering; we need to put a pin in it for now." It's easier to respect someone's boundary when you know exactly how disturbing it is to them for you to cross it. Many of you are frustrated but do not want to hurt each other. Learning how to stop hurting the people you love is an incredible gift that you can give them.

Acceptance

Acceptance is the second A of recovery. They say in recovery circles, "Acceptance is the answer to my problems today." Think about when you feel angry or frustrated or resentful. Does something feel unacceptable to you? When your mom/daughter behaves in ways that drive you absolutely nuts, what if you could pause and understand that's who she is. She's not behaving this way to hurt you (usually), and you don't need to react with intense emotion. Sounds nice, doesn't it? It is.

A few tips for finding acceptance. The most important thing to remember is, you don't have to like something to accept it. Lindsey can't stand that Leslie bothers her about medical appointments, but Lindsey has learned to accept that Leslie cannot control herself around this subject and her reminders are coming from a place of concern. A perspective change is Lindsey's knowing that Leslie's concern is not intended to be harmful, and it welcomes a softer reaction. Acceptance takes practice. Knowing when to pause and hold your tongue is a valuable skill for any relationship. Pausing makes it much easier to calm down and consider another point of view.

It's also useful to remember that situations and people can be resolved in unexpected ways. Whatever is troubling you or your mom/

daughter may change in the future. Bad boyfriends get the boot, people go into recovery, and with professional help, time heals. Acceptance is knowing that you can't control other people and situations, and this provides some freedom to work on yourself.

Action

This is the time when you are clear on your issues and are ready to address them in whatever recovery solutions you choose or deem appropriate. When it comes to actions for recovery, you have many options. We always recommend learning as much as you can about your situation. Has exploring your family history and dysfunction made you realize you need professional help? It may seem frightening at first to talk about your struggles to a stranger, but healing from trauma needs a special kind of help that friends and family members can't provide. Bold choices lead to breakthroughs.

When Leslie attended her first Al-Anon meeting, she sobbed for twenty minutes in front of thirty strangers. It was the first time she had told anyone about the anguish she was suffering from addiction in her family. In a room full of people who were having the same experiences, she was finally free to begin healing from years of pain and trauma.

Trauma Expert Dr. Deborah Sweet, PsyD, on Mother-Daughter Trauma

Lindsey met Dr. Deborah Sweet when she moved to Los Angeles in 2015. Dr. Sweet is a licensed clinical psychologist, trauma specialist, and resiliency coach. With over thirty years in recovery, she is certified in Somatic Experiencing, Havening Technique, Brainspotting, and Attachment-Focused EMDR. Dr. Sweet founded the Trauma

Counseling Center of Los Angeles but now has returned to private practice, which was her first love. She believes everyone needs tools to recover from anxiety, stress, and trauma. Dr. Sweet offered to answer several important questions about how to cope with mother-daughter conflicts that arise from trauma. We are grateful to her for sharing her expertise with our readers.

What Should You Do if Your Mother/ Daughter Won't Take Responsibility?

Dr. Sweet: In thinking about mothers, the most important thing I can recommend is to engage in constant self-care, practice acceptance, and cultivate the inner voice of self-compassion. One of the keywords here is "practice." We practice self-care, we practice acceptance, and we practice listening to the voice of self-compassion.

When a mother won't take responsibility, it is unsatisfying and sometimes devastating. We need to remember we have choices. Many can't or won't see their part. For some, to do this would be to admit that she was wrong or did a bad thing. Their psychology will not allow them to see themselves as bad. Often, they will see themselves as the victim, which removes their ability to take responsibility. Part of it too is to practice not taking her comments personally. I have to take responsibility for my mental health and work with my inner voice.

When we cultivate a loving inner parent, we take the pressure off them to be different than they are. This idea comes from a few sources, one of the most important being ACA (Adult Children of Alcoholics and Dysfunctional Families). They can look at their mother as the vehicle of their birth and know that their loving higher power is their true loving parent. It can take a long time to change our thinking. It can take years. And that's okay.

Understanding why she won't take responsibility and can't help to repair the relationship will only take us so far. We can understand what someone else went through, but in terms of soothing the terrible events, understanding only gets anyone part of the way there. Two other pieces of the puzzle are learning to soothe our nervous systems and finding a spiritual solution. The spiritual solution is not about religion (although it can be), and it allows us to see the big picture. The spiritual solution means "What is good for my spirit?"

I would also suggest finding other mothering or nurturing figures. In other words, find motherly or grandmotherly energy in someone else, find other women who can see you, hear you, be interested in you. When you find other motherly energy, it can take the pressure off your mother. Stop going to her to get this thing she can't provide.

Regarding daughters, we need to notice the words we are using when we think about them. What metaphors are we engaging in? "They are monsters, tigers, or dragons." What are we communicating with ourselves? Often, we get stuck in thinking they can't or won't change. While this may be true, often when we work on ourselves, they seem to change too. Additionally, with a daughter we want to seek to understand. What is going on with this young person? Give what you can, but also take care of yourself. Do not stop doing the things that help you feel good about yourself.

What Is the Best Way to Heal from Mother Trauma?

Dr. Sweet: Be a seeker. Sometimes the answer will come from therapy, meditation, spiritual retreat, art therapy, and of course, books. We have a problem and must come at it from different angles. People think they have an epiphany that happened in an instant. That's usually not the case. It's all these things adding up together and then suddenly, inside you have the freedom you've been looking for.

A lot of progress happens in therapy, but if someone is motivated and seeking ways of looking at the situation, she can have breakthroughs between sessions. If you're not getting what you need from your mother/daughter, you may have to seek it in different places. Find the things that work for you. This part is your responsibility. Your mental, emotional, and mental health is your responsibility. Find ways to express what you are feeling. These could be writing unsent letters, running, working out, dancing, painting or drawing, watching a sad movie, sitting still, and noticing the sensations inside your body. There is so much more to say, but this is a start.

What if You Can't Forgive Your Mother/Daughter?

Dr. Sweet: Do not force yourself to forgive. You'll be ready when you're ready. Notice the things that bring you closer to forgiveness. Practice forgiveness however you can. It is a process. It isn't a one and done event. We are carrying tension and heavy burdens. Sometimes the key is to think about it like finding peace or a lightness. You can say to yourself, "I choose peace," or something similar. Many books have been written on forgiveness. Read everything you can find, but don't pressure yourself to do it. Something that may help is to realize there is a difference in the words you would use between who they were and who they are today. These could be different words. Practice open-mindedness.

Often fear is in the way. Follow the fear. Ask yourself what you are afraid of. Remember someone had to be in pain and fear to do the things they did. Forgiveness is something that is ongoing. You must re-forgive. We replay resentments, and we can replay forgiveness too. How can I be at peace? Sometimes the word "forgiveness" was just too big. Using the Havening Technique with affirmations such as "I can be at peace today," can be a game changer. Dip your toe in the water.

What Should You Do if Your Mother/Daughter Won't Speak to You?

Dr. Sweet: Show up as best you can. Let the other person know you are ready when they are. Leave them to their process. It could take a while. Taking care of yourself and learning to go on with your life are key. I'm a big fan of the unsent letters. Try the three-part letter: an unsent letter to the person (telling them why I'm upset), letter to my loving higher power (sharing why I'm upset), and a letter back from my loving higher power to me.

Practice less identification with the self. Rather than "This is happening to me," think of it as "This is happening," or better yet, "This is happening, and I'm okay." Take a step back. Work on healing yourself. We are complex creatures who need multiple tools to heal these kinds of wounds.

Think About This

Universal traumas affect the mother-daughter relationship in ways you may not have considered. When we asked you to write what you know of your mother's life, you may not have thought about the traumas and life changes she's been through and is experiencing now, just being a female. What about your grandmother? Her experiences affected your mother, and she influenced you. Is there a through line in three generations of experiences? Have you had traumas in common, such as divorces? Did you ever think about how traumas you don't even know about might be affecting you now?

TIME TO JOURNAL

No one's life or history is free of trauma. Before writing this book, Leslie and Lindsey had never shared their traumas with each other. We'd never explored how biology itself, not to mention social injustice, has been traumatic and influenced our behavior in many ways. Moms want their daughters to be safe and may avoid having tough conversations to preserve their innocence. Leslie's mom did not give her even basic information about anything sexual. Grandmothers and moms may not want daughters to know what happened to them in wartime so daughters won't be afraid, wounded, or angry about it. Daughters, too, want to protect their moms (and themselves) from learning things that might hurt each other or damage their love.

JOURNAL PROMPTS

1. Are you aware of any traumas in your family history?

2. Has your mother or grandmother had experiences that have affected them in traumatic ways?

3. Are there divorces in the family?

4. Has reproductive health been a traumatic experience for your mom or grandmother?

5. What about your traumatic experiences? Have you processed or shared your painful experiences?

6. Is this an area where professional help is needed for you and your mom/daughter to heal?

CHAPTER 16

Techniques to
Keep the Peace

Y ou can see from the two T's, triggers and trauma, that it's inevitable for moms/daughters to have areas of annoyance, grievance, hurt, and even rage. After all, whether genetically related or not, you've been connected through many stages of aging while each has had her own positive and negative life experiences along the way. It's normal and natural to have complicated feelings about the relationship. In addition, your mother-daughter relationship is not the same now as it was at any other time in your life. It is constantly changing as you mature. In addition, life events and circumstances create new situations and shifting dynamics. All healthy relationships require a tune-up from time to time.

Whatever stage you're in right now, remember that you're both coping with your own challenges and have different needs. Being a young mom brings overwhelming challenges, and guess what. Being a grandma isn't easy, either. In your middle years, you may have both moms and daughters causing conflict. What does grandma want mom to pressure daughter to do? It's especially challenging because they both can trigger you.

Whoever you are, it isn't easy being you. And getting along with people you love may be a bigger struggle than you anticipated or deserve. We can confirm, however, that life is better when peace prevails. Once you stop the chaos and let your nervous system calm down, you might even find that life can be serene. We provided the writing prompts for homework as a path to explore who you and your mom/daughter are and why you fight. Now we're heading into solutions and conflict resolution with tips that will make all the difference for healing in the future.

When Feelings Could Kill

What do you do when your feelings are out of control? When we had horrific blowups in the old days, we became emotional wrecks for days. We wanted to love each other and were devastated when we failed. Love and rage can get very confusing when you are warring with a mom/daughter. With us, there was family triangulation, hurt feelings, resentment, projection, you name it. We felt ashamed about fighting and angry at each other for starting it, or escalating, or walking out mad. Today, we have tools and sayings at our disposal that return us to peace very quickly even when tensions are rising.

Sometimes just saying, "You may be right; let's let it go for now," works to stop a fight in its tracks. Lindsey was the first to use this phrase, and it always worked. Leslie calmed down right away no matter what was bothering her. We'll provide a list of dos and don'ts for getting along that have worked for many struggling mothers and daughters. From expressions you both recognize as waving the white flag to actual time-outs when your voices begin to rise, we'll also show how to calm down until you can speak safely again.

Stop the Fights Before They Start

How many fights have you had with your mom/daughter where you don't feel she's listening to you? How often have you felt that she doesn't respect you, your choices, your rules? When it comes to family, we feel at home. We can get into the habit of behaving badly, whether that means being irritated or downright nasty. Sometimes it's the people closest to us who experience the worst of us and don't receive the respect they deserve. That's the magic word here, "respect."

Everyone wants to feel respected, especially your mom/daughter. Respect is the key to harmony, so let's consider good old-fashioned respect. We're going to ask you a question, and don't go easy on yourself. Do you respect your mom/daughter? Do you treat her with respect at home? In public? In front of the rest of the family? It matters how we treat each other when we're alone and in front of others. It's not all right to be in the habit of disrespecting your mother/daughter, so let's look at that for a minute.

We all have the right to seek health and happiness. It is a basic human right. As you think about why you might be dismissive, disapproving, or disrespectful, consider whether you are accepting of your mom's/daughter's right to make her own choices. Obviously, this does not apply to moms with daughters who are minors. But even with a child, your degree of respect for your daughter's feelings and choices will affect her later. You want your mom/daughter to feel safe even if you don't agree and have different goals.

Just because you may have different political, religious, or cultural opinions doesn't mean you should argue and try to change your mom's/daughter's ways. The liberal versus conservative views have separated too many loved ones. We've seen many strong feminist moms watch in shock as their daughters choose lives that conflict with their opposite beliefs. We never said it's going to be easy to stay quiet as you watch your mom/daughter do or say things that appall you. How can you be supportive and respectful when you don't feel that way? Where do you begin the arduous journey of kindness and respect?

Techniques for Healthier Communication

Pause: We've already mentioned pause; it's a cornerstone of self-control. Pause every single time you feel the tension rise. We all know when we're about to say something and go too far. Pause before you go there. Play the tape though; is this really what you want to say? Is escalating the situation going to get you what you want? Will you regret what you're about to say? It is a kind of heroism to smile and nod even when you think your loved one is in outer space. Learning to pause before reacting will be especially helpful if you and your mom/daughter have different personality styles and trigger issues. Think about having an angel and a devil on each shoulder. Who are you going to feed with every comment you make?

Listen (stop interrupting): How much are you listening instead of trying to get your point across? Can you be an active listener? You want to be heard and understood by your mom/daughter, so start paying attention to what she's saying. Being a good and active listener means not thinking about how you're going to respond or change their mind. Don't interrupt, don't be on your phone, stay focused, make eye contact, and don't let your judgments about what they're saying trigger a reaction! If need be, give your mom/daughter a few minutes and be silent until the end. Set a timer, and honor that time.

Think before you speak: Okay, you've managed to listen to your mother/daughter for several minutes, and it's time to respond. This is when you can think about what you're going to say. If the same old party lines aren't working, it's time to change them. When you don't know how to respond in a productive way, just say, "Thank you for sharing that with me; I'm going to take some time to consider it." Then before you say anything else, ask yourself whether your response must be said and whether it has to be said by you. This may be a new style of communication for you. Holding back your every thought can feel awkward at first, but the goal is to keep the situation from escalating as well as showing kindness where once you just wanted to have a smackdown and win.

Say what you mean without saying it meanly: When we say hold back, we don't mean hiding our feelings and not telling the truth about what's happening, especially if your mom/daughter is hurting you with her words or behavior. It's appropriate to talk about your issues and conflicts. Honest and open communication, after all, is essential for any healthy relationship. It's how you say it that matters. As you seek solutions for better communication, there will be times when you share things about each other that neither of you want to hear. Can you tell your mom/daughter your feelings without inflicting pain or being mean? We all feel insults deeply, and when someone blames us, it's an insult trigger. It makes us feel angry and defensive. So you want to be sensitive and avoid using blaming and shaming words.

Don't make assumptions: It's so easy to think you know what's in someone else's head, but you don't. The minute one of us sees an unhappy expression on the other during a work call, we immediately assume the bad mood has something to do with us. Your mom's/ daughter's reactions to outside incidents may feel insulting to you or signal that some blame is coming to you. Those annoyed faces, the noises she makes, even swearing are almost never about you, however. This is a perfect opportunity to pause and ask your mother/ daughter what's going on and then listen without interruption.

Ask whether they want feedback: Sometimes we just need to vent and are not looking for solutions. A great tool is asking your mom/daughter if she wants feedback about what's troubling her instead of launching into a list of suggestions that are not welcome. After you're done listening without interruption, you can ask, "Are you looking for feedback or do you just need me to listen?"

Conflict Resolution 101

You're in conflict. It happens all the time, but now we need to know how to get out of it immediately. The three R's to conflict resolution are review, respond, resolve. We have our own version of that, and you will need your own version. Here's what we do when things get out of hand.

Stop yelling and retreat: If things have gone to a bad place, take a step back and agree to discuss this at another time. Sometimes it's fine to agree to disagree. The point is to stop fighting and lessen the dramatics.

Let calm prevail: One of the biggest hurdles in conflict is staying calm. It's not easy when you feel disrespected or triggered, but composure wins every time. Being able to stay calm is mandatory for healthy communication. If you're enraged, don't talk about it until you've had some time to relax your brain.

Find safe spaces: Sometimes the house becomes a battlefield. If the home is not a safe space for tough talks, consider whether walks or another location may be better.

Create boundaries: We wrote about them earlier, and this is where they come in. If there are issues you want off the table, now is the time to create boundaries around them. We try not to bring up the past, or other family members; those are boundaries for us, and sometimes they have to be enforced.

Seek therapy: There's always professional help if that's the safest way to communicate and you both agree.

Get clarity: File this under the review section. Take a moment to make sure you're both on the same page. Sometimes we get so lost down rabbit holes that we don't even know what we're fighting about. If there is an issue, clarify what it is and what is so upsetting about it. Tell your mom/daughter what your fears about the situation are instead of just screaming at her not to do it.

Getting Clarity: What Do You Want from Each Other?

What do you want from your mom/daughter? This is a profound question, and it may have a surprising answer. And yes, it's okay to feel, "She's driven me crazy long enough! I've had it. I just want her to go away." Leslie felt that, and Lindsey wanted to escape, so she did. We both got what we wanted. Relief from each other. As the mom, Leslie was devastated and thought it wasn't fair. It came at a bad time, too. She thought Lindsey's leaving was an unforgivable betrayal.

For Lindsey breaking up with mom was just as painful. She was alone in the world, on her own, and not well either physically or emotionally. It was a difficult time that taught us how to get along without each other. This is important, too. Moms and daughters since the beginning of time have had to get along without each other. For us, being estranged taught us how to be better people on our own. Breaking up was our path to recovery. Sometimes getting away is the best thing you can do for your sanity.

Let's start with what you want. Ask yourself, what do I want from my mom/daughter? We're only talking about emotional needs here. Not money or childcare for life or groceries—just feelings. Emotional means how can your mom/daughter help you feel good so you don't have to be at war. Here are the things that Lindsey and Leslie wanted from each other. All these examples provide emotional satisfaction and happiness, and we didn't have them for a long time.

- **Feeling loved:** When words and actions align.
- **Compassion:** Being empathic, caring what the other feels.
- **Appreciation:** Knowing you are appreciated.
- **Acceptance:** Knowing you are accepted. This is important whoever or whatever you are.
- **Reassurance:** You're okay, and you're going to be okay. We're going to be okay.
- **Peace:** No fighting. No intrusion of space or personal boundaries.
- **Serenity:** Spiritual healing from whatever occurred before.
- **Share knowledge and experiences:** Learning new coping skills, having new experiences together.

As we've seen in previous chapters, your very personalities may clash. Mental health issues and character may get in the way of healthy communication. Many kinds of trauma can also make a healthy relationship challenging. Don't forget warring traditions, beliefs, and identity. But most important of all, where are you on the list of qualities that accept, affirm, and support others? Where are you on the gratitude scale? Do you have qualities you'd like to see in your mom? Do you have a healthy sense of your value and appreciate yourself?

Your next question is this: Is my mom/daughter able to satisfy (any of) my emotional needs? This is where we look back at some of our earlier answers. Is your mom/daughter determined to be right? Is there something about you or your behavior that she can't forgive? Does she have a rigid belief system that means you have to bend to her will? Is she selfish? Is she abusive? On the other side of the spectrum, is she game for self-exploration? Does she like to learn new things? Will she be open to trying something different?

Steps to Manage a Needy Mom/Daughter

- We're all responsible for ourselves. Having problems, sorrows, physical disabilities, addictions doesn't mean your mom/ daughter should rely on you, manipulate you, or guilt you into taking care of her. Being manipulated may be a trigger for you. What should you do?

- If you feel compelled to answer every call and meet every need to the detriment of yourself, you might be codependent and need counseling help. There's no mystery here. A therapist, counselor, or social worker can put your issues into perspective.

- If your mom/daughter is battling addiction, Al-Anon is great for you to learn about what's happening to you both.

- Instead of doing/fixing everything yourself, explore resources for solutions, other people, places, and things that can help to take the pressure off you. What does she need? Who or what else can take care of it?

- Examine your limitations and wishes. What do you like to do? What can you do? What can't you do? What shouldn't you do?
- Practice cutting back. How are you being a doormat? Is your mom/daughter taking advantage of your money, time, chores, or personal space? When you see your pattern of being asked to do too much or you are volunteering to do too much, it's time to cut back. Pick some situations in which cutting back is the healthy choice.
- Yes, whoever you are, it's okay to say, "No, I can't." If making excuses gets you off the hook, use them: have a meeting or have a task that needs urgent attention, someone's at the door, going to the doctor, taking the dog to the vet. You have a life. Don't give it away.

Managing the Pushback

Every time there is a change in the relationship that benefits one of you and seems to step on the toes (or hurt) the other, there is the potential for pushback. What happens when you say no or create a boundary that is inconvenient to your mom/daughter? She has the choice between accepting it with grace, arguing, name-calling, or hitting back. Be prepared for anything. Sometimes the initial reaction isn't what you were hoping for, but that doesn't mean she won't come around with time.

Best Tips

By this point you may understand a little bit more about your mom/daughter. You may have never thought about why your mom was so rigid or loose with rules or other parenting choices. Now you may be considering the reasons why your mom/daughter is the way she is, instead of just being angry about it. How have your culture, finances, and her mother's behavior affected her? What are the traumas and triggers your mom/daughter has experienced? Knowing this should help you find better and safer ways to communicate that will show respect, encourage change, and keep hurt feelings at bay.

Think about personalities and communication styles: As you explore how to communicate better, keep in mind your mom's/daughter's personality and communication styles. If you knew for sure that your mother/daughter would respond with loving kindness if you stopped confronting her and approached her in a softer way, you'd do it, right? Lindsey hates losing her temper because it makes her feel sick after she's calmed down. So when we need to have a tough talk, we prepare and set a time. So much of our conflict erupted when we caught each other off guard or without preparation. Understanding your personality and communication style and your mom's and then making appropriate changes will help.

Don't dwell on or keep bringing up the past: As you learn how to be softer with each other and yourself, do not cause constant tension and anxiety by discussing things that can't be changed. Remember, forgiving and accepting does not mean you have to like what happened, but you can stop torturing each other over it.

Talk about feelings instead of blaming: As you practice giving up the blame game, look inside at the feelings. We talked about saying what you mean without being mean, but how does that work in practice? Great advice we follow is using phrases such as "When you do or say that it hurts my feelings; let's talk after I process my feelings." This implements the all-important pause. It also helps you focus on your own behavior, not what others are doing.

Schedule time to talk: If you are like us, you call each other at the drop of a hat to go over anything. But those impromptu calls are not a good time to go over anything important. If unexpected calls or calls at a certain time of day annoy you, let others know or keep the phone off. Relationship-building takes work, and these little boundaries and changes will help you as you get used to new ways of behaving.

Dos and Don'ts

The Dos and Don'ts are a list we learned in Al-Anon to get along when you're not getting along. The Dos and Don'ts can be hard to keep in practice, but they are so worth the effort. Which ones do you struggle with?

Do:

- Forgive.
- Be humble.
- Take it easy—tension is harmful.
- Play—find recreation and hobbies.
- Keep on doing your best—even when you fail.
- Learn the facts about what you're dealing with.
- Find support.

Don't:

- Be self-righteous.
- Dominate, nag, scold, or complain.
- Lose your temper.
- Keep bringing up the past.
- Wallow in self-pity.
- Make threats you can't keep.
- Be a doormat.

When we understood how negative constantly bringing up the past, nagging, complaining, temper tantrums, and sulking were to our relationship, we began to change. With knowledge comes the ability to make different choices. Now that we know certain subjects are painful for each other we do a more thoughtful job of dealing with them when they come up.

Think About This

Walking on eggshells, stuffing your feelings to avoid confrontation, as well as constant fighting over differences of opinion are unsuccessful strategies for a healthy and satisfying mother-daughter relationship. Solutions for conflict can be achieved by understanding and considering how trauma and triggers play into you and your mom's/daughter's fighting. How does lack of respect play into your relationship? Respect is the foundation of self-esteem and contentment that you both want and need. Which of the techniques we wrote about might work for your mom/daughter now that you know her personality style? How can you practice using these tips and techniques as you work toward better communication?

TIME TO JOURNAL

Here you can explore why you fight with your mom/daughter. What are the triggers that set you off? What happens to the two of you when you fight? Do you drag other members of the family into the battle? How about triangulating and trying to pit others against your mom/daughter? Does one of you do that? What does your body feel like when you become upset or enraged? There are so many things to think about. Do you feel disappointed and heartbroken when you have a flare-up? You may always be hoping that things will be different this time. This chapter provided some techniques that help to lower the heat and bring some sense of safety and togetherness into the picture.

JOURNAL PROMPTS

1. Do you think you fight too much with your mother/daughter? Explain why you think you're fighting? What do you accomplish?

2. Do you constantly fight about incidents from the past? Why can't you let them go?

3. Would you rather win every argument than have peace? Explain the need to win and be right.

4. Do you think you can pause and listen to another point of view to ease your conflict? How will you do that?

5. Do you know what you want from your mother/daughter? Explain.

6. What techniques from this chapter might work for your mom/daughter?

CHAPTER 17

Breaking Up When Necessary and Resources for Extreme Situations

Sadly, sometimes it is the worst-case scenario. You have entered a cycle of despair in your mother-daughter relationship, and none of your tools and boundaries are working. In the worst-case scenario even your mental health professionals can't help you overcome your conflicts. We've been there and know just how heartbreaking it is to feel you can't manage a positive healthy relationship with one of the most important people in your life. You want to give up and get away, but don't despair. This can get better. Maybe it's your mental health professionals who encourage you to take a break, even break up. Maybe it's your gut feeling that you must step back to survive. Are your feelings real and valid? Yes. Whatever you're feeling, there's a reason for it. You can't make your mom/daughter into a different person. You can't fix what's wrong just by fighting about it. But you can disentangle yourself from an impossible situation and thrive.

What brings you to the place of seeming no return? Let's look at a situational reason for a step back. Do you have a grown daughter who lives with you or works for you or is in a tight-knit community that doesn't allow independence of thinking, being, or self-expression? This is a situation that would be challenging to any daughter. We all want to be free to think for ourselves and make our own way in life. This should be a basic human right for both moms and daughters. Imagine a daughter who has reached maturity and longs to be her own person in a situation in which her mom is an obstacle. Say, mom is in a power position and won't share or let go.

In our case, Lindsey had grown up, left home, lived far away in California, had married, divorced, and worked independently. Leslie had followed her lead and embarked on the recovery lifestyle with her. So far, so good. They had taken many positive steps on their recovery journey. They had worked together to produce two documentary films and launched a website. What could possibly go wrong with this dedicated duo? Let's look at the situation. Mom and daughter had the addiction codependency disease and had become enmeshed. Too involved with each other's moods and needs in every way, and we were working together. Too much interaction daily. Not enough appreciation and listening.

For moms and daughters to work together harmoniously, it helps to be equal partners and not to overshare every feeling. Leslie and Lindsey weren't equal partners at the time of the breakup. When Lindsey moved East after six years of independent life in Los Angeles, she moved into mom's New York apartment while Leslie lived in Florida. Suddenly Lindsey's mom was her mom, her boss, and her landlord. That is a toxic situation. When mom is in a power position, it can trigger the awful feeling in a daughter that she's still a child no one listens to. Feelings like this matter, and moms should pay attention to them.

Ideally, moms should not be in a power position over their grown daughters except in certain circumstances. When a daughter is mentally ill, actively using, or must return home because of a divorce, illness, or other catastrophic situation, mom's authority should be respected. It's her home, and the people in it are her responsibility. In many situations like these, mom may well know best. Many moms are kind and patient and compassionate. Kudos to moms like you. It's when daughters don't have any autonomy and moms are self-righteous, rigid, blaming, and emotionally controlling that the relationship can become toxic.

Leslie and Lindsey learned the hard way that when grown daughters are under their mom's influence (whatever the reason) or they're working with mom, they need to be able to express themselves freely and have some autonomy over the situation. Lindsey had a very real and legitimate need to be on her own in her own home with her own income, far from mom's influences. It works best when both mom and daughter support the move and each other. That isn't always the case. It's important to have an exit strategy for which both mom and daughter can prepare. If mom/daughter isn't on board with changes, however, the separation can get nasty. The split can feel like a bitter divorce, and you must work on yourself to heal.

Toxic Moms and Daughters

Both moms and daughters can be toxic when put to the test. We know that because we went from perfectly loving to horrendously toxic. After a separation, we evolved to the better selves we wanted to be. But what does it mean to be toxic? Fundamentally, it's the way your mom/daughter makes you feel and how she affects the quality of your life. For example, what happens when you have a mom who has told you that you're not pretty, not talented, not good enough? You believe her.

If you are abused, you may believe you deserve it. When your mom says you're stupid because you can't make enough money to support a better lifestyle, you may believe you're a useless slug. No one is a useless slug. When your mom turns love on and off like a faucet, you believe something about you is making her do this. She'd love you if only you were . . . better. That is a toxic mom. A toxic mom must be in control of everything and won't listen to reason. She'll ask you what you want and then do the opposite, leaving you frustrated and hurt.

What Happens to Daughters of Toxic Moms?

Daughters of toxic moms need other influences in their lives to learn what's real and what isn't. If there is another caregiver or partner who is supportive and healthy, that helps to provide a positive environment for growth and development. If the caregiver/partner is also controlling and toxic, daughters can have lasting self-esteem issues. How daughters of toxic moms develop also varies depending on socioeconomic factors, level of education, and geography. Where you come from does make a difference.

The most common consequences are low self-esteem, anxiety, depression, and trouble forming healthy relationships (both growing up and in adulthood). Right behind those emotional wounds are trust issues, shame, and guilt. In addition, self-doubt can shade everything daughters do. Leslie and Lindsey had some issues with boundaries, and that's a common result of family dysfunction. For us, that came with people-pleasing, prioritizing other people's needs, and seeking validation from external sources.

Sometimes being a toxic mom is not mom's fault. Her toxic traits might come from another generation far back in time. Repetition of toxic patterns in moms, daughters, and granddaughters is inevitable unless something intervenes to stop it. We talked about generational trauma and how unaddressed trauma and emotional issues can cause unhealthy dynamics from one generation to the next. This is the reason the three A's, awareness, acceptance, and action, are so important. You don't want to pass down the same traits that have made you suffer.

The other spirit crusher for daughters of toxic moms results in the lack of identity formation. Daughters grow up feeling empty inside and don't know who they are or what they want. A daughter who received no validation or love may have trouble developing her own talents and interests even when she's no longer at home. She might struggle with self-expression because she truly believes she doesn't matter. While there are many negative outcomes of having a toxic mom, one outcome for unloved daughters is positive. Daughters who have not been nourished by loving moms often have an extra measure of resilience and grit. When daughters use those survival skills for healing and recovery, they will thrive emotionally, too.

When Daughters Are Toxic

Moms are not the only ones who can be manipulative, controlling, abusive, and toxic. Daughters can act like spawn of the devil, too.

How do they get that way? Of course, plenty of girls grow up and become selfish, uncaring, and downright mean. They're the ones who bully other girls at school and cause chaos wherever they go. Mean daughters may have a character or personality disorder. Let's just say it comes from dad's side of the family. Just kidding. It happens, and no mom in the world can fix daughters who are wired mean. This is one of the worst-case scenarios for moms. When your daughter is toxic, you may fear her for a valid reason. You may want to limit the time you spend with her. If you're in conflict and have no other family or support system to protect you, you're not going to win.

For our purposes, let's focus on loving daughters who have changed. Why do daughters turn on their moms? Here are a few possibilities: Other people, or influences, in daughters' lives have interfered with the mother-daughter relationship. As a daughter, you can be influenced by other people you love and trust who don't like your mom. Plain and simple, it can be anyone who is jealous of the relationship. Someone tried to disrupt Leslie's relationship with her mom. A colleague tried to disrupt Lindsey's relationship with her mom. It's very hard for a daughter to filter out negative talk or gossip about her mom or be asked to choose between two people she loves.

A daughter can be told and believe that her mom is bad in general and bad for her. Who can do that to your daughter? Relatives who triangulate. Your ex-husband, current husband, partner, father, aunts, uncles, siblings. Consider the many influences in your daughter's life. Not everyone in your daughter's life is going to appreciate and support your mother-daughter relationship. Another example is daughters who have moved into new communities with different views or status and believe their moms won't be welcome or fit in. One other category is daughters who don't want their moms to see or interfere with an unhealthy lifestyle or relationships. These examples are for the escape daughters who back away from their moms to avoid conflicts with others.

But how do loving daughters become toxic? We must turn to chemistry for answers here. The brain is easily activated by strong feelings, both love and hate. Surprisingly, there is a thin line between those two powerful emotions. Some toddlers and small children hit their moms and say, "I hate you." Lindsey said this when she was five on the way to school one day, and Leslie worried about it all day. When Lindsey got home, she had forgotten all about it.

A passionate feeling of anger at being thwarted is just as powerful in an adult as it is in a toddler. We tend to believe that love should be steady and unshakable, but our brains are reacting and overreacting to stimuli all the time. Remember issues and triggers that we've talked about before? Our reactions may not appropriately reflect what's really happening, but the emotions of rage are very real, nonetheless. Can we live with the ambiguity that allows feelings of love and hate to coexist in both moms/daughters? This is part of our healing process. Yes, she can hate me and still love me. She may just need some reminders of what we used to be and still can be if we work on it.

Daughters long to love their mothers, and when moms disappoint or hurt them by opposing them in any way, the longing can instantly be replaced by overwhelming rage. That rage can be triggered again and again when no insult by mom is intended, creating a pattern of hurt feelings that demand a fight-or-flight response. Rage in action by a daughter who feels she's been shortchanged or wronged is a dangerous and scary experience.

Daughters also become toxic when brain function has been affected by drug and alcohol use. To protect an unhealthy relationship or addiction, a daughter's brain will turn a loving mom into a toxic hater. Everything Mom says and does to help a daughter can feel like an attack on her very being, and she will feel that her mom hates and wants to hurt her. This, too, is a very real feeling.

When daughters believe their moms are against them, they will project these feelings of anger and dislike onto their moms. "You hate me, so that's the reason I have the right to hurt and treat you badly." Projection is like a get-out-of-jail-free card. It's not her fault if the problem is you. If your daughter is saying that you don't love her, that may well be what she's really feeling about you right now. But like a toddler, it may not be her core feeling.

Fear is one of the reasons that both moms and daughters have difficulty managing their toxic or dysfunctional relationship. Both moms and daughters can be scary when their powerful feelings and wills clash. One thing we haven't discussed in detail is how moms coping with daughters' addiction or mental illness are afraid of what might happen if they don't do what their daughters want them to do. Resentment on both sides builds up. When moms and daughters become enemies, no amount of reassurance that the love is still there works. Your mom/daughter may love you but has lost the ability to access and express gratitude and loving feelings. In fact, you may be experiencing the opposite behavior; your mom/daughter wants to manipulate and control you into being different.

When Conflict Resolution Tools Fail

Some of the tools that we talked about in conflict resolution can heighten tensions when moms/daughters are not ready to understand what's really happening and accept their own part in the conflict. Readiness to change is a crucial component needed to get the relationship on a healthier footing. Creating boundaries with someone who has spent years treating mom/daughter like a doormat can launch real and frightening anger. If your daughter believes you hate her, she will not respond well when you ask her to be kind.

The message here is it's okay to break up or have a separation when the relationship isn't healthy and you're causing each other harm or despair. What's important is finding relief from the storm. When mothers and daughters just can't be loving and kind to each other, it's time to consider another solution. Sometimes damage has been done that can't be undone. Sometimes addiction, mental health issues, or other conflicts make the relationship too dangerous and unsafe for one or both. If that's the case, it's important to keep yourself and your family safe. Let's look at what truly toxic looks like.

Serious Signs to Consider

Deciding to reduce or cut contact with your mom/daughter is serious business and should not be taken lightly. Even when necessary, it is painful and hard work. Here are the signs to look for and consider as you think about how to move forward.

Abuse: If your mom/daughter has been physically, sexually, or emotionally abusive and your well-being is at risk, then she is most definitely toxic.

Ongoing damage to your life: If having conversations or any dealing with your mom/daughter negatively affects your mental health or quality of life, that is toxic.

No remorse: If your mom/daughter can't say she's sorry and has no remorse for anything that has happened, this is a toxic situation.

Toxic patterns: If you are stuck in toxic patterns of disrespect, emotional harm, control, or toxic manipulation, it won't get better without making changes.

Can't respect boundaries: Boundaries are created to keep everyone safe and sound. If your mom/daughter refuses to respect your boundaries, this is a problem.

Damage to self-esteem: If your mom/daughter is one of those nasty criticizers and your heart and soul are broken from constant belittling and undermining, make it stop.

Causes dangerous situations: Alcoholics and addicts are unstable and cause many kinds of disruptions to healthy relationships. There are too many examples to list here, so think anything from allowing domestic violence to take place in the house (or on the mom/daughter) to purchasing or using narcotics in the home, vicious fights with a spouse or partner, any situation in which a mom's/daughter's safety, health, and wellness or mental health is at risk.

How to Break Up with a Toxic Mom/Daughter

As angry as she was, Lindsey still cried every day for months after making the decision to cut ties with her mom. Moms and daughters are bound to each other, and are influenced by each other at every stage. Even when things are awful, breaking the bond goes against every cell in your body. Your brain will change its mind, you will feel wildly mixed emotions throughout the day, you will feel guilty, maybe even ashamed.

Pause and reflect: How is your mother-daughter relationship affecting your current life, mental health, and well-being? If it's clear that you are experiencing harm, despair, or any other detrimental effects, take your feelings seriously. Your experience is real, and we are here to remind you that you matter.

Get a support system: This isn't optional. You will need emotional support and guidance to help you navigate this difficult time.

Trusted friends, family, or professional support can make all the difference on days you don't want to get out of bed. Be sure you don't choose people who dislike or want to harm your mom/daughter.

Professional help may be necessary: If you are not used to understanding and processing your feelings, setting boundaries, and learning new coping mechanisms, this is where doctors, therapists, coaches, and other mental health professionals come in handy. They can help you understand what's happened and how to move forward in healing.

Set the boundaries you want: This is the time to decide how you want to live peacefully. Do you want to limit or cut contact? Try a set of firm boundaries while also establishing consequences for breaking those boundaries? Decide what you want the relationship to look like as you work toward getting your own life back.

Communicate what's going on: Choose the safest method of communication for you and let your mom/daughter know what's going on. Share your boundaries and your reasons for taking a break.

Prepare for anything: If you're dealing with someone who has already been destructive and unstable, this is probably not the moment they are going to change. The reaction probably won't be good, but that's not your problem anymore.

Take care of yourself: How can you nurture yourself and practice self-care? This is the time to focus on healing, self-discovery, self-support, and building new relationships. The goal is empowering, not dismantling, everything about your life.

Resources for Extreme Situations

When your issue is mental illness, abuse, or addiction, you can't fix it alone. The temptation is to break yourself into little pieces trying to fix it, or want to run away, but outside help is needed. Some mothers and daughters have toxic dysfunction. If you're in an extreme situation—for example, personal safety issues, alcoholism, pressing financial problems—look to professionals to help you navigate your options.

Think About This

Not every mother and daughter can peacefully coexist. Both moms and daughters can be toxic. The message here is that it's okay to break up. What's important is finding peace. We know that some mothers and daughters should not be together and should not keep trying. Addiction, mental health issues, or other conflicts can make the relationship too dangerous and unsafe. The goal of this chapter is to provide hope that you can be all right, can survive, and thrive no matter what's happening right now. When you can't be with your mother/daughter, the best thing you can do is take care of yourself and work on improving your own life.

TIME TO JOURNAL

Did you know that love and hate are closely related and you can have both feelings on the same day? Can you live with the ambiguity that your mom/daughter isn't going to have all positive feelings all the time? Are you in a situation in which you feel your mom/daughter is toxic and you can't have a healthy and supportive relationship with her? Here you can consider what makes your relationship difficult or toxic.

JOURNAL PROMPTS

1. Have you identified any toxic behaviors in your relationship with your mom/daughter? What are they?

2. Have you tried any conflict resolution tools that have failed? What were they?

3. Did you recognize any serious signs to consider? Which ones?

4. Do you have an effective support system? Who is in it?

5. Do you think you should talk to a professional or learn more about separation when necessary? Please explain.

6. Make a pros and cons list about the relationship.

STEP 4

Healing and Reconciliation

In Step 3 we explored the way our brains and powerful emotions can get stuck and are triggered again and again by traumas and negative behaviors developed over time. We moved into solutions with tips to take the heat off when tempers flare as well as basic information about conflict resolution and what to do when a break in the relationship is necessary for your sanity. Step 4 brings everything that we've learned about our mom/daughter together and turns the focus on ourselves to move into the stage of healing and redemption.

In Chapter 18 we'll explore what part you play in your mother-daughter conflicts by taking your inventory of fears and resentments to help you understand yourself.

Chapter 19 will show how forgiveness and healing will improve both mental and physical health and give examples of ways to nurture your soul.

Chapter 20 examines what it means to reconnect with purpose and actions you can take to rekindle your mother-daughter love. This chapter reminds us of the five characteristics of healthy relationships and what your healthy relationship can look like.

Chapter 21 focuses on who you want to be, with or without your daughter. This chapter defines the five components of the recovery lifestyle that Lindsey and Leslie each developed on their own to be happy and fulfilled.

CHAPTER 18

Accepting Your Part and Gaining New Perspective

You may feel that your mom/daughter is the problem in your relationship, but what would happen if you considered that you play a part in your conflict? Would the world end? Would you be subject to a prison sentence? Would you be a loser for all time? None of the above. For us, accepting that we each had a part in our emotional warfare and separation didn't end the world, send us to prison, or kill us. On the contrary, admitting that we both contributed to the problem was empowering. It was a sign of maturity and the first step in personal growth that allowed us to take responsibility for our actions.

Remember the response Lindsey received when she started being honest with Leslie? There is a similar kind of relief here. While it can feel embarrassing or shameful to understand how our fears or resentments have driven our behavior, knowledge brings the ability to change. When you understand why you do what you do, you have the power to decide whether you want to keep operating that way. Once you're able to articulate to your mom/daughter, "Hey, I did that because I was scared, embarrassed . . ." then you can have a real conversation. The goal for this chapter is clarity and compassion.

In this chapter we'll show you how to take an inventory of your resentments, fears, and harmful behaviors to help you see what part you play in your mother/daughter conflicts. Taking your inventory is something that millions of people in recovery do regularly to grow beyond old habits. It's a tool for gaining self-awareness and accountability. It's another formula that can shed light on the feelings behind your behaviors. Taking your inventory is very effective in helping both mothers and daughters become less resentful and angry. It was in this process that everything changed for us.

As we examined ourselves while we were apart, we began to see that the other one was not entirely to blame. We had triggered each other, blamed each other, and were dismissive of each other's very real feelings; those patterns had to stop. The goal here is, instead of just complaining about and blaming the other person, to look at our own behavior and accept that we can be hurtful and difficult, too.

When you do an inventory in a recovery program, it is advised that you go over the work with a sponsor, someone in the program who has already done this work and can skillfully and effectively walk you through it. The purpose of this exercise is to reveal your patterns and the part you play in the relationship. We have created a version of an inventory that you can do on your own to see how it works.

How to Take a Personal inventory

Resentment Inventory

Start with a resentment inventory. Make a list of hurts, situations, and traits that caused bitterness or resentment related to your mom/daughter. Describe what happened and how it made you feel. It's good to be thorough here, so take your time. There is no rush, and you want to be thoughtful. We both had resentments about each other that we didn't even know were resentments.

For Lindsey, being pushed into an academically tough prep school was especially challenging while dealing with young, emotional turmoil. Leslie never knew that, and it was within this work that Lindsey was able to see situations like that differently and let them go. Leslie sent Lindsey to the high school she had attended, and it hadn't been as rigorous or fancy in her day.

Leslie found awareness around how self-righteous she sounded when trying to advise or help Lindsey in early recovery and beyond. Leslie had enjoyed her daily martinis but didn't get drunk. She had good eating and work habits. Her attempts to get Lindsey to self-regulate before she was ready felt hurtful and controlling, not helpful.

Examples of Resentment Inventory

- I'm resentful of my mom because she is too intrusive and won't let me make my own decisions.
- I'm resentful because my mom expects me to attend all family gatherings, even with relatives who make me feel uncomfortable.
- I'm resentful of my daughter because she won't stop drinking or take care of her health.

- I'm resentful of my daughter because she lies to me and expects me to help her with everything when she already has enough support. She's a grown-up but doesn't act like one.

Fear and Anger Inventory

Make a fear or anger inventory next. What are your fears, real or imagined, around your mom/daughter? If you're angry, be honest about your anger. You can be furious at your mom/daughter for a million reasons and just want her to be safe and well. As a daughter, Lindsey held back so many details of her life because she didn't want to upset or disappoint Leslie, not because she wanted to intentionally mislead her. There was fear of disappointment under the bad behavior.

On mom's side, Leslie was furious at times with Lindsey over her risky behaviors or lack of self-care, but it never meant she didn't want Lindsey to recover. Look past your current feelings at what your real fears are for your mother/daughter. Explore whether any of your fears have held you back or influenced the way you behaved.

Examples of Fear and Anger Inventory

- I'm fearful that if my mom doesn't help me financially, I'll be in debt. I may become homeless.
- I'm angry when my mom doesn't give me the money I need. I know she could give it to me if she wanted to.
- I'm fearful my daughter will get sick or do something stupid if I don't step in.
- I'm fearful my daughter will not use the money or support I give her in the right way. She's been reckless with money in the past.

Harmful Behaviors Inventory

What are the harmful behaviors that exist in your mother-daughter relationship? This is for you, so be honest. Reflect on how you've treated yourself and your mom. Have you done and said things you regret? Have you caused your mother/daughter harm with any toxic behaviors? Have there been consequences?

For Lindsey, it was helpful to see how enmeshed ideas about finances were holding her back. In learning how to take care of herself financially, Lindsey created her own freedom and independence. In this work, Leslie saw how her spending and lack of high school supervision had affected Lindsey. Awareness of her part in Lindsey's confusion allowed her to find some peace around her actions.

Examples of Harmful Behaviors Inventory

- I complain constantly to my mom about my money problems hoping she'll step in, and I've guilted her into helping me.
- Since my mom drinks, too, I gaslight her by telling her she's as bad as I am.
- I check up on my daughter constantly to make sure she's taking her medicine (doing her homework, getting to work on time, driving safely) even though she's asked me to stop doing that and told me it makes her feel incompetent.
- I constantly tell my daughter what she's doing wrong in her life.

What Patterns Appear

This is the moment to look for patterns in your own behavior. Have your fears and resentments caused you to act in certain ways? Have you behaved in selfish, prideful, or dishonest ways? Have your fears driven you? It was in doing this exact work that Lindsey realized how many fears she had and how they were a driving force in selfish and self-seeking behavior.

Fear of abandonment in a personal relationship might cause your mother/daughter to act in manipulative ways or focus on her needs, which only strained the relationship. It's also a form of self-sabotage that Lindsey didn't want to continue. Without taking the time to do the self-improvement work, she never would have known. We get into patterns of behavior that don't serve us. Until we see the patterns and make efforts to change them, we will keep repeating the same mistakes.

Examples of Understanding Behavior Patterns

- I have been selfish by demanding money from my mom, and I need to learn to support myself. I'm an adult.
- I've been gaslighting my mom about her drinking to take the focus off my drinking, which is much worse.
- I have been selfishly demanding my daughter take her meds (do her homework, get to work on time, drive safely) despite being asked to stop. She is an adult.
- I have beenhurtful in telling my daughter that her choices and behaviors are not healthy.

Time to Reflect

This is the moment for self-reflection and honesty. Look at your patterns to see what you can recognize. Are there behaviors you exhibit every time you and your mom/daughter fight? Do you act the same insecure way in romantic or personal relationships? Are you overwhelmed with fear when it comes to issues around money or food and friends and it's now becoming clear? This is when you should be able to notice the fears, limiting beliefs, resentments, or just bad habits that have caused you to act in ways you regret, aren't proud of, or want to stop.

Examples of Reflecting

- I can see that my fear of not having enough money has caused me to put pressure on my mom, and I have used guilt and shame to get what I want.
- I can see that my fears about my daughter's health (and competence in many areas) have caused me to micromanage and break boundaries.

List the Positives

Recovery inventories always encourage you to list the positives to create balance. This will also help with the perspective shift, which we're about to discuss. When you think about your mother/daughter, what are her good traits? Make a list of anything you think is a behavior that is coming from the heart, even if it annoys you. For example, when Lindsey was able to think about Leslie's controlling behavior as coming from a desire to protect her and keep her safe, it softened her feelings around it. When Leslie understood that so much of Lindsey's hiding her problems came from not wanting Leslie to worry or be disappointed in her, she could react better.

Examples of Reflections

- I can see how my mom's not wanting to bail me out every time comes from a place of wanting me to be self-sufficient and financially healthy.
- I can see how my daughter's resentment of my concern around her health (education, work, driving) comes from a

place of wanting to be independent and from me taking that away from her.

What Do You Like About Yourself?

Mothers and daughters who live in, or have lived in, dysfunctional families, abusive families, trauma-affected families, families with special needs, and any other challenging situations have special skills. These skills were developed by living in difficult environments but can translate into wonderful careers or traits. Often these people make the best caretakers, therapists, friends, mental health professionals, and so much more. When we came into recovery, it was a challenge to name the good things about ourselves. When you've felt bad about yourself and your family for a long time, the pain is deep and not immediately accessible to address.

Now let's consider some of your traits that have come in handy or been sharpened by your experience. For example, Leslie is so sensitive to other parents who are struggling because of her own experiences. Knowing how complicated and difficult it is to parent effectively has made her a valuable support to others who need help. Lindsey has incredible compassion and insight for people in recovery because of her own healing journey. Maybe your experience has caused you to be an excellent caretaker, therapist, friend, or pet parent.

What are your best qualities, and where do you get to use them? This is an important question to consider as we move forward through the rest of this chapter. Make a list of your good qualities and strengths. They don't have to be noble. Leslie realized today that she loves her feet, bunions, and all. Lindsey deeply admires her restraint every time she doesn't say negative things she may be thinking.

Lindsey on Changing Your Perspective

Before my recovery (from anything and every-thing), I had a terrible attitude. I felt victimized, I was exclusive with people, and I lived by the blame game. My recovery journey has improved my attitude. I'm empowered, inclusive, and I feel that coping with my disability has made me stronger. Without recovery practices, I could not have developed into someone who values kindness and an open mind. Did I mention I used to be closed-minded and opinionated? Often about people and things I had no experience with at all.

The problem with being closed-minded is that I was preventing myself from having new and better experiences. Once I accepted that maybe I didn't know everything and began trying new things, I saw quickly how ridiculous being closed-minded had been. Assumptions that I knew best about everything and everyone were stubborn and self-sabotaging.

My inventories revealed that much of my behavior was ruled by fear. I was afraid of not getting what I wanted or losing what I had. I was selfish and self-serving because of that fear. I also had to accept that there was a lot of dishonesty in my thinking. By ignoring toxic behaviors with people and substances, I had created a false narrative about why situations ended badly or weren't working out for me. Inventory work isn't easy, but for me, it was the tool to change the way I saw myself and what had gone wrong in my life.

This is transformational, self-improvement work. Before I knew and understood the damaging impact of trauma, addiction, family dysfunction, and anxiety, I always returned to being unstable and miserable. I'd get triggered and think I was losing my mind. I'd re-lapse and believe I was hopeless. I was always searching for some-thing that I couldn't find because it didn't exist.

When I had the information about myself that I needed to vali-date my life experiences, clarify what was right and wrong, and re-veal where I had become warped, then I could make real changes. Once I knew I was part of the problem, I could stop being the victim. My life became so much better with an improved attitude about my-self, my mom, and others. Having a new perspective allowed me to change the way I saw my history.

When you don't know what's wrong with you, you can't fix it. The work I describe in this book helped me find accountability, per-spective, and a positive mindset. It also helped me be better in all my relationships, not only with my mom. It created a foundation for emotional stability.

Changing Your Perspective

When you've been living in a dysfunctional or painful relation-ship, you get worn down and emotionally depleted from the drama. You may be at your wit's end, feeling that your heart and spirit can't take it anymore. It's normal to feel discouraged, disappointed, even hopeless. It may seem as if everyone is out of control and unfixable. Having these feelings contributes to a negative perspective. With an open mind, however, you can see things from another point of view. Having even a little perspective can make you more empathic and avoid conflict. That's the magic word that we are trying to reduce and avoid—"conflict." Realizing that your perspective needs adjustment is the first step.

At this point, are you learning new things? Are some beliefs you held about your mother/daughter changing? Maybe you thought your mom was a nightmare because she was so controlling about everything, but looking back at her life and her trauma, now you see her vulnerability. Or maybe you're a mom who's been furious with a daughter for not living up to your expectations, but now you can see how your expectations weren't realistic for her. We are working on opening our minds to the idea that maybe everything we think isn't right, and maybe we don't know what's right for anyone other than ourselves.

Consider the idea "Live and let live." The way you talk and feel about any situation is what gives the experience power over you. For example, Lindsey used to feel annoyed when Leslie struggled to make decisions in certain situations. Instead of being annoyed by an innocuous trait, Lindsey now proposes options for decision-making. Since she knows Leslie will struggle, she helps instead of criticizing. We don't stop loving someone because they're not perfect. Lindsey is grumpy in the morning. Everyone knows this. There are times when someone calls, or something happens, and Lindsey's early-morning irritability is unleashed. Her irritability can feel personal, so we must use our awareness to avoid being triggered by it. We have compassion that some mornings are very blue for her.

If you can shift the angle from "Something is wrong with this person" to "How do we support this person when they struggle?", then it will be easier to decide, "Let's not stress Leslie out by decision-making right now" or "Let's not call Lindsey until she has meditated and walked the dogs." You and your mom/daughter are on the same team. When you know a teammate has a weakness, you compensate for them. Mothers and daughters deserve the same respect and patience that a teammate would. Instead of pointing a finger at your mom/daughter for her flaws, how can you support her?

Practice Perspective Building

Empathy: Practicing empathy is the perfect tool for perspective shifting. Try putting yourself in your mother's/daughter's shoes. You may now understand her motivations differently. You already know how frustrated you are with her; now think about ways she might be frustrated with you.

If this suggestion makes your skin crawl, good. You're thinking about it. No one said becoming kinder is easy. It takes practice and continued commitment. Being kind works if you are willing to focus on what empathy means. When Lindsey imagined herself as the mother of an addict, it created an entirely new sense of empathy for Leslie's behavior. It isn't easy being related to an addict, much less the mother/daughter of one. When Leslie first read these pages written by Lindsey and realized for the first time that she'd done some of the same things her mother did, it created a new layer of emotional understanding and compassion for Lindsey.

Ask three people: In recovery, when you have a serious problem, you're sometimes advised to ask three different people for advice. The idea is to get solutions from three reliable people and see where the advice makes sense or overlaps. This is the time to get other viewpoints that can help guide you. They won't all be helpful or work for you, but expanding your audience and getting feedback from other people who have similar experiences will help. Remember, family members may be biased and unreliable as they tend to take sides and may want to cause more drama. So don't engage family members who will make things worse.

Learn and change your tapes: Changing your perspective can also involve paying attention to the tapes that play in your head. Do you have an inner dialogue? What does it say to you? If it is a voice that puts you down, or makes you feel bad, it's not a self-esteem-building inner monologue. This is the reason affirmations were invented. They have been around since the beginning of time.

Use positive affirmations daily: Explore the hundreds of affirmations that are now everywhere and try implementing them. You can write them, say them, think about them, and even tape them to your mirror. The proof is in the punch as they say. Notice the tapes that play in your head, and practice replacing them with your positive response as many times as you need to throughout the day. You can even create your own mantra.

Read and meditate: We will recommend reading and meditating again and again because they provide benefits for both the mind and the soul. Want to learn more about anything? Read. Lindsey read books and articles about how to practice being happy, how to heal from addiction, and how to manage money better. They all helped. Read for pleasure and to learn. Then learn to meditate (if you can), and do it as often as possible. Studies in the last decade, including one from Harvard University, used brain scans to determine that eight weeks of a mindfulness training program called Mindfulness-Based Stress Reduction (MBSR) increased the cortical thickness in the hippocampus, the part of the brain that controls learning and memory and plays an important role in emotion regulation. That means that regular meditation can literally change brain function. Want to be calmer, happier, and more at peace? Meditate. Sing. Chant. Do yoga.

Mindset

Mindset is basically how you see yourself and the world. It's a set of beliefs people hold about themselves defined by culture, disposition, values, and of course experience. If your experience in life, especially with family and your mother/daughter, has been mostly negative, you may have a negative mindset. You may have earned that negative mindset honestly, but it won't serve you long term. If you and your mom/daughter need a relationship overhaul, it's fair to assume there's been some bad blood and you have angry or hurt feelings. How can you prevent those feelings from becoming a narrative you can't rewrite? First, you explored your anger and resentment in your inventories. You know what they are and where they come from.

This is when neuroplasticity and new habits come into play. Neuroplasticity is also known as neural plasticity, or brain plasticity. It is the ability of neural networks in the brain to change through growth and reorganization. This means that brain function is not fixed. That's an exciting piece of the recovery process. Neuroplasticity is when the brain is rewired to function in some way that differs from how it previously functioned. We can change.

How did we come to understand that we have the power to change the wiring in our brains? Interest in the way the brain functions has developed slowly over the ages. Ancient Egyptians thought the brain was a useless organ and was removed during the mummification process. The Greek philosopher Aristotle thought it was a cooling unit for the heart.

In the Middle Ages, philosophers believed that the cavities in the brain filled with spinal fluid housed the human soul. It wasn't until brain imaging became available in the 1970s that mapping of brain activity was possible. Neuroscience is also known as neural science. It is the study of nervous system development, its structure, and how it functions. Neuroscientists focus on the brain and its impact on behavior and cognitive functions.

We now know how the brains of addicts are damaged by substances and alcohol. Brain function can also be rewired by trauma. On the positive side, experiments with the brains of Buddhist monks revealed that their practice of meditation has a profound effect on their emotional lives. Monks, who live a life of study, meditation, and chanting have no anxiety, depression, addiction, or anything like it. Their brain scans reveal enhanced memory, focus, learning, consciousness, and neural coordination. This is how we know the benefits of meditation are real. When you meditate (or redirect your thinking) every day, you can influence the way your brain works.

This should be welcome news to people who find it difficult to connect with others or have relationship problems. You don't have to be a monk or meditate to coax your brain into new thinking habits. Lindsey spent years in therapy and working on somatic practices to rewire her brain and create a better mindset that focuses on positivity, and she can alter her mood and interactions, most of the time.

If your mindset has been battered by years of bad experiences, you can change the way you think to achieve success on this journey. Mindset also has a lot to do with what we want for ourselves and the outcome. A positive mindset will help you across the board—at work, in personal relationships—and it will make this healing process with your mom/daughter much easier.

Tips to Nurture a Positive Mindset

Any type of self-improvement takes practice, and creating a healthier outlook and mindset is no different. Don't be discouraged if changes don't happen overnight. It takes years to develop dysfunctional and unhealthy behaviors, and it takes time to rewire them. A therapist of Lindsey's recommended a book called *The Happiness Advantage* by Shawn Anchor. This book uses positive psychology and provides a list of activities to perform for several months to help promote a happier mindset. The book focuses on gratitude, so we'll start there.

Happy people feel grateful for what they have. In tough times with your mom/daughter, find things to feel grateful for in your own life. Even if it starts small with your morning coffee or a beloved pet. In our experience, anguish and anger fade when you feel gratitude. We talked earlier about surrounding yourself with positive, supportive people. Their outlook will influence yours. As you foster positivity with supportive people, limit your time with people who insist on staying negative. Negativity is contagious, and you don't want it as your constant companion.

Coping with failures or setbacks is a great way to nurture a new mindset. Almost every day something is going to go wrong. How do you feel about big and little problems? Are you hashing them over endlessly with your mom/daughter? Instead of having a pity party or falling into hopelessness, this is your chance to practice healthy self-talk, reassuring yourself that hurdles come up in every situation.

Take a moment to feel the disappointment, but don't live there. Change the subject if your mom/daughter can't stop talking about failures or unhappiness. It can be annoying to have someone always tell you to look on the bright side, so find your own words for "We're going to be all right."

Look for inspiration in people, places, and things. We are always surprised by how inspired we get from watching a great movie, reading a book we can't put down, taking a walk, going somewhere new, listening (or participating) in something spiritual, visiting animals, gardens, or whatever else makes your heart soar. Staying inspired by positive people, peaceful places, and other beacons of light will add some glow to this time in your life.

Think About This

Many of us are so used to feeling or thinking in a certain and fixed way, that those feelings and thoughts are all we have. They may come from our mothers, our traditions, or our culture. We may not realize how negative or unhealthy rigid thinking can be. After years of fighting with your mom/daughter, we know how hard it is to stay positive and have a cheerful and hopeful outlook on the relationship. The science, however, shows that we can change the way we feel and see things, even if our situation doesn't change. If you've seen trees in a hurricane, you know it's the trees that bend with the wind that survive. In relationships, it's shifting perspective and learning our own part in conflict that help us to accept responsibility, let go of the past, and move forward with a more positive outlook.

CHAPTER 19

Forgiveness and Healing

Alexander Pope, poet of the Enlightenment, wrote a treatise about patient safety in 1711, and one line has stuck: "To err is human, to forgive is divine." The Bible, of course, talks about forgiveness, and the reasoning there goes something like this: God forgives, so when humans forgive, they are acting in a godlike manner. More modern philosophies about forgiveness, however, are not so lofty in their reasons for forgiveness. New thinking centers around the impact that rage and resentment have on your mental and physical state.

We must turn to biology and hormones again to understand why anger presents such a threat to our emotional and physical health. As we have indicated before, the root cause of anger is often hurt feelings, a strong sense of unfairness, embarrassment, and humiliation. What happens physically is the amygdala part of your brain ignites the fight reflex, and in an instant you're ready to rumble. It's a literal flash flood as blood rushes from your gut to your muscles, getting you ready for a fight. Your heart rate and respiration speed up. Your body temperature rises, and you begin to sweat. A tickle to your amygdala, and that's what anger does to you physically.

It's not only your brain that reacts when you're hurt and angry. Your adrenal glands, the endocrine glands on top of your kidneys, produce and release cortisol, the essential hormone that regulates the body's stress response. Cortisol is important because it affects every organ in your body, and quite simply producing too much of it can make you sick. Just as exercise and other pleasurable activities release feel-good endorphins, rage and chronic anger flood your system with cortisol, the feel-bad hormone that makes you anxious, stressed, and irritable. When we say anger can make you sick, here are some symptoms produced by high levels of cortisol in your body. This is normal in crisis, but the brain can't always tell the difference between a perceived threat and a real one.

- Rapid weight gain, mainly in the face, chest, and abdomen.
- A flushed and round face.
- High blood pressure.
- Osteoporosis.
- Skin changes (such as bruises and purple stretch marks).
- Muscle weakness.
- Anxiety, depression, or irritability.
- Increased thirst and frequent urination.

These are the physical results of too much cortisol in your system. We know and have lived with people who have chronic anger, and we have seen the signs of a red face, high levels of irritability, anxiety, high blood pressure, and roller-coaster depression. When you or a loved one has symptoms like the ones listed above, though, you probably haven't heard any doctor prescribe anger management or forgiveness.

The chronic release of cortisol in your body adds to anxiety, depression, high blood pressure, and even affects your cardiovascular health. It also affects personality and relationships, even the outcome of situations you care about at work and at home. In addition, chronic anger negatively affects personal relationships since no one enjoys being around angry people.

Anger also reduces your ability to make smart decisions. Ever regret doing something when you were angry? Join the club. Anger affects your behavior, making you more aggressive and reactive. Over time, anger and rage can also hurt your self-esteem and sense of self. Is it clear that there are no benefits to holding onto hurt feelings and anger about the past?

Anger, especially toxic anger, can feel like a mental prison from which there is no relief. Reflect for a moment on how many people you have strong, negative feelings about—it could be your mom, daughter, other family members, friends, colleagues, or anyone else in your sphere. Who brings the rage, and how many people in your life make you feel that way? Can you get over it?

Have you ever thought that forgiveness is a gift you give to yourself? As Martin Luther King Jr. said, "Forgiveness is a catalyst creating the atmosphere necessary for a fresh start and a new beginning." New beginnings don't happen overnight because enlightenment does not immediately bring behavioral changes. You forgive others because it helps you find peace but only when you're ready for peace.

As we've said before, you don't have to like what happened or condone it to forgive. There's also no timeline with forgiveness. We needed a couple of years to calm down and explore our own pathways to peace. By the time we reconnected, we were ready. We had stopped thinking about the bad things and remembered only the positive things. We were happier, didn't have the flash anger habit, and were both able to sit calmly and listen to each other, even when it made us uncomfortable at first.

Practicing Forgiveness

There are many reasons that may appeal to you for forgiving your mother/daughter over time, but it may feel out of range right now. Lindsey never wanted to be angry at Leslie and vice versa. Had you asked either of us during bad times if we could magically make it better, would we? The answer would be yes. If you feel the same, know that there are some best practices to get you in the spirit of promoting a forgiving mindset. You don't have to be there now; just be open to the idea that forgiveness is a good thing that may help you feel better someday.

Forgiveness can appeal to people for different reasons. It may be an important component of your religious beliefs and practice. You may want to feel peaceful and have physical well-being. If your goal is healthier brain function and feelings of well-being, forgiveness is an act of self-care and self-love. While the pain of past traumas may remain, it can become more manageable. Someone once said to us, "Holding onto resentments is like drinking poison and waiting for the other person to die." If you care about yourself and your well-being, this can be a reason to forgive. Another benefit is improved self-esteem. It feels better to forgive and heal than it does to be angry and seethe.

One other benefit of forgiveness is perspective and mindset, which we mentioned in Chapter 18. Forgiveness for yourself and whoever hurt you helps you see people and the world differently. It is harnessing this powerful compassion and understanding that transforms us into wonderful friends, therapists, sponsors, basically inspiration to others who have similar problems. Forgiveness breeds hope.

Tools for Forgiveness

Writing: When it comes to recovery work, there is nothing as direct as writing. Get your feelings out in a safe way by journaling or writing a letter you won't ever send! A great recovery assignment Lindsey once got from a sponsor was to write a letter from God to yourself. She wanted Lindsey to see a situation from God's perspective. What does God (Spirit, the universe) want you to learn from this experience? If you can't write, you can direct your pain into other forms of self-expression below. Some people just don't like writing as much as we do.

Forgiveness meditations: There are podcasts and YouTube videos for this if meditation practice is something that interests or works for you. We've shared about what a fantastic tool meditation is for all recovery and healing, and forgiveness meditation is no different. We always think of a practice by starting with one to three months to see what kind of effect it's having. Psychologists say it takes thirty days to start a healthy habit or end a bad one. You can't kick an addiction in thirty days, however. And we'd say it takes us three months for habits to become ingrained.

Seek support: Join support groups in person or online. Reaching out is easier for some people than others. You can't tell someone whose brain functions on anger, resentment, and hurt feelings to become a joiner. It just won't happen. But using some of the other tools to reduce stress and trauma that we have mentioned can open your mind to the value of support from others. Whatever you are dealing with, there are other people dealing with it, too. If you think therapy would help, try that. Do not keep bringing up your problems with your mom/daughter to people who can't support you in the right way. Rather, seek out unbiased, positive people who understand what you are going through.

Practice compassion: Are you able to accept other people for who they are? If not, try it. Listen to other people who are struggling, and see how these problems look from other angles. Be encouraging and loving to the people who are in your life right now. Do you say you're sorry when you make mistakes, bump into people, or other little ways we slip up throughout the day? Saying "I'm sorry" is a powerful gift.

Pray: Whatever your religious or spiritual beliefs, this is for you. If you don't have any spiritual beliefs, or a religion, you can move on. You don't have to pray to any special God for prayer to benefit your life, and you don't have to pray to create space and a pause. Lindsey was mad at God when she found recovery. At first, she prayed to the ocean, then to the dogs; you get the idea. Prayer is another action and tool that create space and a pause. You can focus your thoughts and ask the universe for what you want. For a few minutes every day put your intention out there and envision what you want to happen. Even the words "Help remove these feelings" have worked for us.

Listen to podcasts about forgiveness: There are many pastors, mental health professionals, self-help gurus, and others who talk about forgiveness. Don't just listen to us; listen to the experts and light shiners on how to inspire forgiveness.

Healing

Sometimes you don't even know you need to heal. Being stuck in conflict is often rooted in a belief that there is no way out. You may have lived in a place of misery and dysfunction for so long you don't know anything different. Your emotional unhappiness colors how you feel about everything every day. For us, the mindset of pulling up your bootstraps and not telling anyone about your problems and pain created a tough exterior. We were what is called very well defended, which created barriers to healing.

We're sure many of you are well defended, too. When you're used to being tough and self-sufficient, accepting that you may need to ask for help is unthinkable. Asking for help may seem to you weak and something that "other people do." We know because we were the queens of "I'm fine" and "I don't need help." That is, until we did need help.

To heal you must learn to be kind to yourself. It's hard to explain unless you've felt it, but when you have unresolved trauma and emotional triggers running the show, you often feel hopeless, crazy, and out of control. The only way forward may be through an effective process of healing. As Lindsey mentioned earlier, the only time she was treated for suicidal depression was when she was going through that terrible time in her thirties and fighting with her mom.

When you are a survivor of any kind, learning basic self-care, self-love, and self-acceptance is a challenge. At the start, it feels silly and embarrassing to have needs. It makes sense when you know you've been pushing those little girl's feelings and needs down for decades. But give it time as you get to know yourself again.

What is healing exactly? Healing literally means the process of becoming sound or healthy again. How does that sound to you? It was the prescription we needed. We were done with despair and drama and wanted to be sound and healthy again. The healing process for you will depend on where you are on your recovery journey.

If you are like us, mental health and addiction education as well as therapy may be your first step. Learning how to measure your feelings and manage them will help take care of you during stressful times and will serve you for the rest of your life. Finding our way through the most painful and emotionally challenging times gave us the strength we needed for healing to occur.

We both had a strong desire to get better. Who are you and who you want to be are good questions to ask yourself. If you have been accommodating for years and holding onto bitter resentment, this is the time to discover who you were before the conflicts began and find your way back to that person. What did you love and have to give up? Who are you without your misery? What do you like to do? What do you like to eat? We were so enmeshed that we no longer knew who we were without each other or how to take care of ourselves on our own.

Tools for Healing

The feel-good chemicals: We've already talked about how different chemicals affect our brains and mood. Did you know that you can produce your feel-good chemicals any time you want?

- **Oxytocin,** the chemical that helps increase love in our bodies, can be nurtured by acts of kindness or helping others, gratitude, physical touch with humans or animals, or positive social interactions.
- **Dopamine,** the "reward" or "increase drive" chemical, can be increased by achieving a goal, reading good books, getting enough sleep, or eating something you enjoy; even cleaning the house and pausing social media will help.
- **Serotonin,** the mood booster, is helped with nature and sun

exposure and eating healthy foods (remember the gut-health connection). Calm breathing, getting enough rest, and exercise help, and it's been reported that supplements can help as well.

- **Endorphins,** the stress relievers, our final feel-good chemicals, are increased by regular stretching and exercise. Some more of our favorite endorphin boosters are laughing, singing, dancing, taking baths, meditating, basically any activity where you are having a great time.

- Healing requires new habits, but if you implement some of these in your daily life, they will improve your mental health and well-being.

Professional help/trauma recovery/support groups: You know what these are now. Your options for recovery are limitless. Therapists, social workers, marriage counselors, addiction specialists, and other mental health professionals who have seen it all can help you. Twelve-step programs have been a godsend for millions of people. Many rehabs and outpatient facilities for addiction and trauma have recovery retreats or weekends, which can also be eye-opening.

Religion: If religion is comforting to you, this is a good time to use the comfort you have relied on in the past. We believe that having a strong faith is an important component of recovery health.

Brain healing: We wrote about neuroplasticity and how it is possible to rewire the brain; you can do that work with the following activities: yoga, meditation, chanting, reading, writing, sound baths, Reiki, massage, walking in nature, daily exercise, good nutrition, breath work, animal therapy, affirmations, Tai Chi, and gratitude.

Get creative: Art therapy is practiced in every recovery facility for a reason. Painting, drawing, making music, or any art form helps calm the brain and soothe anxiety. Even puzzles, coloring, and board games provide focus and distraction to enhance your emotional spectrum.

Foster or rescue animals: When Lindsey moved to Los Angeles, one of the first things she did was get a dog. Then she got another dog, this time a rescue to calm her anxious dog. That didn't work out as expected. Both dogs were anxious, but the good intention was there. Lindsey's dogs provided everything for her—entertainment, exercise, caring for something other than herself, and a safe way to love and be loved. A daily connection to something that requires you to be present and vigilant, especially with a rescue dog, is healing.

Think About This

The takeaways in this chapter include all the reasons forgiveness is important for your own physical, mental, and emotional health. Toxic anger floods your body with the feel-bad hormone and can cause surprising physical illnesses. Anger also affects other relationships and life in general, casting a negative haze over everything. Forgiveness releases the default reaction of rage and brings peace. It is a process that takes time, but there are tools you can use to rewire your brain. In the healing arena, this may be the first time you've considered it for yourself. Healing may not be something you thought you needed or wanted. However, we all need a little healing, and with practice it might become something you enjoy.

JOURNAL PROMPTS

1. How do you feel about forgiveness? Do you forgive easily? Does your family have feelings about forgiveness? What are they?

2. Have you been forgiving toward your mother/daughter? Has she been forgiving toward you? Explain.

3. Do any of the tools for forgiveness appeal to you? What might you try from that list? Can you schedule it into your life?

4. Have you ever thought about healing before?

5. Do you think you or your mother/daughter needs healing?

6. What from our list of tools will you try? Can you make a schedule you will stick with?

CHAPTER 20

Reconnecting with Purpose and Rekindling the Love

During this journey of self-discovery, we've learned some universal truths about moms and daughters. Top of the list is that we never stop longing for mom's love. Moms and daughters may disagree, fight, hold onto hurt feelings longer than we should, act out our rage, separate, and even break up, vowing never to speak to each other again. Our reasons for conflict and discontent are as varied and nuanced as we are. Some of us have endured unbearable betrayal, devastating abuse, and even total abandonment; others are still hurt by constant demands, indifference, or neglect in childhood; and still others are just constantly annoyed by personality and cultural differences. Never underestimate the power of annoyance or the chronic anguish of a primal love lost.

As we learned in Step 3, no matter what has caused your mother-daughter relationship discontent, more than any other human desire you want the love of your mother/daughter. Even when the bond seems to have been damaged beyond repair, the longing for the mom-daughter connection and acceptance endures.

Here's where we take all the things we've learned and written in the first three steps and begin doing something different. We have explored our mother's/daughter's and our stories, personalities, communication styles, areas of conflict, triggers, trauma, need for boundaries, techniques for keeping the peace, accepting our part, forgiveness, and healing.

We've learned how our emotional, memory-storing right brain can be imprinted with complicated bitter feelings that may not reflect what really happened. Emotions as we've said before are feelings, not reality. Furthermore, much as we want to recover from lingering painful feelings and resentments, the reasoning powers of our left brain can't do it by sheer will alone. While our emotions are real, they do not serve to inspire the relationship we long for. We need to create new patterns of thinking, reacting, and behaving. In the simplest terms we want to relax our aggression-vigilant reflexes and become emotionally sober.

Emotional sobriety means being able to balance powerful destructive feelings that can easily overwhelm us with effective reasoning, perspective, strategies for self-regulation, and positive thinking. With awareness and practice, we can develop emotional sobriety to change our self-talk and curb hair-trigger reactions. Remember, everyone needs help with this. In taking this journey of mother-daughter discovery, our goal is to help other mothers/ daughters gather the new thoughts and tools they need to forge a more positive and satisfying relationship.

Before we reconnect with purpose, do you have some insights you didn't have before? We keep asking this question to keep you thinking. Do you have some compassion where before you only had frustration and rage? We started Step 4 with the challenging task of looking into our contribution to our mother-daughter relationship issues. If we're honest, we can pinpoint ways our own behavior exacerbates the conflict and keeps negative feelings alive. Have you taken the forgiveness step seriously? We'll repeat this truth: forgiveness is a gift you give yourself, and it doesn't mean you condone what happened.

You won't immediately reap all the benefits from your reading and writing. Just like planting a tree, emotional change takes nurturing and time. There is no such thing as failure. If your mom/daughter is not able or ready for the kind of loving relationship you long for, understanding and taking care of yourself will be the solution you need to find peace. One abandoned, heartbroken mother we know learned to manage her loss by creating an award-winning garden. Literally, Alice (not her real name) filled her world with flowers when her daughter refused to speak to her and took the grandchildren. She learned how to let go of her grief through nurturing plants. Everyone needs a welcoming garden for their love. Alice's love for her daughter and grandchildren will always be there, waiting for a change of heart.

What Kind of Relationship Do You Want?

Let's explore what change you'd like to make. You have taken this journey because you want a better relationship with your mom/ daughter. To reconnect with purpose, we now return to the question of what kind of relationship you want. Here again, we're all different. There is no satisfactory one-size-fits-all when it comes to any relationship. Monthly checkups, calls, and emails might be a welcome change for some mothers and daughters. Others might long for those yearly family holidays to be less stressful, even pleasant. That means the communications leading up to reunions must be pleasant, too. Many moms/daughters want to see each other weekly, and some need phone or face time every day. What do you need, and what can you tolerate?

When we began to reconnect with purpose, we did not know if a loving relationship was possible. Without any contact for almost four years, Leslie wanted to know what Lindsey's life was like and be assured that she was all right. Lindsey missed her mom and wanted to restore the happy relationship they once had. But Leslie wanted an apology first for the hurt Lindsey had caused while Lindsey wanted to make living amends. How did we compromise? Compromise is a key factor in improving any relationship. What do you want?

- Daily loving interactions.
- Weekly phone calls or video calls..
- Monthly check-ins.
- Peaceful holiday reunions.
- Yearly recognition.

Reconnecting with purpose for us meant removing the obstacles that prevented us from safely being together. Some of the pain points we've touched on include moms/daughters not accepting each other as individuals, moms/daughters not respecting each other, moms/daughters who lack healthy coping mechanisms for trauma and pain, moms/daughters being unable to express appreciation and gratitude, moms/daughters who dominate and control, moms/daughters who can't listen or be safely honest with each other, moms/daughters who can't apologize for past traumas and hurts, and moms/daughters who can't accept apologies. A few of these hurdles may resonate with you.

How do you get over your obstacles? You may not agree on many things, but most of you do have the desire to get along, be kind, and loving. Here's where you put your actions where your desire is. With a new perspective and intention, you can feel and act differently for a better result. You can approach this goal several ways. Just make sure you don't tackle your issues head-on with a still resentful mom/daughter. You'll just get into an argument.

Instead, remember what you want to accomplish and begin to lay a new foundation for trust. For example, just saying you love a mother/daughter when you haven't acted loving in the past won't be convincing. You can and should say it, but your actions must match your words. What are some ways to show your love and appreciation in a genuine way?

Be prepared to diffuse, deflect, back off, and compromise. For example, if your mom/daughter feels that you do not appreciate her, express your appreciation and gratitude in ways she hasn't seen before. What did Lindsey do? She began sending greeting cards. She sent flowers on Leslie's birthday. She sent videos of her dog; Leslie is a dog lover. These gestures demonstrated to Leslie that Lindsey was thinking about her in a positive way and was connecting in a safe way. What is your mom's/daughter's language of love? What makes her happy? Here are some simple gifts that cost nothing to give and are always welcome.

- **Compliment her:** Offer sincere compliments and acknowledge what's good and unique about her.
- **Actively listen to her:** Be present and give your undivided attention to your mom's/daughter's feelings, thoughts, and experiences.

- **Give emotional support:** Offer encouragement and empathy during difficult or challenging times. Offer congratulations when your mom/daughter is doing well, too.
- **Celebrate her:** Celebrate her special days, achievements, milestones, and successes. Show that you're proud of her.
- **Express gratitude:** Let her know that you appreciate and are grateful for the positive things she has provided. Say thank you.

Speaking of gratitude, everyone wants to be appreciated. For moms/daughters in recovery, showing up when you say you will is an important step toward rebuilding trust. Showing up instead of flaking will lessen the pain of cumulative disappointments that have developed over time. Show your mom/daughter in recovery you support her recovery by not drinking around her. Leslie joined both AA and Al-Anon to get a better understanding of addiction and recovery. Lindsey doesn't drink. Leslie, who used to love martinis, has been sober for fifteen years. Make family reunions about food and games, not alcohol. Our family got closer when alcohol left the party.

Can you stop harping on the same old subjects? Bringing new topics to the conversation is another way to show you're trying. What are safe and engaging subjects that you can talk about? Not marriage, partners, children, finances, or jobs. Our first conversations after our separation were often about old friends and experiences that weren't triggering. We avoided tough subjects that wound us up, and still do. We don't rehash old grievances. Talk about music, activities, good memories from the past, what you're having for dinner. Here are some communication tips that inspire trust.

- Don't judge. Creating a safe space means being

nonjudgmental. Don't criticize anything about her. Criticism hurts, and the wounds linger.

- Share your knowledge and skills in a fun way without pressuring her to do what you think is best.
- Smile and laugh together. Let go of your grievances and grudges, and lighten up your verbal exchanges.

Speaking of verbal exchanges, keeping your mouth shut when you have a negative thought is one of the best ways to build trust. This is all about you, and it requires some self-control. Here's where you don't say what you think or offer advice she didn't ask for. New subjects of conversation can rejuvenate a stale relationship. Lindsey shared her experiences with Buddhism and yoga. Leslie shared her interest in Rotary. Both now share these positive, spiritual, and service activities. Any form of shared activities, spiritual practice, volunteering, or helping others will bring satisfaction in the relationship.

Five Characteristics of Healthy Relationships

Let's look at five characteristics of healthy relationships. This is the foundation of any effective, functional, and satisfying relationship. To rekindle the love there are only five commandments to follow. Can you and your mom/daughter follow these?

HONEST COMMUNICATION AND RESPECT

Mothers/daughters are respectful of each other. That means not interrupting, not arguing, not putting each other down. Respect is being able to listen and find common ground even when you don't agree. Respect is keeping the boundaries your mom/daughter asks for. When your mom/daughter is upset, you ask this one question: Do you want me to listen, advise, or give you a hug? Give only what's asked for.

ACCEPTANCE OF EACH OTHER

Acceptance that both of you are individuals and both have value is profoundly important. Whatever circumstance you're in or conflicts you face, acceptance of your mom/daughter and her separate self, feelings, and life experiences is key to both her and your well-being.

HAVING LOVE AND COMPASSION

When mom/daughter is struggling with drugs, alcohol, or a disability, love and compassion take on a new meaning and have a special role to play. Having compassion also relates to poor choices, mistakes, and unhealthy relationships. Life is hard. Both moms and daughters have experienced traumas that shaped their behavior. Offer words that show your support.

INVOLVEMENT AND COLLABORATION

Mothers/daughters who share some parts of their lives—activities, work, praying, serving others, and playing together—are healthier than those who don't. If this isn't possible, stick with the other characteristics.

HEALTHY COPING SKILLS

Because life is not always easy or simple, mothers/daughters need both individual and family coping skills to use during difficult times. Here again emotional sobriety means not relying on someone else for love and support. Practicing self-love and self-support creates healthy independence.

Rekindling the Love

Very small gestures can bring about big changes. Rekindling the love starts with you. Don't ask for an apology. Leslie didn't know that her insistence on an apology was a form of blaming and shaming. Remember the good things you had (or want for the future), and slowly take the steps to get there. If you're reaching out after a break, be sure your mom/daughter is ready to reconnect. Rekindling the love can start with random acts of kindness. Help with a chore without being asked. Be nice on the phone. Send some cards. We don't know anybody who doesn't love to get greeting cards and photos. Let your mom/daughter know you're sending positive vibes her way. Over time your gestures will send a powerful message.

Leslie sent an email: "Let's meet for coffee for an hour and not talk about what happened." We didn't meet for coffee since we lived on opposite coasts, but we started talking on the phone weekly. No fights, no drama. We began sharing videos and information. Holding the pose of kindness, compassion, and acceptance was crucial for us. We're highly reactive. In our new relationship, we knew we had to listen without fighting back. We had to hear things we didn't like without making excuses. We couldn't risk relapsing into old habits. Our goal was to keep our expectations low, be patient, and maintain the boundaries we needed to make our relationship safe for each other. Then we wanted our newfound closeness to be fun and useful. Here are some ways for you to rekindle the love like we did.

- **Affirmations:** Use affectionate terms. Say I love you, I'm proud of you, I like what you're doing with your children, job, house.
- **Physical affection:** Give her hugs and kisses. There's nothing like a hug from a mom/daughter to lift a mood and create warm feelings.
- **Thoughtful gestures:** Remember her birthday, her anniversary. Send a tiny meaningful gift that she doesn't expect.

Bring back the memories with actions that affirm what was positive in the past. Every mom/daughter has at least a few happy memories. What did you do together that once brought joy? It could be a hobby, a sports activity, travel, or movie nights with popcorn. Divorce or teenage years may have damaged those memories, but you can restore them, bring back positive emotions, and make new memories. How? Share photos. Create a mom-daughter scrapbook. It doesn't have to be in book form. You can create videos of vacations by adding photos and animating them into a flipbook. You can enjoy the hunt of finding the images to add to your scrapbook. You can also get connected by creating a scrapbook of what you're doing now. Some of our relatives take pictures of both the food they prepare at home and the food they eat at restaurants and while traveling. Create your own food blog. Everybody has to eat.

What activities can you do to bring back the love? If you enjoy collaborating, here are some projects that bring joy to moms and daughters we know. Collecting family recipes and creating a cookbook to share is both enjoyable and can be a gift to the whole extended family. Lindsey and Leslie are working on their recipe book now. Share your values by helping others. There are a million ways to make a difference in your mother-daughter relationship, your family, and your community by helping others.

Mom/daughter knitters make hats and socks for the homeless or military service members abroad. Quilters make quilts for refugees and dog beds for shelter dogs. One daughter's gift to her mom was a book and slideshow of quilters and quilts in their family, going back generations. Some lovers of sewing make dolls and stuffed animals for children in cancer hospitals. Remember your Girl Scout days?

Fundraising for causes is all about your values and compassion for those in need. Lindsey and Leslie do this in Rotary service and with their addiction prevention programs for teens. You can also explore new places, travel, and go on road trips. You can take up gardening or tennis or sing in a choir.

Here's a last hint of what moms and daughters can do. You can rekindle the love by starting a business together. Bakers and caterers, diner owners, bloggers, and publishers. Movie makers and lawyers. Invent a product. You name it. Anything fathers and sons can do mothers and daughters can do, too. Don't be afraid of failure. Failure can be a good teacher for becoming successful.

Think About This

The takeaways from this chapter should include that you must be patient with this process. Don't expect yourself, or anyone else, to be able to change overnight. Patience with the process is imperative. Understanding what you want and what healthy characteristics will look like for you and your situation will also help you focus on this process. Use your new tools to help you work toward your own happiness; they can help your mother/daughter be happy too.

TIME TO JOURNAL

This is a good time to let your imagination go to the good place. What would life look like in a perfect world, or if all your interactions went smoothly? There's power in vision work, and there's power in writing things down. The universe doesn't know how to help if you don't give instructions.

JOURNAL PROMPTS

1. What kind of relationship do you want to have?

2. What do you want your interactions to be like?

3. Are there any gestures that would be meaningful to your mother/daughter?

4. Are you someone who brings up the past a lot?

5. If so, do you think you could practice letting that go?

6. What might be some good activities that you can do together?

CHAPTER 21

Creating the Lifestyle You Love

The most important thing we learned on this journey of self-discovery is that as much as we love each other and want to be connected, we are two people at different stages of life, each with our own needs and desires. Awareness of our own worth, separate from each other, brought us the understanding that neither of us can think or compensate for the other's vulnerabilities, and neither is responsible for the other's health and happiness. We can support each other and be kind to each other, but our lives are our own. Is that a new idea for you?

In the same way you and your mom/daughter are eternally connected, each has choices to make about how to live your life. When you feel comfortable about who you are and what you want, you can begin to create the lifestyle that you may only have dreamed of. You don't have to have a mansion or move to Tahiti to achieve real and lasting happiness. You can reclaim your serenity, heal your heart, and take care of yourself wherever you are.

It's brain work, and while it's sometimes difficult, brain work is also fun. Use your imagination to define what you want. Your outcome, health, and happiness are in your head. This was what we learned about healing and redemption. Your mom/daughter has her own higher power, her own path, and her own experiences, so we're going to leave her alone for now and focus on ourselves. Let's get back to basics and consider what we need to be happy.

In this final chapter, we're going to show you how we created our recovery lifestyle and give you a few ideas to start one yourself. Remember, we are planting seeds, not suggesting a complete overhaul, unless a complete overhaul is what you want. Just remember that evolution is gradual and should be flexible. A recovery lifestyle is a living, evolving adventure filled with a variety of communities with which to connect, traditions to begin, activities to engage you, hobbies to develop, and people to enjoy.

Lindsey's Recovery Lifestyle

After I got sober, life was harder than I expected. Being sober is not fun when you're struggling with the most important things in your life: romance, finances, and family. I adopted the concept of a recovery lifestyle after having to rebuild my entire life around a whole new set of goals and principles. I had to find ways to feel fulfilled and content, to be supported in my recovery, to reach my potential, and to thrive. People in recovery have many challenges. It took years to imagine and then create a balanced life with emotional sobriety.

Experience of what worked and didn't work led me to a universal recipe for wellness that can enhance anyone's life. Even adopting

a few of them can improve your life. For me, the five components of a recovery lifestyle are spirituality, nutrition, fitness, self-
improvement, and advocacy. Your recovery lifestyle might look a
little different, but with a mix of these in your life, you have the tools
you need for happiness.

Spirituality

We'll start with spirituality because it can be your anchor for personal satisfaction and a catalyst for personal growth. Spirituality also
plays a role in emotional and physical health. Where does spirituality come from? Do you ever feel there's something missing in your
life but don't know what it is? Do you wish that you could connect
with something that's deeper than your everyday life? Or do you
have a feeling that there's something bigger going on in your life?
Spirituality adds a level of satisfaction to everyday life. But what is
it exactly?

Some people may think that spirituality is like a religion, but
there's a big difference. Religion is organized around a specific set of
beliefs, rituals, and practices. Worship is commonly conducted with
regular services in a church, synagogue, or mosque. To bring spirituality into your life, however, you don't have to follow any rules or beliefs. Spirituality relates to the practice of developing a sense of peace
and purpose that includes connection with other people. Spirituality
is often considered to be an important domain of overall health. It
is sometimes measured in connections: to yourself, to others, to nature, and to the transcendent.

Spirituality is an important component of recovery because in the
hard work of healing after years of substance abuse, people must find
purpose in life itself to sustain sobriety. For me, learning the tools to

think and act beyond myself brought new meaning to life. I learned how to live with humility and peace, as well as additional ways to be of service toward others. Adding spirituality to my life created an environment of peace during a time of uncertainty and strife with family. In fact, my mom and I both developed our spiritual lives in different ways. Here are six ways to bring spirituality into your life.

Meditation: Meditation is about slowing down. It is a way to be quiet and still and detach from problems, chaos, or whatever makes you sad. Plan a few minutes in the morning to just breathe. There are many online aids to meditation. If you can't meditate, find another way to get quiet before your day begins.

Mindfulness: Mindfulness is a way to become aware of your five senses and bring feelings and thoughts together. When you're mindful, you go about your day finding pleasure in what you smell, taste, touch, hear, and see: the smell of rain, the taste of your morning beverage, the blessed touch of a hug, the sound of your favorite music, the sight of a bird in flight. Let your senses bring positive feelings to you wherever you are. When you find beauty around you, peace follows. Every moment of positive mindfulness reinforces a happiness habit.

Emotional intelligence: As you go through your day, put names to your feelings. I'm excited, sad, frightened, happy, hopeful. You get the idea. When your feelings are negative, calm them down with mindfulness before they escalate into negative reactions. Emotional intelligence can become a habit, too.

Gratitude: Bring gratitude into everything you do and speak. Gratitude keeps you grounded. Grateful people have more contentment than complainers.

Connect to others: There is nothing more comforting than being around people who enjoy or believe the same things you do.

Nutrition

The second piece of the recovery lifestyle pie is nutrition. Nutrition is more than having a healthy diet. It is also about enjoying your food while giving your body the fuel it needs to operate at its best. What you eat affects your mood, how your body feels, and of course your health and weight. Did you know that small changes in your eating habits over time can lead to huge results? Eating and cooking should be enjoyable, especially for those who have struggled with eating disorders or just healthy eating in general.

The first step to healthy nutrition is to explore what kind of eating habits serve you best. The food that you consume and when you consume it both affect your body and mind. Foods can make you sleepy or alert, energetic or comatose. Talking to a nutritionist and getting educated on what foods will be best for your health are a good start. Also, people in addiction recovery should consider the amount of sugar and caffeine they consume. Sugar and caffeine are intoxicants that can make your day a roller coaster of highs and lows.

Exercise

After spirituality and eating, what my body likes is endorphin-producing exercise. It's free, and almost any kind of exercise can make you feel good. The benefits of physical activity to your mental health and wellness are too many to list here. I love exercise because it makes me feel great and gives me something to do, and I have always found communities of friends through my exercise programs. If you are not comfortable with exercise, start slowly with activities such as walking. The point is not to force yourself to do things you hate but to find physical activities you enjoy, which make you feel better and enthusiastic.

Self-Improvement

You wouldn't be here in this very last chapter if you didn't believe in self-help. Again, let's take the focus off your mom/daughter and ask you to consider the areas in your life in which you'd like some improvement. That's why you're here, and it's work that only you can do. Your mom/daughter can't fix your emotional health. You and your brain are in control of the outcome. You can create the outcome you want. Would you benefit from learning more about trauma and triggers, or maybe our story makes you feel comfortable seeking professional help? Start contemplating a self-improvement goal and the actions you need to take. If you struggle getting things done, check in with a friend who will hold you accountable before and after you promise to take an action.

Advocacy

While at first advocacy may not seem like the cure for misery and dread, it provides perspective and purpose. We know families who have lost children to gun violence or addiction who redirect their grief to help others or make societal changes. Making your personal issues your cause helps you and others. Advocacy for addiction recovery and mental health changed the course of my life and career. Becoming a recovery advocate allowed me to turn my biggest deficit, addiction, into an asset. Not only was I freed from the secret keeping, but using my story and knowledge to help others became a worthwhile and rewarding part of my recovery.

If there is a cause you care about, from a particular disease experienced by a family member or animals to the environment, to education, to helping at-risk kids, this is a good time to get involved. It gives you purpose outside yourself and a community of people interested in being positive and making change in the world. You can change your life and the lives of others just by asking yourself what's the kindest thing you can do right now.

 ## Leslie's Recovery Lifestyle

After many years of being an addict's mom, I had a form of PTSD. Many mothers will relate to the daily fear and anguish of coping with a loved one who has trouble managing life safely. It doesn't have to be drug use that brings worry and extra responsibility to moms. It can also be a daughter's failure to launch or any one of the other issues we have discussed. Moms can over-worry and be over-involved. For me, every time the phone rang, I was terrified of impending crises. I didn't want the phone to ring, ever, and was not able to feel happy, be with people, or enjoy my life. There was always some kind of incident and drama to deal with. When Lindsey cut me off, however, I didn't immediately find peace. I grieved just as much as any mother whose daughter had passed away and was gone forever.

I had a therapist at the time who asked me what I wanted, just as we are asking you. I wanted a quiet life, but I also wanted to feel good about myself. I wanted to be the creative person I used to be. I wanted to feel happy and hopeful again. With Lindsey out of the picture, I had the opportunity to travel past the pain of our broken relationship and rediscover myself without being judged or found wanting.

Suddenly, I didn't have to think about Lindsey every minute and the services or emotional support I had to provide to keep her alive or safe or healthy. As Lindsey was free to live her own life, I was free to live mine. Freedom didn't feel good at first. It wasn't easy to let go of my hurt and damaged self-esteem as a "failed" mom. Nor was it easy to accept that I was on my own with the work we had started together, the advocacy mission we had to lift the stigma of addiction and help other families. I felt very alone, but I did carry the work on because I thought it was more important than my own hurt feelings. I also missed the fun and funny side of my daughter.

Then, without any planning or goal setting, I came alive again. I slowly stitched together exactly the recovery lifestyle that Lindsey has described. I created a new life for myself. Of course, I was like Greta, the daughter of an alcoholic mom who moaned and complained, "Why is she doing this to me? Doesn't she love me after all I've done for her?"

No answers came my way. Even if Lindsey had wanted to tell me, she didn't have the words then to explain. And the truth is her answers really weren't my business. She had her path to follow, and I had to find meaning and purpose in my life without her. As an adult, there are just some things you must accept as beyond your control and, yes, get over it. Detach and let it go. I had to let my daughter go. Letting go was my final job as a mom.

Where did that detachment leave me and my broken heart? Moms often have broken hearts, at least once in our lives. We're not all guaranteed happy endings. So what do we have if we don't get our happy ending? After many tears and much feeling sorry for myself, I slowly realized I still had everything I needed for a productive and satisfying life. I had myself, and I mattered. I also had friends and family for whom I could cook, a garden I could cultivate, a piano and music to play. I was over sixty, but I wasn't done with life. I met someone new, started playing golf, returned to Pilates and then tai chi. For a while I saw a therapist. Then a personal trainer came into my life. Every two weeks I had a massage. I wrote articles and mentored other moms who were suffering like me. I became a grandmother. Three times. All girls, perfect in every way.

And that wasn't all, I worked on a few new books, sat in the sun. Like Alice, who developed her garden when she lost her daughter, I learned I could be happy on my own whether my daughter returned to me or not. I had been forced to overcome profound grief once before when I lost my mother at the same time as I became a mother myself. Forty years later, with much water under the bridge, I was still needed, still valuable, still vibrant. No matter what happened, I was all right. Spirituality made me kinder. Nutrition kept me cooking. Exercise was my mood and sleep medicine. Mindfulness made me love the taste of food, the sound of music, the sight of clouds and blooming flowers, the touch of cool water on my skin, the smell of baking bread. I'm baking bread right now. Advocacy continues to give me purpose and community.

When I was a young woman, I admired the wild manes of the gray-haired ladies in long skirts who walked barefoot in the sand, baked bread, made jam, played the guitar with grandchildren, and danced in the moonlight. I'm a seventies girl, after all. My wish was to be like them when I grew up. It still is. So my last words (in this book anyway) are to get simple and go back to basics. With the revelations about who you are, where you came from, and how you arrived where you are right now, you can use the tools of recovery for a happier and healthier life. Your last homework assignment is . . . whatever you want it to be.

Recommended Reading

The Happiness Advantage: How a Positive Brain Fuels Success in Work and Life by Shawn Achor

Codependent No More: How to Stop Controlling Others and Start Caring for Yourself by Melody Beattie

12 Essential Insights for Emotional Sobriety by Allan Berger, PhD

12 Smart Things to Do When the Booze and Drugs Are Gone: Choosing Emotional Sobriety Through Self-Awareness and Right Action by Allan Berger, PhD

Rising Strong: How the Ability to Reset Transforms the Way We Live, Love, Parent, and Lead by Brené Brown

Emotional Sobriety: From Relationship Trauma to Resilience and Balance by Tian Dayton, PhD

Treating Adult Children of Relational Trauma: 85 Experiential Interventions to Health the Inner Child and Create Authentic Connection in the Present by Tian Dayton, PhD

The Body Keeps the Score: Brain, Mind, and Body in the Health of Trauma by Bessel van der Kolk

Mother Hunger: How Adult Daughters Can Understand and Heal from Lost Nurturance, Protection, and Guidance by Kelly McDaniel

Parenting from the Inside Out: How a Deeper Self-Understanding Can Help You Raise Children Who Thrive by Daniel J. Siegel and Mary Hartzell

Healing in Your Hands: Self-Havening Practices to Harness Neuroplasticity, Heal Traumatic Stress, and Build Resilience by Kate Truitt

Overcoming Underearning by Barbara Stanny

Grit by Angela Duckworth

Drop the Rock by Bill P., Todd W., and Sara S.

What People Are Saying About Leslie and Lindsey Glass

Praise for Leslie and Lindsey Glass

"Leslie and Lindsey Glass's new book, *The Mother Daughter Relationship Makeover*, is certain to make a major contribution to the understanding of what can go wrong, and right, with this most important relationship. Thousands of mothers and daughters wish they could have a relationship like theirs. This high-achieving duo is charming, compassionate, accepting, and open not only with each other but with everyone they touch."

—**Leonard Bushel,** author of *High: Confessions of a Cannabis Addict* and editor/publisher of the *Addiction/Recovery e-Bulletin*

"Lindsey and Leslie Glass are incredible resources when it comes to anything recovery related. They have devoted their lives to raising awareness of the many issues regarding addiction, recovery, and prevention. They are talented writers and filmmakers, and have used their talents as recovery advocates to address the stigma that still exists regarding addiction. It's been our pleasure to work with them because they're the genuine article. We wish them continued success, and look forward to any future collaborations."

—**Ken Pomerance,** co-founder of InTheRooms.com

"Lindsey and Leslie Glass have created a wealth of creative and user-friendly recovery and self-help content that inspires thousands of people every single day."

—**Marisa Ravel,** owner of Laserkitten

Praise for *The Secret World of Recovery*

"Important film! *The Secret World of Recovery* is a documentary that anyone dealing with addiction and recovery issues should see. Lots of important information about what recovery really means and how people get into long-term sobriety. I recommend this very highly to people who want to know more about dealing with alcoholism and addiction in the family."

"We watch this DVD in our facility. The clients really enjoy it and it makes for quality discussions. *The Secret World of Recovery* is informative, interesting, and refreshing. The educational pieces are engaging and appropriate for our clients. It is inspiring and it instills hope, laughter, and fun into the hard work of recovery."

"*The Secret World of Recovery* is a must-see for family members of those struggling with addiction as well as the addict themselves; a good documentary."

—**Amazon reviewers**

Praise for Lindsey Glass's *100 Tips for Growing Up*

"*100 Tips for Growing Up* is beautiful."

"It's simple and relatable."

"It's interactive. I just love the notes to self."

"Recovery content like this is brilliant."

—Amazon readers

"The tips are easy to digest, and the place for journaling after every tip is a great way to hardwire healthy behaviors into the brain. My patients love it."

—**Michael Fitzgerald,** director, Acute Care
Behavioral Health Program

Praise for the Healthy Teen Project: The Teen Guide to Health

From Parents

"Our whole family read the book and will cherish our son's contest experience forever."

"Our son has gained so much confidence from creating art for the mental health contest; he's a different person."

"We learned a lot about anxiety and stress in teens, and our daughter used her project for her college application, and for mentoring students at college when she got in."

From Students

"I was surprised by how much I didn't know about health and mental health. Parents should read it, and teachers, too."

—**2021 contest winner**

"I learned about brain function and physical health (from the book), made a video about it, entered the contest and won $5,000. It was a joy for my whole family."

—2022 contest winner

"Doing a project about influences on the teen brain changed my life and habits. Social media is no longer my friend."

—2023 contest winner

From a Participating Art Teacher

"The hundreds of students who have participated in three years love this book and project. We have few opportunities that provide health education, and none that use art as a stimulus, so this is unique. At the end of the year, families of teens from different schools enjoy seeing the exhibition from other students. The winners will never forget their experience. And having Leslie teach a class brings real excitement to the classroom."

From a Participating Afterschool Program

"Our students are leadership mentors, and this program inspires them to learn more about mental health and what they can do to help others. We have contest winners every year."

Praise for Leslie Glass Mysteries

"Glass delivers what her fans have come to expect—page-turning suspense and dynamic characters . . . to sum it up in one word: chilling."

"Welcome to Portland . . . Glass's most provocative character, tracked by the deadliest killers you never want to meet."

—reviewers on Goodreads

Praise for the Novels of Leslie Glass

"Sharp as a scalpel . . . scary as hell. Leslie Glass is Lady McBain."

—Michael Palmer

"Nobody writes crime mysteries quite like Leslie Glass."

—Romantic Times

"Brilliant . . . skillfully done."

—Tampa Times

"Truly fantastic."

—New York Post

About the Authors

Leslie Glass is a journalist, novelist, playwright, and documentarian. In her writing career of more than four decades, she has worked in advertising, publishing, magazines, documentary filmmaking, and theatre. For twenty-four years, she served as Trustee of the Leslie Glass Family Foundation, which she retired in 2018. Leslie has served on many organization boards including, the Middle States Commission of Higher Education and the New York City Police Foundation. Since 2011, Leslie has concentrated on creating educational tools for life skills, family wellness, and teen addiction prevention. With her daughter Lindsey, she developed the popular website Reach Out Recovery, publishing self-help books and more than 1,500 original articles about addiction, recovery, and family relationships. Leslie is also the author of fourteen novels, including nine *USA Today* and *New York Times* bestselling crime novels featuring NYPD Detective Sergeant April Woo, the first female Asian-American detective in mainstream American fiction. Leslie lives in Sarasota, Florida, where her passions are Tai Chi, golf, cooking for friends and neighbors, and the Rotary Club of Sarasota Bay, where she developed the "What Makes You Healthy" wellness education and art program for teens based on her book, *The Teen Guide to Health.*

 **Lindsey Glass** is an author, screenwriter, and recovery/mental health advocate. She has worked in publishing and film as well as in the non-profit world for over two decades. She has coproduced two documentaries on addiction recovery and is cofounder of the popular wellness website Reach Out Recovery. Lindsey has written dozens of articles about recovery, relationships, and wellness that have been read millions of times worldwide. A passionate advocate for those suffering with addiction and mental health issues, Lindsey is the president of ROR Empowerment, the non-profit arm of Reach Out Recovery. Since 2012, Lindsey has worked tirelessly to develop tools and provide access to information about recovery and emotional wellness including: programs, books, workbooks, and curriculums. Lindsey's book *100 Tips for Growing Up* is used in life skills and empowerment programs and has been taught in recovery and sober living facilities, including Homeboy Industries. Lindsey cares deeply about social issues. She lives in Southern California where she is a member of Rotary International, a practicing Buddhist in the Soka Gakkai, and a passionate dog enthusiast.